EVERY DAY GOD'S WAY

365 DEVOTIONS ON HOPE

PUBLISHING GROUP

NASHVILLE, TENNESSEE

978-1-4627-9428-7

Published by B&H Publishing Group
Nashville, Tennessee

4 5 6 7 8 9 10 • 22 21 20 19 18

SEARCHER OF HEARTS

This wondrous knowledge is beyond me. It is lofty; I am unable to reach it —Psalm 139:6

There is no escaping God. Hagar, running away from Sarah's cruelty, met God in the wilderness and exclaimed, "You are El-roi," for she said, "In this place, have I actually seen the one who sees me?" (Gen. 16:13). Jacob fleeing from his brother Esau, saw in his dream a ladder from earth to heaven and, waking, cried, "Surely the LORD is in this place, and I did not know it" (Gen. 28:16). And our psalmist, reviewing the possibilities of flight from God's presence, declared, "Where can I go to escape your Spirit? Where can I flee from your presence?" (Ps. 139:7).

Who would want to get away from God? Why do we run from Him? Even those who are lost—those who do not know Him—cannot escape the presence of our loving God. He is our only hope and comfort, our sole cause for constant, renewing joy. For God pursues us that He may bless us. His vigilant pursuit is the expression of His love.

Father, You alone know what is best for us. Strengthen our faith that we might trust Your perfect will. Help us to know Your presence and to rejoice in Your unfailing care.

THERE IS NO ONE LIKE YOU

There is no one holy like the LORD. There is no one besides you! And there is no rock like our God. —1 Samuel 2:2

There are striking similarities between Hannah's song and the song that Mary sang after the angel had told her that she was to be the mother of the Savior. Mary spoke for herself, for Hannah, and for all of us, when she said, "Surely, from now on all generations will call me blessed, because the Mighty One has done great things for me, and his name is holy" (Luke 1:48–49).

The best school of theology is experience. We may read everything that has been written about God and yet still fail to know Him. But when He enters our lives, forgives our sins, saves our souls, answers our prayers, changes our circumstances, and fills life's cup to overflowing with His goodness, then we can say, "There is no one besides you!"

It was the gift of a child that inspired the praise of Hannah and Mary. It is the gift of a Child—Mary's Child—that prompts our own hearts to sing. For in Jesus Christ, God comes near to us, in power to bless and in love to save.

■

Lord, thank You for the gift of Jesus, our Savior and our only hope. Open our hearts and minds to receive by faith this extravagant gift of relationship with You.

PRINCIPLES FOR LIVING

*"Don't think that I came to abolish the Law or the Prophets.
I did not come to abolish but to fulfill." —Matthew 5:17*

We need to be careful what worldly terms we apply to the Lord Jesus. Some call Him merely a great teacher and even a revolutionary leader—but the extravagance in these terms obscures the truest truth of our Savior: He came to us because He dearly loves us. Everything He did here on Earth—His ministry, crucifixion, death, and resurrection—was all done "for the joy that lay before Him" (Heb. 12:2).

And although Jesus denounced the traditions of men, He respected the eternal truths preserved in the ancient Scriptures. To Him, these were foundations upon which to build: unchanging principles that Christ followers must use as starting points for a fuller knowledge of God and of His will.

Today, the Ten Commandments are considered good material for a movie but unnecessary for life. But Jesus said of them, "For truly I tell you, until heaven and earth pass away, not the smallest letter or one stroke of a letter will pass away from the law until all things are accomplished" (Matt. 5:18).

*Help me understand your instruction,
and I will obey it and follow it with all my heart.
Help me stay on the path of your commands,
for I take pleasure in it. (Ps. 119:34–35)*

GOD'S APPOINTED KING

Ask of me, and I will make the nations your inheritance
and the ends of the earth your possession. —Psalm 2:8

Many kings and dictators have dreamed of claiming this promise. Some rulers and politicians of today have made their bid to rule all the nations of this earth. These leaders have set themselves "against the LORD and his Anointed One" (Ps. 2:2). If they are striving to lead without God's guidance and help, if they aren't submitted to His ultimate will, then their efforts will, ultimately, be thwarted— if not in this age, well, then certainly in the age to come.

God has turned away from all such selfish leaders. He has already appointed the King who shall one day rule over the nations. His anointed One is Jesus, His own beloved Son. He entered the world first as a little infant, depending upon Mary and Joseph to care for Him. He will return to this earth again. The second time He will come to judge the living and the dead and reign as God's appointed King (2 Tim. 4:1–2).

■

"Our Father in heaven, your name be honored as holy. Your
kingdom come. Your will be done on earth as it is in heaven"
(Matt. 6:10–11). Please strengthen and renew our faith to trust
You more today, and to submit to Your good and perfect will.

A SUFFERER'S FAITH

But I know that my Redeemer lives, and at the end he will stand on the dust. —Job 19:25

Never is faith more beautiful and meaningful than when it comes from the heart of one who suffers. Through the ages, the experience of Job has been a comfort and strength to those in pain. Anyone can express faith when all is well, but it takes one with a genuine experience with God to say what Job said in the midst of his time of agony. There was no doubt in the mind of Job about his Redeemer. He could say, even in his suffering, "I know."

A pearl is formed at the cost of suffering on the part of an oyster. A grain of sand works its way inside the shell, and in this suffering, a calcium deposit is secreted to cover the offending object. After many long months of suffering, a beautiful, valuable pearl is made.

So it is in the life of one who has a strong faith in God. Pain only helps to make that life more beautiful, an encouragement to others in their own time of need.

■

Father God, please give us faith to carry us through times of suffering and disappointment and transform them into blessing. May we "rejoice as [we] share in the sufferings of Christ, so that [we] may also rejoice with great joy when his glory is revealed" (1 Pet. 4:13).

THE REDEEMER FORETOLD

"The Redeemer will come to Zion, and to those in Jacob who turn from transgression." This is the LORD's declaration. —Isaiah 59:20

One of the proofs of the divinity of Christ is the fact that His entrance into the world was prophesied hundreds of years before He came. His coming as Redeemer is the summary of all the promises and many prophecies of the Old Testament.

It should be a source of strength to the faith of Christians that the Savior's coming was not some hasty afterthought on the part of our Heavenly Father. His entrance into this world in the flesh was in the mind of the Godhead in eternity—before the world was made. God "has saved us and called us with a holy calling, not according to our works, but according to his own purpose and grace, which was given to us in Christ Jesus before time began (2 Tim. 1:9).

The Scriptures say He will come to Zion (sometimes used to refer to the Church Christ established) because it is on that holy hill that the Savior will be proclaimed as King.

For centuries the Jews were strengthened in the midst of countless trials by the hope that one day the Messiah would come. Today we look back on His coming two thousand years ago, even as we long for His second coming sometime in the future.

■

*Father God, please strengthen our faith
in this Savior who died for us.*

THE SAVIOR GIVEN

For my eyes have seen your salvation. —*Luke 2:30*

Ancient cities usually had watchmen to warn the people of an approaching enemy and to announce the coming of friendly visitors. At times a person would call out, "Watchman, what is left of the night?" hoping for a reply (Isa. 21:11).

Simeon is pictured as a watchman put in a special place and told to look for a certain sign and then announce it to the world. The day came when he saw that sign, the child Jesus. He announced his discovery and then asked to be relieved of his post that he had occupied so long, content that his task was done. What a privilege to have such an opportunity as this! Think of the thrilling experience Simeon had of actually seeing the long-awaited Messiah.

The Holy Spirit is speaking to many people every day and telling them of the Messiah who has come. Most of these people not only do not thrill at the good news, but actually turn away from Christ and reject Him. Yet He gave His life for us all. He is available to all, and He pursues all (see Ps. 139).

God, thank You for the gift of Your Son. May others come to know the truth of the gospel and receive Jesus as Savior.

PROMISE OF THE COMFORTER

But the Counselor, the Holy Spirit, whom the Father will send in my name, will teach you all things and remind you of everything I have told you. —John 14:26

For God's people of old traveling through the wilderness, His presence was expressed in the pillar of cloud by day and of fire by night. The wilderness road might have its dangers for some, but for those who marched under the sign of God's presence no harm could befall them.

For Christ followers, the needed assurance of God's presence, companionship, protection, and power, is not above or around us but within us. "But you do know him, because he remains with you and will be in you," said Jesus of the Holy Spirit (John 14:17). If we are called upon to carry some heavy load, He shares the burden with us. If we need courage to stand against the tide of the times, He strengthens us beyond our powers. If we are in need of wisdom to understand the way that we take, He becomes the source of understanding and counsel.

Why is it that we know so little of the Spirit's help? Is it because Jesus failed to fulfill His promise or because we fail to recognize and honor the heavenly guest within us?

■

Lord, we pray that the Holy Spirit may become better known to us as we learn to listen to Him and yield to His will.

SPIRIT OF TRUTH

*When he comes, he will convict the world about
sin, righteousness, and judgment. —John 16:8*

The Holy Spirit achieves many things in the human heart. The
first of these is conviction, that deep disturbance of the that
which produces repentance. Without conviction, a Christian
profession is nothing better than a snowy cloak thrown over a
trash heap. The Holy Spirit reveals our sin and makes it real to
us. This kindness leads us to repentance and also relationship
with our God (Rom. 2:4).

> If we walk in the light as he himself is in the light,
> we have fellowship with one another, and the blood
> of Jesus his Son cleanses us from all sin. . . . If we
> confess our sins, he is faithful and righteous to for-
> give us our sins and to cleanse us from all unrigh-
> teousness. (1 John 1:7, 9)

The Holy Spirit enables us to have the mind of Christ, so
we can walk in fellowship with Him. He becomes the Spirit
of Truth to us, revealing our true condition as sinners, working
repentance in our hearts, cleansing us through faith, and unit-
ing us in fellowship with our Lord. "The Spirit himself testifies
together with our spirit that we are God's children" (Rom. 8:16).

*Jesus, thank You for the gift of the indwelling Holy Spirit. Please
grow our faith that we may be attuned to the Spirit of Truth,
trusting what He has to say, and following His lead in obedience.*

PROTECTED BY THE BLOOD

The blood on the houses where you are staying will be a distinguishing mark for you; when I see the blood, I will pass over you. No plague will be among you to destroy you when I strike the land of Egypt. —Exodus 12:13

Have you ever noticed how all great dramas—whether of page, stage, television, or film—are a mixture of both tears and laughter? In a similar way, great religious experiences seem to blend great fear and great faith.

While the successive plagues afflicted only the land of Egypt, even in Goshen, where the Israelites lived under divine protection, the stench and the horror breached its borders. The promise of Israel's release from bondage carried its own condition: obedience. The sacrificial lamb must be chosen and prepared. Those to be delivered must be aware of their danger and so ready themselves for faith to mark a great religious experience.

In such a manner does the sinner's fear thrust him at last, in faith, upon the promises of God—of the blood of the Lamb of God—to work in us a great deliverance from the bondage of sin. Thanks be to God, "For Christ our Passover lamb has been sacrificed" so that we might live (1 Cor. 5:7).

Lord Jesus, thank You for Your unimaginable sacrifice, and for Your complete and perfect work on the cross.

A SHADOW OF THINGS TO COME

For it is impossible for the blood of bulls and
goats to take away sins. —Hebrews 10:4

A sledge hammer is not an appropriate tool for adjusting a fine watch, even though the watch badly needs regulating. More than a teaspoon is needed to bail out a leaky boat, however zealously the spoon is applied.

The problem and need for taking away sins has long stirred the sensitive conscience. Rite and sacrament, incantation and sacrifice have somehow made their appeal, enlisted their devotees, and all had their moment. But over every one of these means hangs the shadow of futility: the power of sin is unbroken, the stain of sin remains.

The law prescribed an eye for an eye, pain for pain, suffering for suffering, and life for life. Yet sin remained. The machinery of sacrifice demanded the offering in blood and flame of the perfect gift for the imperfect giver. Yet the power of sin was undiminished. Only of Jesus could it be said, "Here is the Lamb of God, who takes away the sin of the world!" (John 1:29). "But this man, after offering one sacrifice for sins forever . . . has perfected forever those who are sanctified" (Heb. 10:12, 14).

■

Let us give thanks to God for His unspeakable gift.

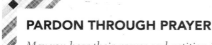

PARDON THROUGH PRAYER

*May you hear their prayer and petition in heaven
and uphold their cause. —1 Kings 8:45*

In describing God, much has been said of His "all-seeing eye."
Less noted, but no less real, is God's "all-hearing ear." No noise
of battle deafens Him. No private sigh of suffering escapes His
hearing. The sounds of the very soul in tribulation, distress, or
supplication, whether framed in words or tears, come readily
to His ears.

Nowhere are Solomon's wisdom and insight recorded more
arrestingly than in his dedicatory prayer for the temple. He
besought God's hearing for His people's prayers in whatever
circumstance and need the future might bring. To Solomon, all
of life seemed to turn on a divine axis. For Israel to fall before
future invading conquerors would be evidence of national sin
against God. Similarly, drought, pestilence, privation, and captivity would confirm the nation's estrangement from God. But
for the sins that God's eye sees, His ear awaits His people's
prayerful petition for pardon.

> Therefore the LORD is waiting to show you mercy,
> and is rising up to show you compassion,
> for the LORD is a just God.
> All who wait patiently for him are happy. (Isa. 30:18)

■

*Father forgive me for the wrongful attitudes of my heart
that lead to my sin in action. "May the words of my
mouth and the meditation of my heart be acceptable to
you, LORD, my rock and my Redeemer (Ps. 19:14).*

A CALL TO REPENTANCE

"I will judge each one of you according to his ways." This is the declaration of the Lord GOD. "Repent and turn from all your rebellious acts, so they will not become a sinful stumbling block to you." —Ezekiel 18:30

Our modern-day culture seems to condone, if not encourage, anything that makes us "happy," with, perhaps, one caveat: "as long as nobody gets hurt." Or rather, as long as you don't get caught.

To the contrary, the prophet declares that man, in rebellion against God and disobedient to the moral law and His will, is not judged by the prevailing standards of society. He is writing his own sentence of spiritual death to be confirmed by divine judgment. Scripture tells us that fear of God alone will determine our eternal fate: "Don't fear those who kill the body but are not able to kill the soul; rather, fear him who is able to destroy both soul and body in hell" (Matt. 10:28).

Truly, there is nothing we can do to save ourselves. But there is good news for those who call on the name of Jesus Christ. "For [we] are saved by grace through faith"—not the works of our own hands (Eph. 2:8–9). Jesus promises, "Therefore, everyone who will acknowledge me before others, I will also acknowledge him before my Father in heaven" (Matt. 10:32). Thanks be to God.

Thank you, Jesus, for Your sacrificial gift of grace. May other hearts turn to You and receive the gift of salvation.

THE BOOK OF THE LAW

When all Israel assembles in the presence of the LORD your God at the place he chooses, you are to read this law aloud before all Israel. —Deuteronomy 31:11

The book of the Law was the will of God spelled out in plain, understandable speech. God gave it to Moses; Moses gave it to Joshua; after the death of Moses, it was Joshua's responsibility that the people have it in their minds and hearts, "that they may listen and learn to fear the LORD [their] God and be careful to follow all the words of this law" (Deut. 31:12). It is the highest wisdom to know and do the will of God.

The Christian who knows the grace of God in Christ Jesus learns to love the book of the Law. It is not a hard compulsion that burdens him, but a light that illuminates his moral path. The moral and spiritual values that guided Israel still call to men saying, "Your eyes will see your Teacher, and whenever you turn to the right or to the left, your ears will hear this command behind you: 'This is the way. Walk in it'" (Isa. 30:20–21).

The book of the Law points to the way of salvation by grace; it is solid pavement upon which the child of grace may walk. "Abundant peace belongs to those who love your instruction; nothing makes them stumble" (Ps. 119:165).

God, we humbly ask for seeing eyes, hearing ears, and an understanding heart to follow You.

INTERPRETERS OF THE LAW

*They read out of the book of the law of God, translating
and giving the meaning so that the people could
understand what was read. —Nehemiah 8:8*

Many people claim that they do not understand what they read in the Bible—that they need an interpreter to make them see its meaning. Jesus said that there is an interpreter whose services are available to all of God's children.

When we try to do the interpreting in our own understanding, we want details laid out for us. But when the Holy Spirit interprets, He guides in simple truths. Jesus said, "When the Spirit of truth comes, he will guide you into all the truth. For he will not speak on his own, but he will speak whatever he hears. He will also declare to you what is to come" (John 16:13). In plain speak, the Holy Spirit helps us make sense of God's Word. He enables us to understand its meaning and its application for our attitudes and our acts.

God's truth is not just a philosophy for the purposes of discussion, but it is a way of living, and to be further understood must be obeyed in action. With the Holy Spirit leading us, we can all learn to be great interpreters of God's Word, and by His gentle guidance, we can also learn to obey it.

*Lord, we pray for more intimate experience of the presence
and work of the great interpreter, the Holy Spirit.*

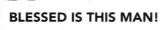

BLESSED IS THIS MAN!

*His delight is in the LORD's instruction, and he
meditates on it day and night. —Psalm 1:2*

Blessedness is more than happiness. Happiness may be derived from toys or earthly experiences—at least a sort of temporary happiness. But blessedness has its roots in reality, and a divine reality at that. Still, not all happiness is blessedness.

How happy—how blessed—is the one who detests evil and clings to what is good (Rom. 12:9). "His delight is in the LORD's instruction." May we seek out the Word of God and commit to reading and studying it, making it the passion and drive of our very lives. Making God's Kingdom our priority (Matt. 6:33), seeking truth in His Word—these are pursuits that will not return void (Isa. 55:11). What comfort—what joy!—to know God will meet us in His Word.

To be such a blessed child of God, we must not only resolve to make the Bible our chief book for reading every day, but we must also pray for a heart to hear the Father's voice in its words. We grow in relationship with Him as we return again and again to His all-sufficient Word. Surely there is blessing and abundance in feasting on this daily bread—on every word that comes from the mouth of God (Matt. 6:11; Deut. 8:3).

*Father God, make us hungry for Your Word.
Teach our hearts to seek You first.*

CHRIST IN ALL THE SCRIPTURES

Then beginning with Moses and all the Prophets,
he interpreted for them the things concerning
himself in all the Scriptures. —Luke 24:27

"Christ is the answer." We've heard this before, but without personal experience, it is an empty message. It is only a good battle cry if it is understood. Christ is the answer, but only as He reveals Himself in Scripture. Jesus spoke of "everything written about [Him] in the Law of Moses, the Prophets, and the Psalms" (Luke 24:44). Then He opened the understanding of His followers. He does the same for us, by the Holy Spirit. And when He does, we see that all of Scripture points to Jesus Christ.

The Law, the prophets, and the psalms refer many times to the Lamb of God that takes away sin. Every animal slain for sin yielded its blood to be sprinkled on Israel's altar for atonement and forgiveness. In Isaiah 53 the prophet unveils the most superlative view of Christ in sacrificial glory; He shows both His substitutionary dying and His resurrection. The years of Jesus' time on the earth were already cast in a pattern presented clearly in the Old Testament. The New Testament accounts of His life and ministry are the fulfillment of prophecy foretold and yet to be fulfilled.

■

Lord, please open my mind and heart to understand Scripture,
to seek and find Jesus Christ throughout Your Word.

GOD'S PURSUIT

They received the word with eagerness and examined the Scriptures daily to see if these things were so. —Acts 17:11

Sometimes, we are slow to believe that Scripture has a personal and practical application, and slower still to walk in its teaching and promises. There is a certain degree of acceptance; that is, we believe and walk according to Scripture—as long as it lines up with the world's "common sense."

But God pursues us for relationship—not just to give us a moral code for living. And one of the primary ways He pursues us is through the written Word, which His Holy Spirit inspired men to write.

We would never have approached God in prayer if God had not first sought us. "God proves his own love for us in that while we were still sinners, Christ died for us" (Rom. 5:8). "We love because he first loved us" (1 John 4:19).

When our hearts turn to Jesus and receive Him as Savior and Lord, it is always the work of the Spirit. It's His kindness that leads us back to Him (Rom. 2:4). The Holy Spirit leads us to pray and to search God's Word. His guidance leads us to our ultimate joy: relationship with our Creator God.

■

God, give me a heart to search the Scriptures daily. Grow my faith more and more each day.

RESPECT FOR PERSONALITY

*But I tell you, love your enemies and pray for those
who persecute you, so that you may be children
of your Father in heaven. —Matthew 5:44*

Personality is God's image reflected in us. We, so far as this earth is concerned, are the object of God's love and affection. And in this lost and broken world, our sin has marred His image within us. Even so, God's love for us sets out to restore us, and His image—one He respects—for His glory.

God commanded, "Do not take revenge or bear a grudge against members of your community, but love your neighbor as yourself; I am the LORD" (Lev. 19:18). There can be no true love where there is no genuine respect. To exercise such respect and love we have to go beyond the surface of the personality that we see. We must love and respect the person that God created as His image bearer.

"Love the Lord your God with all your heart, with all your soul, with all your mind, and with all your strength. The second is, Love your neighbor as yourself. There is no other command greater than these" (Mark 12:30–31).

We "all have sinned and fall short of the glory of God" (Rom. 3:23). Still, "we are his workmanship, created in Christ Jesus for good works, which God prepared ahead of time for us to do" (Eph. 2:10). By God's grace, may He teach us to love His image in others.

■

*God, teach me to love well and respect others. Help
me to see You and Your goodness reflected in them.*

THE CHRISTIAN'S RULE

Therefore, whatever you want others to do for you, do also the same for them, for this is the Law and the Prophets. —Matthew 7:12

The spirit of the Golden Rule is love, love for self that reflects in love for others. We cannot treat others with respect due them until we realize that, in spite of our faults and limitations, we ourselves are of infinite worth in the eyes of God. When we understand that Christ first loved us and that He has great expectations in us, we can understand why He requires us to have confidence in our fellow man.

God created us for His glory and calls each one of us by name (Isa. 43:7). He sees our souls as valuable—so valuable that He sent Jesus to save us. God knew nothing of this world is of gain without a relationship with Him (Mark 8:36). And so He came to rescue you; and so He came to rescue me.

We love others not because they are lovely and lovable, but because Christ dwells within each of us. Through Him we can see the value of others and love them in spite of their faults and limitations. We "do not owe anyone anything, except to love one another, for the one who loves another has fulfilled the law" (Rom. 13:8).

Lord Jesus, help me to love my fellow man as You have loved me.

COMPANIONS OF JESUS

Suddenly, two men were talking with him—
Moses and Elijah. —Luke 9:30

An old man who had recently lost his wife said to a boy upon the death of his father, "Son, your father will be closer to you in many ways than he has ever seemed before. The curtain which separates this life from life after death is very thin, even though we cannot see through it."

The disciples did not seem particularly startled by the fact that Moses and Elijah were alive and interested in the redemptive work of the Lord Jesus. On that mountaintop heaven and earth came wondrously close. The curtain of the future has not been pulled aside for us to give any complete understanding of the nature of the life that Christians enjoy after death. But we are assured by many Scriptures that life, not death, has the last word.

The truth that we often think of as an Easter text is our assurance for every day in the year. To Martha, Jesus declared, "I am the resurrection, and the life: he that believeth in me, though he were dead, yet shall he live: and whosoever liveth and believeth in me shall never die. Believest thou this?" (John 11:25–26 KJV).

Pray today for a trust in the promises of God which
will furnish strength in the hour of testing.

MANY MANSIONS

In my Father's house are many rooms; if not,
I would have told you. I am going away to
prepare a place for you. —John 14:2

No other words have comforted the bereaved and encouraged the fainthearted more than the wonderful words of Jesus. To His sorrowing disciples, and to us, He gave two blessed assurances. First, the preparations for our future life are more than adequate. Second, wherever we do not have definite information, we can trust God. He is our blessed assurance.

A person face-to-face with death, in his own life or in the passing of a loved one, may rest in the assurance that God's provisions are adequate. To depart is to be with Christ, and to be with Christ is far better (Phil. 1:23). The questions we have that seemingly go unanswered need not trouble us. Of those unsolved problems, Christ has said, "I would have told you." When we cannot understand, we can still trust.

> Blessed assurance, Jesus is mine!
> Oh, what a foretaste of glory divine!
> Heir of salvation, purchase of God,
> Born of His Spirit, washed in His blood.
> This is my story, this is my song.
> Praising my Savior all the day long.
> —Fanny Crosby

Thank You, Lord, for the loving provision of
Your Son and our Savior, Jesus Christ.

A KING'S OBEDIENCE

So David did as God commanded him, and
they struck down the Philistine army from
Gibeon to Gezer. —1 Chronicles 14:16

David had a great army at his command, yet he relied more on God's promises than his own military forces. He sought and received God's counsel and was obedient to it. He believed that God's promises were true, that what God said God would do. David's obedience to God led to the complete defeat of Israel's chief enemy, the Philistines, for the duration of his reign.

Sometimes we hesitate to attempt a mighty task by ourselves. But there is no need to hesitate to try something, to step out in faith, when God is by our side. If experience has taught us anything, it's that our efforts alone can achieve very little. But when we realize that it's not our effort but God's grace and power that really matters, then we are bound to believe God's promises too. "For nothing will be impossible with God" (Luke 1:37).

David could have relied on his own strength and his great army to defeat the enemy. Instead, "David did as God commanded him." For us as Christ followers, obedience to God is the fruit of our faith.

■

We thank You, heavenly Father, for Your promise
of help in all of life's circumstances.

HEALED BY A LOOK

So Moses made a bronze snake and mounted it on a pole. Whenever someone was bitten, and he looked at the bronze snake, he recovered. —Numbers 21:9

The story of the fiery serpents and the bronze serpent may seem incredible to some people today, but it helps us to understand what the Bible means when it says that God delivered His people "with a strong hand and an outstretched arm" (Deut. 26:8).

We must understand that life is not a simple unfolding of the natural order. God's presence is evident in history, and through history He reveals Himself and achieves His purposes. Those purposes, however, relate to us only as we give the response of faith.

The Bible and human experience both testify to this great fact: all the resources of God are available for His children. We need only give trustful response. Our lives are healed of their sicknesses when we turn outward from self and upward to God. There was no magic in the bronze serpent. There was no healing in an image. The power and the healing were in God then and they still are today.

■

Turn our hearts to You, Father. May our nation be led to look to You for Your resources and strength. For all strength and power belongs to You, Lord (Ps. 62:11).

THE GREATEST COMMANDMENT

He answered, "Love the Lord your God with all your heart,
with all your soul, with all your strength, and with all your
mind;" and "your neighbor as yourself." —Luke 10:27

"Just as love for God begins with listening to his Word, so the beginning of love for the brethren is learning to listen to them."

This statement is in the writings of Dietrich Bonhoeffer, a pastor hanged by the Nazis. Refusing asylum outside his native Germany, he was active in the Confessional Church and the Resistance until his arrest in 1943. The Sunday after Easter, 1945, he had just finished preaching to fellow prisoners at Flossenburg when two men entered. "Prisoner Bonhoeffer, come with us."

"This is the end," Bonhoeffer said to a friend, "but for me it is the beginning of life."

Such calm anticipation of death was a part of Dietrich Bonhoeffer's deep involvement in a full life of love toward God and his neighbors. He understood that there would be "suffering in this world" (John 16:33), but anticipated the life to come.

And by God's grace, Bonhoeffer may well have been strengthened by the apostle Paul's words: "My goal is to know him and the power of his resurrection and the fellowship of his sufferings, being conformed to his death, assuming that I will somehow reach the resurrection from among the dead" (Phil. 3:10).

Lord, we humbly ask that You would grow in us a faith
and willingness to obey Your greatest commandment.

GOD'S KINGDOM FORETOLD

Say among the nations: "The LORD reigns. The world is firmly established; it cannot be shaken. He judges the peoples fairly." —Psalm 96:10

On March 23, 1743, Handel's immortal oratorio, *The Messiah*, was sung in London for the first time. Present were many of the nobility of England, including King George II. As the first notes of the climactic "Hallelujah Chorus" sounded, and the words, "For the Lord God omnipotent reigneth," were heard, the king stood to his feet and remained standing until the final thrilling declaration: "And He shall reign forever and ever. Hallelujah!" Instantly upon the king's arising the audience was also on its feet. And so began a precedent of the audience standing whenever this chorus is sung.

Such a tribute should be more than a polite gesture to the music of Handel. It is an acknowledgment of Him who is King forever. Psalm 96 was sung at an annual "coronation service" in the temple at Jerusalem. The people of Israel, the nations of the earth, and finally all the natural world were summoned to exult in Him. Surely He is worthy of our praise.

So let us join with all the saints and sing to Him a new song. Let us bless His name, and proclaim His salvation. May we never tire of declaring His glory and His wonderful works. Amen.

■

Lord, we pray that the kingdom of this world may soon become the kingdoms of our Lord and of His Christ.

AN EVERLASTING KINGDOM

"In the days of those kings, the God of the heavens
will set up a kingdom that will never be destroyed,
and this kingdom will not be left to another people.
It will crush all these kingdoms and bring them to an
end, but will itself endure forever." —Daniel 2:44

Over the door of the Cathedral of Milan is this inscription: "All that pleases is but for a moment. All that troubles is but for a moment. That only is important which is Eternal." Whoever first wrote that took a firm stand on a vital matter. Find out what is enduring, give yourself to that, and you will have the secret of life's best use. And among these eternal things, says the inscription, neither pleasure nor trouble can be included.

Few lessons are harder to learn. We run after the things that please us, and run from the things that trouble us. But these are seasonal, temporal, while the kingdom of God is everlasting.

It was knowledge of the eternal nature of His kingdom that gave Jesus such confidence in the face of bitter opposition and disappointing results. "Heaven and earth will pass away," He said at the end of His earthly ministry, "but my words will never pass away" (Matt. 24:35). To His eternal kingdom we rejoice to belong.

■

Father, we ask for the wisdom to know the difference between
the temporal and the eternal, and a faith toward the everlasting.

A CROWN REFUSED

Therefore, when Jesus realized that they were about to come and take him by force to make him king, he withdrew again to the mountain by himself. —John 6:15

It takes strong determination to turn down an honor that looks plausible but deflects us from the highest, truest truth. It must have been a sore temptation to Jesus to permit the multitude whom He had fed to lift Him to their shoulders and go marching down the mountainside shouting that He was their King, that under His leadership they would become masters of their own destiny! The disciples evidently were taken in by the prospect, for the Gospels record that Jesus had to send them away before He could dismiss the crowd. Then He retired to pray. Did He feel at this point that the tempter who had "departed from him for a time" (Luke 4:13) in the wilderness had now returned in full force?

He refused this crown because acceptance of it meant abandoning the cross, turning from the sacrifice through which our redemption was to be made possible. It would have been to save Himself and to lose us instead. Only Jesus Christ, God's only begotten Son, would have the courage to spurn this easy victory and popular acclaim, and instead turn from escape and run toward His unfathomable sacrifice—all for us, "the joy that lay before Him" (Heb. 12:2).

It is only by Your grace, Jesus, that our hearts can turn and follow You. Strengthen our faith that we would reject any offer that turns us from Your purposes.

CHRIST, THE CENTER OF OUR FAITH

For there is one God and one mediator between God and humanity, the man Christ Jesus. —1 Timothy 2:5

"Aren't all religions seeking the same objective?" some people ask. "Isn't it true that what makes a good Christian makes another a good Jew, or Muslim, or Buddhist?"

Such a line of thought is nowhere suggested in the New Testament. Christ is not just the center of our faith; He is the only means by which any man comes to God.

Jesus said, "I am the way, the truth, and the life. No one comes to the Father except through me" (John 14:6). "There is salvation in no one else, for there is no other name under heaven given to people by which we must be saved" (Acts 4:12). These are not exceptions; they are examples of the New Testament's claim.

Does this imply that all other religions are wholly false? No, other religions share much with the teachings of our Christian faith. Some speak of God as our Bible does. Some are aware of the misery of life on Earth apart from God, even as we are. Some express the longing of man for salvation and his hope for life beyond death.

But the one thing which no other religion can offer is a Savior by whose death and resurrection all who put their trust in Him may have everlasting life.

Lord, give us courage to preach the unsearchable riches of Christ Jesus, that those who are lost may find abundant life in Him.

A NEW HOPE

For we know that if our earthly tent we live in is destroyed, we have a building from God, an eternal dwelling in the heavens, not made with hands. —2 Corinthians 5:1

The wind blows; you cannot see it, but the strength of it is there. It is something you cannot see, but you know it exists.

The butterfly unfolds itself from an ugly cocoon that once held an unsightly fuzzy caterpillar. No one denies the presence or the beauty of the butterfly, even if we did not see its metamorphosis with our own eyes.

A tiny seed buried deep in the ground grows into a mighty plant. An unexplainable, undeniable fact!

And just by the simple act of yielding our hearts to Jesus, we experience unsurpassed happiness, peace of mind, desire to serve, and desire to do God's will. Those who know Christ Jesus have felt and experienced this transformation in their own lives. It is as unexplainable and as real as the wind, or the butterfly, or the seed.

For those of us who have received Jesus' gift of salvation, the hope of a resurrection and eternal life is as real as all these other transformations. And so it is with great joy that we anticipate His coming glory and our eternal home with Him.

Thank You, God, for the promise and joy of knowing there is a resurrection after this life.

TOWARD A MATURE FAITH

But grow in the grace and knowledge of our Lord and Savior Jesus Christ. To him be the glory both now and to the day of eternity. —2 Peter 3:18

The orchid plant, though slow-growing and often un-comely as a show piece, may take as long as seven years before it reaches the maturity that produces that gorgeous blossom known as the "queen of flowers." Sometimes during its growth, the leaves may become so wrinkled and unlovely that only the expert grower would consider it worth saving. The fact is that the orchid conserves all its strength and loveliness for the day of maturity, when it will blossom forth in sheer perfection, as if by magic.

Growing in grace and in the knowledge of our Lord is a slow but sure process that reaches maturity through daily fellowship with Him through the years. Only experience in praying and receiving God's answers through trial, persecution, hardship, and all of life's ups and downs brings us to a mature, abiding, dynamic faith in Him.

When we stay close to Jesus, our faith will never remain at a standstill. It blossoms into maturity.

Lord, help me to remain steadfastly close to You. Help me to be still, to abide in Your presence.

ATONEMENT

But he was pierced because of our rebellion, crushed because of our iniquities; punishment for our peace was on him, and we are healed by his wounds. —Isaiah 53:5

For two thousand years, devout Christians have interpreted Isaiah 53 as an accurate portrayal of the sufferings of Christ in making atonement for man's sins. The purpose of atonement is to bring into a state of reconciliation, to make "at-one" those who previously were alienated from one another. Many people have thought that the purpose of Christ's atoning death on Calvary's cross was to reconcile God to man. However, we now see that the primary purpose of Christ's atonement was to reconcile man to God, and that, as Paul said, "in Christ, God was reconciling the world to himself, not counting their trespasses against them, and he has committed the message of reconciliation to us" (2 Cor. 5:19).

At the heart of all atonement is vicarious suffering, one person suffering voluntarily in order to redeem, reclaim, and bless another. But in order for such suffering to be effective, it must be accepted by the one for whom the sacrifice was made. And so as Christ followers, we should plead with our fellow man, even as the apostle Paul did, on the basis of Christ's suffering, "Be reconciled to God."

▪

Thank You, Jesus, for going to the cross to reconcile me to Yourself. I pray that others will come to know You and be reconciled to You, thanks to Your atoning death. I pray they, too, will become "at-one" with You.

THE CROSS CALLS US

I have been crucified with Christ, and I no longer live, but Christ lives in me. The life I now live in the body, I live by faith in the Son of God, who loved me and gave himself for me. —Galatians 2:20

In the ringing words of today's text, the apostle Paul gave his testimony that he had indeed been crucified with Christ and that he was alive unto God through Christ Jesus.

The cross calls us to be crucified with Christ. For Christ followers, the experience of the cross does not call for physical death but it does call for us to die to our own flesh. The cross also calls for us to be alive unto God. Following His crucifixion with Christ, the apostle Paul experienced a more definite awareness of Christ and a more complete identification with Christ than he had ever known. So vivid was this relationship with Christ that Paul was able to declare "Christ lives in me."

For those who trust in Jesus, the way of the cross leads home. It does not lead to death and destruction but to life abundant and life eternal.

Lord, I pray that all Christians will experience both death to sin and the indwelling presence of Christ.

LOVE FOR GOD'S BOOK

*I have your decrees as a heritage forever; indeed,
they are the joy of my heart. —Psalm 119:111*

You can learn a lot about people by observing the kind of books
they read. In a bookstore, young boys and girls will hurry toward
adventure books, brides-to-be might examine bridal magazines,
while pastors might browse in the Bible study section.

But the Bible is not just another book to be selected on the
basis of interest. It is THE Book. It is not simply what some
great and good men have said about God. It is what God is
saying to us, His people, through His Word.

You can learn a lot about a person's faith by observing their
treatment of the Bible. Do we keep it carefully tucked away on
a bookshelf, only to be referred to from time to time? Do we
only come to God's Word in times of crises? If so, we are miss-
ing out on life with the living, active Word of God (Heb. 4:12).
If it seems confusing, we need only to approach Scripture with
an open mind and prayerful spirit. If we ask God for help in
discerning His Word, He promises to reveal its meaning to us
(John 14:13–14).

Truly, this is the secret to a new life in Christ Jesus. May
the words of the Bible, the living Word of God, reach us and
penetrate our hearts and minds. May we be changed through
studying it.

*Thank You, God, for continuing to reveal
Yourself through Scripture.*

LOVE FOR OTHERS

*The one who loves his brother or sister remains in the light,
and there is no cause for stumbling in him.* —1 John 2:10

Have you ever analyzed your reasons for loving someone? Is
it because they are physically attractive? Because the person
is kind and considerate? Because they are a person of character and strength? In other words, do you love someone solely
because of their appealing qualities? Such is the way of human
love.

But some people are not very lovely. They may be unattractive in personality. Perhaps they are questionable in character. They may have repulsive habits. Or they just rub us the
wrong way without our being able to say why.

The Christian way is to love, not because of, but in spite
of. Christian love has a reason, but not a reason found in the
loved. Rather, it is found in the nature of the new life Christ.
We love because we are children of God. We love "because he
first loved us." We love because we see our brothers and sisters
through the eyes of the gospel of Christ. When all's said and
done, this is the sure mark of Christian character: "The one
who loves his brother or sister remains in the light, and there is
no cause for stumbling in him" (1 John 2:10).

■

*Lord, help us to recognize our opportunities to express our
love for one another, and in so doing, glorify Your name.*

CHRIST REIGNS

They said with a loud voice, Worthy is the Lamb who was slaughtered to receive power and riches and wisdom and strength and honor and glory and blessing! —Revelation 5:12

During the reign of Charles II over England, John James, an early Baptist minister, was hanged, and drawn and quartered. He was accused of a treasonable statement against the king, presumably because he had preached the ultimate Kingship of Jesus Christ.

In all ages and in every nation, Christians have declared the sovereignty of Christ. They are not discouraged that the conflict between good and evil seems to go on as long as the world lasts. They are not deceived by the apparent strength of the forces of evil. They know that the final victory belongs to the Lord (Ps. 3:8).

The certainty of Christ's sovereignty strengthens our faith in the face of conflict that goes on in our relationships and within our own hearts. We sometimes find ourselves torn between good and evil, between the will of God and the will of our own flesh. But we need not fear. With Christ as our King, we can fight any battles we face in this life with the confidence that evil will ultimately be overcome.

■

The victory belongs to You, Lord! May You reign supreme in all of my heart, mind, and life.

INVITATION FROM THE MASTER TEACHER

*"Take up my yoke and learn from me, because
I am lowly and humble in heart, and you will
find rest for your souls." —Matthew 11:29*

Give me your tired, your poor,
Your huddled masses yearning to breathe free,
The wretched refuse of your teeming shore . . .
—Emma Lazarus, *The New Colossus*

This classic invitation, inscribed on the base of the Statue of Liberty, has brought hope to many entering this country to begin a new life. Jesus issued a similar but greater invitation in our text for today, an invitation without geographic, racial, or national boundaries.

Jesus invites us to put on His yoke. We may have seen pictures of oxen or water buffalo laboring under a heavy wooden yoke. Surprisingly, Jesus used the yoke as a symbol of the Christ follower's surrender to Him as teacher and Lord. This is paramount to our lives, as Christians: dying to ourselves so that Christ may reign.

Do you find yourself weary? Are the burdens you're carrying weighing you down? Are you stuck? Then turn to Him and find the rest He waits to give you. "Humble yourselves, therefore, under the mighty hand of God, so that he may exalt you at the proper time, casting all your cares on him, because he cares about you" (1 Pet. 5:6–7).

*Lord, I humbly ask for the rest of soul that can
only come with complete surrender to You.*

SYMBOLS OF STRENGTH

Finally, be strengthened by the Lord and by his vast strength. —Ephesians 6:10

We often hear the phrase "a self-made man." In the Christian life, there are no self-made men. We begin the Christian life letting God remake us, and we continue it by depending, not upon our own resources, but upon God's. People who boast of their own strength, and those who complain endlessly about their inadequacies, have not learned the key to the Christian life.

The key to the Christian life is found in our text for today. It is true that Paul admonishes us to strengthen ourselves with Christian armor, but first he tells us to consider the source of our armor. We must look to God for strength before we even begin to dress for battle.

In John Milton's *Paradise Lost*, the devil is pictured as a gigantic figure with tremendous power. Adam and Eve are small by comparison, physically and mentally inferior. So it is today. When we seek to resist Satan in our own power, we are like a man fighting a tank with his bare hands. Only God is stronger than Satan; we must fight in his strength, or we need fight at all.

Lord, give me the strength to overcome Satan in the temptations of the day. Help me to stand and say to the enemy, as the archangel Michael did, "The Lord rebuke you!" (Jude 9).

THE SECRET OF STRENGTH

I pray that he may grant you, according to the riches
of his glory, to be strengthened with power in your
inner being through his Spirit. —Ephesians 3:16

From what we know of the apostle Paul, we may believe he was far more concerned with his inner man than with what the world thought of him. But we find just the opposite in today's culture, even among the Christian community. We spend the most of our life feeding, clothing, and amusing the outward person.

Why should the inner man be more important to Christians? The answer is in our text today. It is from the Holy Spirit within us that we draw our strength for the Christian life. Just as an electric light bulb is almost worthless until lit from within by an unseen power, so Christians are quite ineffective until the unseen Holy Spirit completely indwells their inner being.

So no matter our outward affliction or appearance; the Holy Spirit is at work in our hearts, transforming us day by day to be more like our Savior (2 Cor. 3:18). "Therefore we do not give up. Even though our outer person is being destroyed, our inner person is being renewed day by day. . . . So we do not focus on what is seen, but on what is unseen. For what is seen is temporary, but what is unseen is eternal" (2 Cor. 4:16–18).

■

God, help me not to be distracted by this world.
Instead, grant me a greater concern for the
condition of my heart, mind, and soul.

CHRISTIAN FAITH IN MODERN CULTURE

Do not be conformed to this age, but be transformed by the renewing of your mind, so that you may discern what is the good, pleasing, and perfect will of God. —Romans 12:2

Conformity has become a keynote of our society. Americans buy big cars one year and little ones the next because that is the thing to do. We furnish our homes with the latest in home decor and dress ourselves in the latest season of fast fashion—because everyone else is doing it. Unfortunately, we can carry this habit of conforming over into our spiritual lives. If it is fashionable to go to church on Sunday morning, we go then, but no more. Some of us allow culture to dictate our spiritual lives as well.

Conforming Christians have hurt the cause of Christianity immeasurably. Christianity purports to be a religion that transforms lives; but when unbelievers see no transformation, their skepticism is understandable.

Mahatma Gandhi, the great spiritual leader of India, although never professing to be a Christian, saw in the teachings of Christ a pattern for a nonconforming life. Gandhi was willing to sacrifice all, even his life, for those things in which he believed. If we are not willing to be different because of our beliefs, we cannot expect the world to think our cause very important.

■

Lord, please give me the conviction and courage to be different for the sake of Christ, making Your name great in a lost and broken world.

THE GREAT ILLUMINATOR

Now God has revealed these things to us by the
Spirit, since the Spirit searches everything, even
the depths of God. —1 Corinthians 2:10

How much do we know of "the deep things of God"? Most Christians live on the surface of spiritual experiences and never explore those depths of truth where rich treasures are to be found.

God has given us His Holy Spirit to help us to know these things and benefit from them. He leads us to have a stronger devotion to the Lord Jesus and a deeper hunger for insights into the divine Word.

Not all can experience these blessings for they have no appetite for them. But this should never be true of us as Christ followers. Our hearts should always desire to know more of Him and to abide in His presence.

This desire can be satisfied through the Holy Spirit. "God sent the Spirit of his Son into our hearts, crying, 'Abba, Father!'" (Gal. 4:6). God is speaking to us by His Spirit even now. Stop your fighting, we will hear Him and know that He is God (Ps. 46:10).

■

Lord, we ask that Your Holy Spirit may show us the deeper
things of God and enable us to lead others to Jesus.

THE COMING DAY OF THE LORD

But I am not ashamed, because I know whom I have believed and am persuaded that he is able to guard what has been entrusted to me until that day. —2 Timothy 1:12

When someone puts their valuables in a safety deposit box in the vault of a bank, they trust that those items are safe. The person can count on finding them when they go back to the bank, no matter how much time may have passed.

Paul had committed his life and soul to Jesus, and he knew he could trust his treasure in Jesus' hands against "that day"— any day, every day, and especially the coming day of judgment.

> How did he know these things? Because of the words of strong assurance that Jesus Himself had spoken. "My sheep hear my voice, I know them, and they follow me. I give them eternal life, and they will never perish. No one will snatch them out of my hand. My Father, who has given them to me, is greater than all. No one is able to snatch them out of the Father's hand. I and the Father are one." (John 10:27–29)

In the double grip of Father and Son, Paul was safe for time and eternity. And so are we.

■

Lord, we ask that our faith be strengthened, so that our sense of security in Christ may stir us to share the gospel.

WHO IS MY NEIGHBOR?

*"Which of these three do you think proved
to be a neighbor to the man who fell into the
hands of the robbers?" —Luke 10:36*

The lawyer who asked Jesus how he could inherit eternal life was well acquainted with the demands of the Jewish law. He claimed ignorance, however, as to how far his responsibility went in carrying it out. We, too, may be tempted to seek ways of escape from responsibility in an equally subtle manner. We may, for example, forget about the personal application of this parable by directing our attention to the seeming faults of the lawyer.

We can also evade the issue by thinking about the priest and the Levite who were too callous to relieve human suffering when they saw it. We may even thank God that we are not as unfeeling as they are—and fail to see those same faults in ourselves.

We need to face some searching questions about parallel situations today. What about the family who needed help but we were too busy to go help them? Did we pass it off as the responsibility of others when our pastor told us about the needs of the church or on the mission field? To fail to recognize that the story of the good Samaritan carries a command and a caution for us today is to turn a deaf ear to the Master's message.

*Lord, make my heart willing and my mind alert to
the opportunities I have to be a good neighbor.*

THE EXAMPLE OF JESUS

For I have given you an example, that you also should do just as I have done for you. —John 13:15

Jesus had taught His disciples on many occasions that the greatest is always the one who serves most unselfishly, but His words had never penetrated their hearts. Luke tells us that while they were in the upper room with the Master, there as "a dispute also arose among them about who should be considered the greatest" (Luke 22:24).

And so it was essential that they receive a lesson on true love that they would always remember. They had not heeded His words, but they would never forget His demonstration of selfless love when He washed their feet. His lesson was for us, also.

Yes, "faith, if it doesn't have works, is dead by itself" (James 2:17). But empty acts aren't what Jesus is calling us to. "The sacrifice pleasing to God is a broken spirit. [He] will not despise a broken and humbled heart (Ps. 51:17).

Wherever He is calling us to serve, He's calling us to do so, first and foremost, with love. In everything, God desires and conspires to win the hearts of His children.

■

Father, grow in me the selfless love You modeled for us in Your Word.

THE CHEERFUL GIVER

Each person should do as he has decided in his heart—not reluctantly or out of compulsion, since God loves a cheerful giver. —2 Corinthians 9:7

When it comes to giving to God, the question that often comes up is, "Where should we draw the line?"

There are some who draw a protective line around their worldly possessions. Others can be impulsive and inconsistent in their giving. They may give freely today, and then go for a long period of time before giving again, when it's convenient. The truth is, even as people who love Jesus, we can find it easy to spend lavishly on ourselves, but a good bit harder to give to God a very small portion of what we have.

God wants us to become cheerful givers because that is the kind of giver He is. When we step back to consider the entire course of our lives, we can trace another line—one of God's faithful provision. Learning to see His faithfulness, the abundance of gifts He freely gives, will no doubt grow in us the desire to give. It's in sharing our finite resources with the Church that we get to participate in the divine and infinite work of the Lord.

Sometimes we forget that we belong to a Father in heaven, we live like orphans hoarding His gifts (Exodus 16), fearful we can only count on ourselves to provide. But the truth is that we are sons and daughters of the King, who has infinite resources and gives generously.

■

Lord, please loosen my grip on my worldly possessions, and free up my heart to be generous with what You've given me.

SEEK TRUE RIGHTEOUSNESS

*But seek first the kingdom of God and his righteousness, and
all these things will be provided for you. —Matthew 6:33*

Solomon, given the opportunity to request whatever he most
wanted, asked for wisdom and knowledge that he might wor-
thily fulfill the duties of a king. And he got his wish—but, with
it, God gave him much more.

> "God said to Solomon, 'Since this was in your
> heart, and you have not requested riches, wealth,
> or glory, or for the life of those who hate you, and
> you have not even requested long life, but you have
> requested for yourself wisdom and knowledge that
> you may judge my people over whom I have made
> you king, wisdom and knowledge are given to you.
> I will also give you riches, wealth, and glory, unlike
> what was given to the kings who were before you,
> or will be given to those after you.'" (2 Chron.
> 1:11–12)

We may grasp at whatever material gain we want, but sooner
or later God, in His kindness, shows us that those things will
not satisfy us. That's why He tells us to seek His Kingdom
first, and then all things and opportunities will fall into place
according to His good and perfect will for us. When we put
first the interests of God's Kingdom, we gain so much more:
a desire for the things of eternal significance—things that are
"imperishable, undefiled, and unfading, kept in heaven for
you" (1 Pet. 1:4).

■

*Lord, I am grateful that You know what I truly
need. I pray to desire Your best for my life, and
to seek Your purposes before all else.*

CALL TO DISCIPLESHIP

Calling the crowd along with his disciples, he said to them, "If anyone wants to follow after me, let him deny himself, take up his cross, and follow me." —Mark 8:34

As children, we used to play the game of follow the leader. As we grew older, but not much wiser, this ceased to be a game and more a part of life. Only now we weren't walking fences or balancing a stick on our chins; unconsciously, we mimicked each other's conduct, at times, even when we didn't agree with it. No one knew why; it was simply the thing to do.

We weren't actually following the leader now—after all, no one really ever knew or saw the kid up front. Instead, we were "following the follower," the one just ahead of us.

This may still be true for us today; but it shouldn't be if we know Jesus. He calls us to follow—to follow Him so closely that we will learn to do what He did, learn to love how He loves, and learn to take up our cross.

It is good to surround ourselves with wise men and women who love Jesus, but when it comes to living life well, we need not look further than His example.

Jesus, give me a heart that chooses to follow You. And please strengthen my faith to actually do so.

PARABLES ON DISCIPLESHIP

"For which of you, wanting to build a tower, doesn't first sit down and calculate the cost to see if he has enough to complete it?" —Luke 14:28

An undisciplined life is an unexamined life. It knows no peace. Like a flooded river, it spills over its banks and works havoc in the valleys it was meant to irrigate. A river is at peace only as it stays within its appointed limits. The undisciplined life knows neither its origin nor its destiny. It can neither define its present nor plan its future. It has nothing to hang its heart upon, no one in whom to confide. Things happen to it, but it causes little to happen with intent. Wanting only to be free, to be full, and to be secure, it remains empty, enslaved, and apprehensive.

But as disciples of Jesus Christ, we are called to be disciplined. It's important to know our limitations, and to live and work within them. It's good to know our beginning and our end. As Christ followers, our lives are "hidden with Christ in God" (Col. 3:3)—He supplies us with what we need. His ultimate goal for us is the sea of eternity. As children of God, we are not simply creatures of this time—we bear an eternal family resemblance.

■

Lord, "Search me, God, and know my heart; test me and know my concerns. See if there is any offensive way in me; lead me in the everlasting way" (Ps. 139:23–24).

REWARDS OF DISCIPLESHIP

*"[He] will not receive a hundred times more, now
at this time—houses, brothers and sisters, mothers
and children, and fields, with persecutions—and
eternal life in the age to come." —Mark 10:30*

Life has only two roads: away from God and toward Him. At
first glance, one is more inviting that the other. One way is
level, shaded, well-paved, offering at each turn and bend an
increasingly pleasant view. But it leads nowhere in particular
and at journey's end there is nothing but disappointment, dis-
illusionment, and death.

The other way might be, at times, tortuously uphill, rocky
and steep. But it leads to God and lasting satisfaction. But the
traveler does not journey alone; his Lord is with him. And he
endures as God endures, finding in life significance, meaning,
and purpose—and quite possibly, adventure:

"You reveal the path of life to me;
in your presence is abundant joy;
at your right hand are eternal pleasures." (Ps. 16:11)

These are the questions we need to answer: Where am I
headed? Is my face or my back toward Christ? What am I seeking? Is it permanent or will it pass away? Am I permanent, or
will I, too, pass away?

■

*Lord God, please make Your way known to me that I may
follow it in faith and even see it as a great adventure with You.*

INDIVIDUAL RESPONSIBILITY

"If I want him to remain until I come," Jesus answered,
"what is that to you? As for you, follow me." —John 21:22

What we call grace is God's overture to us. What we call faith is our personal response. Life without God is like dwelling in a dark and lonely room, with only one window—and even that with a drawn shade. In the darkness, things are grotesque and obscure, and even a whisper becomes a shout. Outside the room the sun shines even on the window with the drawn shade. But the occupant inside does not know it. Yet the warmth of the sun will penetrate. The grace of God is like that. And what we call faith is the response of the dweller in the darkness as he goes to the window and raises the shade, allowing the light of the love of God to shine within.

There is no substitute for that individual response. Others may be nearer the window but we can only raise it for ourselves. Each in our own way has to respond to the grace of God for ourselves. And the light of the love of God will come flooding in, inviting the dweller in the darkness out into a brighter world.

■

Lord, may we respond to Your gift of grace this
day in whatever way You present it to us.

THE KINGDOM TRIUMPHANT

*The seventh angel blew his trumpet, and there were loud
voices in heaven saying, The kingdom of the world has
become the kingdom of our Lord and of his Christ, and
he will reign forever and ever. —Revelation 11:15*

In this last book of the Bible we are in the presence of great
mystery, and at the heart of the mystery is God Himself. We
cannot fully know Him (Can you hold the ocean in your
hands?), but we can increasingly love Him. Though we may
not comprehend Him, we may yet know Him—responding to
His commands and committing our lives to His keeping.

As Christ followers, are we asked to do more than this?
Our understanding of God may be incomplete, but it is nei-
ther blind nor ignorant, for we know what Christ is like, and
He has said, "Have I been among you all this time and you do
not know me, Philip? The one who has seen me has seen the
Father. How can you say, 'Show us the Father'?" (John 14:9).

This Christ, who is the image of the invisible God, is victorious. His kingdom is an everlasting kingdom. The tides of
history remove the works of men, and, for all their seeming
strength, empires and dominions rise and fall. But Christ has
triumphs yet in store, to be shared by those whose trust is in
Him.

■

*Father, I ask for faith in Your future and in Jesus
Christ, whom You've appointed Lord of the future.*

DEDICATED MINDS, COMMITTED HEARTS

Set your minds on things above,
not on earthly things. —Colossians 3:2

The human mind is a wonder in and of itself, designed by our Creator God. Modern psychology is stressing more and more the importance of what the Bible has been telling us all along: the mind exercises a tremendous influence on the body; the two are very much connected.

Jesus said, "Love the Lord your God with all your heart, with all your soul, and with all your mind" (Matt. 22:37). And in doing so, we are to set our affections (minds) on things above (Col. 3:2).

Surely, there are plenty enough distractions in this world; but just as Jesus Christ was not of this world, neither are we (John 17:16). Which is why Paul says, "Do not be conformed to this age, but be transformed by the renewing of your mind, so that you may discern what is the good, pleasing, and perfect will of God" (Rom. 12:2).

As Christ followers, we're called to spiritual discipline, to "take every thought captive to obey Christ" (2 Cor. 10:5). "For where [our] treasure is, there [our] heart will be" (Matt. 6:21). So we must ask ourselves, "What do I treasure? Where does my mind wander off to? What do I meditate on?" For whatever it is, that is our heart's true affection, what we truly love.

Lord, Your thoughts and ways are higher, better than mine. Help me to treasure what You treasure. May my mind be dedicated to You. May my heart learn to love You best.

PRACTICAL INSTRUCTIONS

*In all your ways know him, and he will make
your paths straight.* —Proverbs 3:6

The book of Proverbs is a veritable treasure house of wisdom. This particular passage abounds with precious promises to those who follow after God and are committed to His ways. Among the rewards promised are length of life, peace, understanding, and guidance.

To those who acknowledge God in all their ways, light and direction will be given. To acknowledge God means more than to profess with the lips a vague acquaintance with Him. It is much more than subscribing to a creed or giving intellectual assent to a proposition. An acknowledgment of God implies a faithful endeavor to find and to follow His will. It means we are aware of our constant need of His divine hand to lead us and a willingness to follow where He leads.

Jesus promised this world bring trouble (John 16:33), but we cannot navigate our circumstances on our own. He alone is able to untangle the messiness of life's threads. But we don't have to. We can trust in Him and His knowledge, rather than our own understanding (Prov. 3:5). In doing so, we acknowledge that He is God, and we are not.

■

*Lord, we ask that we may be given wisdom, courage,
and faith to acknowledge God in all we do and say.*

DEDICATED POSSESSIONS

Everyone whose heart was moved and whose spirit prompted him came and brought an offering to the LORD for the work on the tent of meeting, for all its services, and for the holy garments. —Exodus 35:21

The Christian concept of stewardship rests upon the idea that God owns everything and that we, His children, are merely trustees. All that we have comes from God and to Him we are responsible. Our time, our talent, our money—our all—are His.

The basic theological premise of the Old Testament is that God is the sovereign Creator and is therefore the Lord of all creation. It is also clearly pointed out that God has entrusted to man much that He has made. Whatever we call our own, therefore, whether much or little, is to be dedicated to God. This simply means that our possessions should be placed at His disposal to be used of Him according to His will and purpose. This, of course, involves giving, and giving is primarily a matter of the heart.

In today's reading, we saw the Israelite community bring what they had to give to the Lord. What is even more important is that they did so after their spirits were made willing.

Father God, we ask for hearts that are willing to give our best for You.

THE GREAT INVITATION

*See! I stand at the door and knock. If anyone hears my
voice and opens the door, I will come in to him and
eat with him, and he with me. —Revelation 3:20*

Dwight L. Moody, the famed evangelist, used to say that he
did not claim to understand all the mysteries of God's elect-
ing grace. He refused to be drawn into debate concerning the
questions of predestination and fore-ordination. He said that it
was his thought that when Jesus appeared to John on the Isle
of Patmos, He wanted to make it unmistakably plain that He
meant for all to come. That accounts for the "everyone who
believes in him will not perish but have eternal life" (John 3:16).

Certainly no one will be denied who will accept the Savior's
willingness to enter if he will but open the door. This knock is
for all who will hear and heed the voice of Jesus Christ. He will
not enter, however, until we open the door. He will not come in
as an uninvited guest and will not force His way in. But once
He enters the door of our heart, a fellowship will begin that
will endure through all eternity.

This is beyond the sweetest invitation ever given on Earth.
To heed His invitation is to have abundant and eternal life. To
reject it means ultimate and complete loss forevermore.

■

*Jesus, crack my heart wide open that I might share the
gospel—Your incomparable invitation—with all the world.*

A REFORM THAT FAILED

"Why do you call me 'Lord, Lord,' and don't do the things I say?" —Luke 6:46

Josiah was a good king. He set about to cleanse his kingdom of its iniquity. He led his people to renew their vows and to enter into covenant with God. A great reform movement swept the land as a consequence. The reformation was short-lived, however, in spite of the good intentions of the king. It failed because it was not rooted deeply enough in the hearts of the people.

Mere reformation is never enough by itself. It is not sufficient merely to depart from evil. We must do good. To turn away from something without turning toward something or Someone creates a spiritual and moral vacuum into which evil comes pouring out like a flood. Our condition then becomes worse than it ever was before.

The people of Josiah's kingdom failed to keep covenant with God. To confess with our lips and to deny with our lives is hypocritical. It is worse than useless to call on the Lord's name, and then refuse to do His bidding. Reformation apart from regeneration often results in degeneration. It has been suggested that to call Jesus "Lord" is orthodoxy; to call Him "Lord, Lord," is piety; but to call Him "Lord, Lord" and then disobey Him is hypocrisy.

■

*Lord, forgive me for when I've called upon You
with my lips without obeying You in my heart
and action. I repent of this hypocrisy.*

ANSWERING GOD'S CALL

*So Abram went, as the LORD had told him, and
Lot went with him. Abram was seventy-five years
old when he left Haran. —Genesis 12:4*

The Bible is always its own best commentary. In that great roll of the heroes of faith, in Hebrews 11, we are told of Abraham that "he went out, even though he did not know where he was going" (Heb. 11:8). He did not lack divine promises and assurances, but the test of his faith was in his willingness to leave his home in Ur of the Chaldees without any precise knowledge of his ultimate destination. Each successive day, he believed, would bring its own guidance from a loving, all-wise God, who knows the end from the beginning. In God's own good time, life's goal would be reached and life's reward enjoyed.

The world has little but mocking laughter for this pilgrim philosophy. It demands to see where it is going. It reckons security in terms of facts and has little patience with the child of God who walks by faith, not by sight. And even we who know the Lord are sometimes weaned away from that childlike trust by which we first entered the Kingdom and must eventually attain the crown. We must find encouragement in God's goodness, remembering His past faithfulness, so that we may have courage for today.

*Lord, I humbly ask for a stronger faith in You.
Give me eyes to see Your faithful work in my life.
And thank You for loving me so well.*

GOD'S PROMISE RENEWED

*Abram believed the LORD, and he credited it
to him as righteousness. —Genesis 15:6*

After some great sorrow or trial, we're inclined to say, "I could never have faced life if I had known in advance what was going to happen." Is this an acknowledgment of the weakness of our faith? God had sufficient confidence in Abraham to tell him calamitous news before it happened. As yet no son was born to the patriarch; the first star of the myriads promised had yet to rise in his sky. And yet here was God telling him that those descendants he had yet to see would go on to spend 400 years in slavery!

God knows and reckons with the mighty forces that stand between His children and the realization of His purposes for them. He has no uncertainty as to the final outcome. "You will be hated by everyone because of my name," said Jesus to His disciples; "But the one who endures to the end will be saved" (Matt. 10:22). He tells us the worst, but He also tells us the best. As believers, we are not promised a life that's a picnic. Satan will see to it that the road to heaven is fraught with difficulty and danger. But God is pledged to bring every trusting child of His to the safety and joy of the promised land.

■

*Lord, please grant me a faith that will
not shrink in the face of trial.*

GOD OF THE IMPOSSIBLE

Is anything impossible for the LORD? At the appointed time I will come back to you, and in about a year she will have a son" —Genesis 18:14

Do we believe in miracles? As lovers of God's Word, we must. The Bible is worthless if its records of supernatural events are untrue. Some skeptical souls may doubt them; but the believing heart accepts God's miraculous presence throughout history—all the way from the division of the Red Sea to the virgin birth of Jesus—displaying the victory of the supernatural over the natural.

Sarah probably believed in miracles, in general terms. She would scarcely have shared Abraham's long wanderings if she had not also, in some measure, shared his faith. But believing that miracles happen is one thing; believing that they will happen to us personally, is another. Our circumstances, we tell ourselves, are different; our problems are unique, our plight beyond remedy. But our shallow laughter of unbelief is drowned out by the glorious assurance of God's voice: "Is anything impossible for the Lord?"

Lord, please grow in me the ability to say, out of deep experience, "No, nothing is impossible for You, Lord."

FAITH'S GREATEST TEST

Abraham answered, "God himself will provide the lamb for the burnt offering, my son." Then the two of them walked on together. —Genesis 22:8

The practice of holding for ransom contains a concealed tribute to human nature. The kidnapper operates on the belief that somebody cares enough for his victim to pay heavily for their release. With all his perversion of mind and hardness of heart, he recognizes that there is such a thing as protective love.

Abraham loved Isaac as his son, and with peculiar intensity, because all the promises of God were centered on the young man. If Isaac had died under sacrificial knife, it is questionable whether his physical suffering could have equaled the mental and spiritual anguish of Abraham.

Some critics of atonement question the action of a loving God for inflicting suffering and death on His innocent Son, Jesus. But Paul had deeper insights. He saw that, "in Christ, God was reconciling the world to himself" (2 Cor. 5:19). God the Father was no passive onlooker at Calvary. As it was of Abraham and Isaac, so it is of the divine Father and Son: "The two of them walked on together."

■

Lord Jesus, grow my faith so that I might desire to participate in "the fellowship of [Your] sufferings," for Your glory and the good of others.

SEEKING THE HEAVENLY LAND

*For he was looking forward to the city that has foundations,
whose architect and builder is God. —Hebrews 11:10*

The history of exploration is an epic to thrill the heart. Brave men have faced terrible odds, and endured bitter disappointments, to satisfy their longing to set foot in lands that were once unknown. Columbus showed a commendable spirit of determination in his effort to enlist royal patronage for his voyages. It is a pity that many early explorers wasted their time and other people's money searching for the nonexistent—the lost continent of Atlantis, for example, or the site of the Fountain of Youth.

Abraham was not in this company. The land for which he sacrificed home and security, becoming a wanderer for many years, was as sure as the promises of God. Canaan, with all its rivers of milk and honey, was not his destination. Earthly gain is never the ultimate destination for God's faithful children. Sometimes it is found. Sometimes it eludes our grasp. But, at journey's end, for all who go forth at God's command, there is "the city that has foundations, whose architect and builder is God."

◾

*With heaven in our hearts, Lord, help us to live for You,
and to share the gospel of our Savior with others.*

A DIVIDED HOME

"Suppose my father touches me. Then I will be revealed to him as a deceiver and bring a curse rather than a blessing on myself." —Genesis 27:12

What causes a home to be divided? In reality, there are many reasons. Usually the reasons could more properly serve to produce unity, should the responsible parties so desire. The twin sons, Esau and Jacob, could have brought happiness and solidarity to the home of Isaac and Rebekah. Instead, the father selected the firstborn as his favorite, and the mother chose the cunning Jacob to receive her special love and affection. And in the end, a deceitful mother helped to create hatred between the twin brothers.

What causes a home to be united? The reasons are, likewise, many. One is the sharing of a common goal. A husband and wife are two separate persons, but their goals for the children must be one if the home is to remain united. An important goal is expressed by Paul in Ephesians 6:4: "Fathers, don't stir up anger in your children, but bring them up in the training and instruction of the Lord."

Lord, we ask that You lead us to establish and strengthen our homes upon You. May we desire to make Your name great within our own families as well as our communities.

A STOLEN BLESSING

So Jacob came closer to his father Isaac. When he touched him, he said, "The voice is the voice of Jacob, but the hands are the hands of Esau." —Genesis 27:22

Jacob reluctantly obeyed the instructions of Rebekah, his mother, deceived his father, and received the blessing. Rebekah remembered the message of the Lord given to her before the birth of the sons: "And the older will serve the younger" (Gen. 25:23). But she apparently determined that it would be necessary for her to intercede, even to the point of persuading Jacob to steal the blessing, thereby forcing Esau to fulfill God's message to her. She did not realize, nor did Jacob at the time, that it was God who had already decreed that Jacob should be the chosen one.

Is it not true that we often try to run ahead of the Lord and strive for things to happen according to our plans? Do we sometimes act and then hope we have followed God's will rather than seek His will before acting? Jacob stole a blessing from his father, which was intended for his brother. But he did not steal the favor of God. "So then, it does not depend on human will or effort but on God who shows mercy" (Rom. 9:16).

Lord, we need Your grace and mercy to be with us. Without Your presence, this life is empty, as are our plans apart from You.

A LOST OPPORTUNITY

*When Esau heard his father's words, he cried out
with a loud and bitter cry and said to his father,
"Bless me too, my father!"* —Genesis 27:34

As compared with his father Abraham and his son Jacob, Isaac
was not an outstanding character. He was actually a bridge
between these two. And now we have the account of his son
Esau, who, like his father, was not very ambitious. He was
a sportsman who seemed to have had little time for spiritual things. Esau would probably have said that his mother
Rebekah, in concert with her favorite son Jacob the schemer,
caused him to lose his opportunity to receive the blessing. But
God, who sees beyond time and circumstances, had known
the two and had chosen Jacob, who later became a spiritual
leader.

We can lose opportunities for useful service when we desire
to receive spiritual blessings rather than be a spiritual blessing
to others. Our Savior, Jesus Christ, is the perfect example of
this. "He emptied himself by assuming the form of a servant"
(Phil. 2:7). As Christ followers, may the deepest desire of our
hearts be to serve others in Jesus' name and for His glory.

Father, we humbly ask for "the mind of Christ" in serving others.

A VISION AND A VOW

"When Jacob awoke from his sleep, he said, "Surely the Lord is in this place, and I did not know it." —Genesis 28:16

The important turning point in Jacob's life did not actually come when his aged father bestowed the blessing upon him. It actually came in the vision, as he responded to the presence of God. Now he was away from the divisive influence of Isaac and Rebekah. He was ready to assert himself as an individual and was responsive to the message of God.

In *Studies in Genesis*, Dr. B. H. Carroll writes "There is evidence of [Jacob's] conversion, his keen sense of divine presence and realization of the import of divine communication, his recognition, as if for the first time in his hitherto unworthy life, of his relation to God and the fixed purpose that came into his heart from that time on to serve God, to honor God with the first fruits."

The important turning point for us as Christ followers is the moment of convergence when we see ourselves as sinners; we see the Lord Jesus Christ as our Savior; we turn from our lives of sin and shame; and embrace the life of faith in Jesus. This is the moment we are ready to make our own vow to commit our whole lives to Christ's lordship.

■

Thank You, Jesus, for pursuing my heart. I pray today for my friends and family who have not turned to You in faith. Give me the courage to share the truth of the gospel with them.

BLESSING THROUGH SUBMISSION

"I am unworthy of all the kindness and faithfulness you have shown your servant. Indeed, I crossed over the Jordan with my staff, and now I have become two camps." —Genesis 32:10

A strange and marvelous spiritual transformation came to the life of Jacob. This one who deceived his father and brother to guarantee a parental traditional blessing, now humbly prays to God, "I am unworthy of all the kindness and faithfulness you have shown your servant." He is now willing to submit himself to God's plan, in order that it might be fulfilled in his life. He is now seeking the favor of God, rather than attempting to steal it.

As a result of this transformation and persistence to do the will of God, Jacob, whose name literally means "a supplanter" is given a new name, "Israel," meaning "a prince of God." And God did bless him and guide him, and assured him, "Do not be afraid to go down to Egypt, for I will make you into a great nation there" (Gen. 46:3).

When we humbly submit ourselves to do the will of God, we are assured of His spiritual blessings. Life will not be easy, as it was not for Israel. It is not the easy life but the eternal spiritual values that bring true happiness.

∎

Thank You, Father, for the abundant mercies You've provided in my life. Truly, You are good Father, caring for me in ways I could never ask or think (Eph. 3:20).

REUNITED WITH GOD

But Esau ran to meet him, hugged him, threw his arms around him, and kissed him. Then they wept. —Genesis 33:4

There are not many scenes described in the Old Testament which could provide a more touching emotional scene than the one in today's text. This is the same Esau who said, "The days of mourning for my father are approaching; then I will kill my brother Jacob" (Gen. 27:41).

And yet it is not the same Esau, nor the same Jacob, who stole his blessing. Each is now concerned for the other's welfare. Jacob comes to Esau not as his lord, but as his servant, offering him a blessing. And so he gives God the credit for his heart's transformation: "Because God has been gracious to me and I have everything I need" (Gen. 33:11). The dramatic scene of their reunion is enlarged by the presence of Leah, Rachel, the twelve sons, and the servants with their children, plus a host of animals.

We who have the joy of being in a family with brothers and sisters are truly blessed by the Lord. We may be separated most of the time, but the same love and devotion, though flawed and imperfect, abides where there is a shared faith in Christ.

■

Lord, I humbly ask that You make me a spiritual blessing to my own family.

WHY DOES GOD LET IT HAPPEN?

Look, his ego is inflated; he is without integrity. But the righteous one will live by his faith. —Habakkuk 2:4

The prevailing attitudes of Habakkuk's day can still be found in our own culture today. Have you ever been asked the question, "Why does God allow those who reject Him to live in luxury and command such power in the world?" Habakkuk went directly to God for the answer to this question. Of this encounter, author Kyle M. Yates writes: "When his doubts arose and he could not reconcile a bad world with a good God and a righteous law, he refused utterly to dismiss his doubts without an answer. He was honest and fearless and dogged in his determination to find the solution to the perplexing and conflicting problems."*

Habakkuk waited patiently for God's answer. And in essence, God's answer was this: Even though those who do harm exist now, and seem to prosper, their sin contains the seeds of their own destruction. If they remain in their sin, they will surely fall, while the righteous by faith will live on forever. The "faith" mentioned in verse 4, is not merely some abstract term. It speaks of a very real, deeply rooted faith in God.

***

Lord, I pray for all those who love Jesus and call on His name, that they may remain steadfast despite discouragement; and for those who remain dead in their trespasses, that they may turn from their sin to the living Savior, Jesus Christ.

* Kyle M. Yates, *Preaching From the Prophets* (Nashville: Baptist Sunday School Board, 1953), 152–53.

THE FOLLY OF FAVORITISM

Now Israel loved Joseph more than his other sons because Joseph was a son born to him in his old age, and he made a robe of many colors for him. —Genesis 37:3

The opening words of the Lord's Prayer set the stage for a proper relationship between parents and children. "Our Father" means that He is wholly Father to each one of us. The Father gives a complete and special love to each of us, which makes all of God's children individual and yet equal.

Israel was the child of a mother who showed favoritism toward him in relation to his brother Esau. Now "bringing the fathers' iniquity on the children and grandchildren . . ." (Exod. 34:7) as Israel made Joseph the apple of his eye.

Favoritism tends to create snobbery in the favored and resentment in the unfavored. The coat of many colors is a symbol of a common folly.

How can we stop a sinful succession of favoritism today? The clue to success is to examine our hearts and admit our true feelings of resentment or pride related to favoritism. Then, we must let Jesus, the One who became a servant, wash away our wrong attitudes, and renew our hearts and minds to align with His.

■

Father, help me to love all members of my family in a special way, so that none will feel neglected.

GOD'S OVERRULING PROVIDENCE

And now don't be grieved or angry with yourselves for selling me here, because God sent me ahead of you to preserve life. —Genesis 45:5

Have you ever heard the statement, "Whatever happens is best"? Well, it's not a biblical truth; it comes directly from Stoic philosophy.

Whatever happens is not necessarily best. Misery, injustice, and sin are all about us in much that happens. God has not willed these things, and they are not best. It was terribly wrong for Joseph's brothers to sell him into slavery. But in the end, God replaced Joseph's bloodstained coat of many colors with royal robes because Joseph was obedient to His will.

But very quickly it must be added that God's overruling providence steps in to help make all things work together for the good of those who love God (Rom. 8:28). The sin of Joseph's brothers was transformed into an instrument to help save them all (Gen. 45:4–8). The Bible teaches that God has a plan and a purpose which will be fulfilled in history (Isa. 14:24).

The ultimate truth is that the greatest tragedy in life is in our never knowing Jesus Christ as our Lord and Savior. Life apart from Him, lost and broken in our sin, is a life of darkness. But even this serves to contrast and highlight God's purposes and His faithfulness.

◼

Lord, we ask that our lives might be found in Your will, so that what we do will have eternal significance and serve to make Your name great.

GOD'S CHOICE FOR LEADERSHIP

The LORD replied to Moses, "Take Joshua son of Nun, a man who has the Spirit in him, and lay your hands on him." —Numbers 27:18

Moses, after serving as God's leader before the people of Israel for forty years, was being discharged. Nothing had been done or said about a successor. Here was an army in the field about to change leaders. This could be hazardous. Some men cannot endure the sight of their successors, but Moses earnestly desired to see his in place before he died. So he sought the appointment of a new leader.

Only God knew who had the ability, wisdom, and valor to lead the people. "The LORD replied to Moses, 'Take Joshua son of Nun, a man who has the Spirit in him, and lay your hands on him'" (Num. 27:18).

Before the congregation and the priest Eleazer, Moses "laid his hands on [Joshua], and commissioned him, as the LORD had spoken through Moses" (vv. 22–23) The outgoing leader, because of his experience and relationship with the Lord, comforted, strengthened, and encouraged the new leader.

When a church, or any part of it, needs a man to entrust with high responsibilities, "the God who gives breath to all" (v. 16) can bring forth the man who's being called into service.

God, I humbly ask that You would give me eyes to see and recognize Your will at work, and to help others to do the same.

CONTINUING PRESENCE

The LORD spoke to Joshua: "Today I will begin to exalt you in the sight of all Israel, so they will know that I will be with you just as I was with Moses." —Joshua 3:7

In prayer, Moses had spoken to God and now was listening. "Confer some of your authority on him so that the entire Israelite community will obey him" (Num. 27:20). Then as a father bestows his knowledge, character, spirit, position, and wealth upon his son, Moses turned to Joshua in front of the people and taught him to listen to God, and to receive Him.

Later, "The LORD spoke to Joshua: 'Today I will begin to exalt you'" (Josh. 3:7). Events then began to take place that would have brought joy to the heart of Moses.

The ark of the covenant became the symbol of the presence and leadership of God, instead of the cloud. The twelve bearing the ark of the covenant touched the flooded Jordan River, and it banked high. Below, the river ran dry. With jubilation, the people crossed and gathered stones from the floor of the river to make an altar to honor God.

Then the people observed their new leader more closely, and heard him sounding out orders to the forty thousand fighting men, "On that day the LORD exalted Joshua in the sight of all Israel, and they revered him throughout his life, as they had revered Moses" (Josh. 4:14).

◼

Thank You, God, that Your presence is always with me, that, because of Jesus, it will never leave me.

POWER THROUGH PRAYER

So the LORD listened to Elijah, and the boy's life came into him again, and he lived. —1 Kings 17:22

One of the great words of the New Testament is "power." It's derived from the same Greek word from which we get "dynamic" and "dynamite." God's power has endured through the centuries—from creation through Elijah's experience with the dead boy, through the New Testament, and to the twenty-first century today.

How do we make contact with God's dynamic spiritual force? How do we experience the power and presence of God? By prayer, meditation, and supplication. "Whatever you ask in my name, I will do it so that the Father may be glorified in the Son" (John 14:13). If we desire power for service, we have only to ask God for it.

Don't forget that there are two sides to prayer—the talking side and the listening side. You've probably heard it said, "The trouble with most people is that they talk too much." We're all capable of spending so much time talking to God in prayer, that we aren't able to hear God speaking to us. When we stop striving and fighting and worrying, we will be able to hear Him and know that He is truly God (Ps. 46:10).

Lord, I pray that Your presence would be the most palpable and Your voice the loudest in my life.

THE SNARE OF ENVY

Everyone with a proud heart is detestable to the LORD; be assured, he will not go unpunished. Iniquity is atoned for by loyalty and faithfulness, and one turns from evil by the fear of the LORD. —Proverbs 16:5–6

It is easy to grow jealous of another because they have gained more success, recognition, or wealth. Yet, the good fortune of a friend ought to make us happy.

Saul became insanely jealous of David. Young David was youthful, energetic, and intelligent. He was quiet, never putting himself forward. Yet the people hailed him in the streets, praised him for his courage, and blessed him for his greatness. They compared him directly to Saul and found Saul wanting:

> "As they danced, the women sang:
> Saul has killed his thousands,
> but David his tens of thousands." (1 Sam. 18:7)

This was more than Saul could stand. His jealousy and envy produced wild desires in his heart to destroy David.

But God protected David. Twice, Saul's javelin missed David. Then David decided to go away until Saul's wrath was appeased. Throughout his whole life, David proved his certainty of the Lord's protection and His ultimate sovereignty.

■

Lead us as You see fit, God. That way we will remember You alone are God, and always be grateful for Your unending care and guidance.

PORTRAIT OF A PROPHET

John wore a camel-hair garment with a leather belt around his waist and ate locusts and wild honey. —Mark 1:6

Every stroke of the divine narrator's brush makes more vivid the prophetic picture. Like the prophets of old, John was disciplined in his personal habits. Like Elijah, he wore the simplest of clothing and ate the plainest of food. His speech was blunt, like Amos, piercing the heart like a spear. He was as fearless as Jeremiah and as earnest as Isaiah. He broke the silence of four long centuries. The crowds came to see him and hear his message, and the excitement was intense.

He was prophetic in the truth he declared. It was a message of judgment and hope. He came announcing "a baptism of repentance." When a Gentile became a Jewish proselyte, he underwent three things: circumcision as a mark of entering the covenant, sacrifice as an atonement for his sins, and baptism as a symbol of his cleansing from all the pollution of his past life.

The Jew was familiar with baptism, that is, the baptism of the Gentile. But John came demanding the baptism of the Jew as well. He was called to prepare the people. He told them, "One who is more powerful than I am is coming after me. I am not worthy to stoop down and untie the strap of his sandals. I baptize you with water, but he will baptize you with the Holy Spirit" (Mark 1:7–8).

The good news has come! The gospel is true! Repent, believe, and receive Jesus' gift of salvation.

■

Lord Jesus, thank You for pursuing my heart and for Your gift of salvation. I ask now for clean lips and pure motives, so that I might speak truth in love to others.

PUTTING JESUS FIRST

"He is the one coming after me, whose sandal strap I'm not worthy to untie." —John 1:27

Nothing so reveals our true nature as what we believe ourselves to be. We may think of ourselves as valuable, a person of character, a redeemed child of God, or nothing much at all—a worthless worm of the dust. We may make the mistake of assessing our worth the way the world does, in terms of money or personality or service. But the way we view ourselves matters because it determines how we'll live our lives.

John the Baptist thought of himself as a voice crying in the wilderness, a road-builder for the King. He was not the Messiah, nor Elijah, nor one of the prophets. He was a forerunner, making ready the road that the King of heaven might enter in.

A rabbinic saying makes it clear that a disciple may do anything for his master that a servant does, except untie his sandals. That was a service too lowly even for a disciple. But John said, "There is one coming whose shoelaces I am not worthy to untie."

As Christ followers, we must receive before we can give. We must humble ourselves before God before we can be useful. We glorify the Father in our submission to His will.

The resources of heaven are available to those who put Christ first.

■

Lord, please grow in me a willing mind, a responsive heart, and a submissive will.

COURAGE TO SPEAK GOD'S TRUTH

*"Herod feared John and protected him, knowing
he was a righteous and holy man. When Herod
heard him he would be very perplexed, and yet
he liked to listen to him." —Mark 6:20*

There is not one promise in the New Testament that offers Christ followers exemption from the sorrows, the sufferings, and the difficulties of life. Instead, we're warned, almost bluntly, that the price of discipleship includes self-denial, cross-bearing, and sacrifice.

There are, it has been pointed out, two ways of gaining followers. You can bribe them or challenge them; appeal to the heroic or the base. Jesus never sought disciples under false pretense. Again and again He urged men to count the cost and weigh the alternatives of following Him (Luke 14:25–34).

Sometimes it's costly to speak the truth. It's easier and far less embarrassing to condemn the messenger, like our pastors, than to reform our own lives. But John preferred lonely Machaerus to condoning evil, and death to falsehood. He spoke with his life as well as with his lips.

As Christ followers, we must have the courage to stand up and be counted as those who love Him. With Christ, it is not *both and*, but *either or*. You cannot serve both God and the things of this world (Matt. 6:24). Neutrality is not the mark of God's child.

John spoke the truth in love, even at the price of blood.

Jesus, give us the gift of courage to live up to Your convictions.

COMMENDED BY JESUS

This is the one about whom it is written: "See, I am sending my messenger ahead of you; he will prepare your way before you." —Matthew 11:10

It has been said that everyone has their god. Some worship their bodies, some their appetites, some their wallets, and some their own cleverness and sense of self-sufficiency. And there are those who, like the apostle Paul, are the "servant of Christ Jesus" (Rom. 1:1).

Not only do we have our own personal gods and idols, but we also have our own personal system of values. There are the standards of earth and the standards of heaven; the evaluations of God and the evaluations of men.

In the eyes of God, John stood tall. "What did you go out into the wilderness to see?" Jesus asked the crowds. "A reed swaying in the wind? What then did you go out to see? A man dressed in soft clothes? See, those who wear soft clothes are in royal palaces. What then did you go out to see? A prophet?" (Matthew 11:7–10). But John was more. He was the herald of the King. Of John, Jesus declared, "Truly I tell you, among those born of women no one greater than John the Baptist has appeared" (v. 11).

As Christ followers, we march to the beat of an unseen drummer, pattern our lives by His standards, think in terms of eternity, and long for His divine approval: "Well done, good and faithful servant" (Matt. 25:21).

■

Lord, make me sensitive to Your Holy Spirit, and please give me an appetite for the things of God.

FAITH TO FINISH THE JOB

The residents of one city will go to another, saying: Let's go at once to plead for the LORD's favor and to seek the LORD of Armies. I am also going. —Zechariah 8:21

God's work is always important, whether it consists of feeding a child, plowing a garden, building a church, or comforting those who grieve. We can fold laundry or bake bread or sweep floors to the glory of God.

One of the glories of work is that it is one of the few things we really can give to God. Our talents are gifts, and while the materials may come from other hands, our labor is our own.

Skill and speed and dexterity are not equally endowed between us. We can watch as someone uses their gifts and talents, and instead of praising God for them, we yield to jealousy, resentment, and futility. Talents may be varied, but opportunities are not. No matter the gifting, we can faithfully serve God—not by our strength or by might, but by the Spirit of God (Zech. 4:6).

> There is nothing better for a person than to eat, drink, and enjoy his work. I have seen that even this is from God's hand, because who can eat and who can enjoy life apart from him? For to the person who is pleasing in his sight, he gives wisdom, knowledge, and joy. (Eccles. 2:24–26)

Lord, please give me a grateful heart and a willing hand, and the faithfulness to do Your will.

A GUEST OF JESUS

And he brought Simon to Jesus. When Jesus saw him, he said, "You are Simon, son of John. You will be called Cephas (which is translated 'Peter')." —John 1:42

Jesus Christ is so real in many people's lives that they feel His presence in the room with them. Some may feel extremely close to Him in the still quiet of the night, among the trees on a mountainside, standing on the shore of the thundering ocean, or while singing His praises with other believers at church.

This is as it should be. An absentee god, or the historical Jesus, is not the real one, but merely a cheap idol.

Paul was right: "He is not far from each one of us" (Acts 17:27). It is God's presence with us that marks us as His children. Indeed, He knows us by name and promises to never leave or abandon us (Exod. 33:12–17; Heb. 13:5). And as writer C. S. Lewis suggests in *Letters to Malcolm: Chiefly on Prayer*, God may be far more present in our lives than we can imagine:

We may ignore, but we can nowhere evade the presence of God. The world is crowded with Him. He walks everywhere incognito. And the incognito is not always hard to penetrate. The real labor is to remember, to attend. In fact, to come awake. Still more, to remain awake.

■

Lord God, I know You are always near. I pray for increased awareness that You are with me.

BREAKFAST WITH THE MASTER

"Come and have breakfast," Jesus told them. None of the disciples dared ask him, "Who are you?" because they knew it was the Lord. —John 21:12

Faith is meeting. We may know about God, believe the historical facts about Jesus Christ, give mental assent to the Bible as the Word of God. None of these is faith. Faith is always a response by a living human being to a living God.

What is it like to receive the revelation of God? Well, imagine a man lying on his back in the rain. His mouth is wide open, ajar. What if we receive God as we might take in rain this way. This is not a perfect illustration. We know God only as He has made Himself known: through Jesus Christ. But we receive Him directly, into our hearts.

Faith is our response to God, acknowledging that we are His subjects, and dependent on His care and love. To walk by faith is to depend on God each moment that we become aware of Him.

Lord Jesus, I want to live with You as my constant guide. Help me to look to You daily for assurance and direction.

NO LONGER HESITANT

Nicodemus (who had previously come to him at night) also came, bringing a mixture of about seventy-five pounds of myrrh and aloes. —John 19:39

Joseph of Arimathea and Nicodemus were hypocrites, not in the accepted sense of trying to appear better than they really were, but in that they tried to appear less interested than they really were. It was not that they had made a profession of faith and were failing to live up to it, but they had a Christian faith that they were choosing not to show.

But when they saw what their indifference had cost, that Christ had been crucified, and that they had in a sense helped crucify the Master, they were then given the courage of their own convictions. They were no longer hesitant. If only we could see what our delay and indifference is costing those we come in contact with, or how it is hindering the Kingdom.

"Therefore, everyone who will acknowledge me before others, I will also acknowledge him before my Father in heaven." (Matt. 10:32)

Lord, help us to be true to our highest convictions, even when it may be unpopular. Even when it costs us something.

JOHN HERALDS THE CHRIST

John answered them all, "I baptize you with water, but one who is more powerful than I am is coming. I am not worthy to untie the strap of his sandals. He will baptize you with the Holy Spirit and fire." —Luke 3:16

In ancient times, when a king was going forth to survey his lands, men were sent on before to prepare the way. Often, a new road would be cut, trees leveled, bridges built, highways mended.

John the Baptist, as the herald of Christ, prepared men's hearts by creating an atmosphere of expectancy by making men and women aware of their sin, calling them to repentance, and helping them to feel their need of a Savior.

We are invited to be a herald of Jesus Christ as well, preparing the way for His coming. Our Savior wishes to come into the hearts and homes of all people. But make no mistake: God will accomplish His will with or without us (Isa. 46:8–11). Still, out of His goodness, we are invited to participate in His divine plan of reconciliation, and commissioned to share the gospel to those the Lord sends our way (Matt. 28:16–20).

Lord, I pray that You will use me to help create in the hearts of all my acquaintances a conscious need for Christ.

THE ONLY SAVING NAME

*"There is salvation in no one else, for there is
no other name under heaven given to people by
which we must be saved." —Acts 4:12*

Today's text points out that there is only one saving name
known in this world. It is not the name of a celebrity, politician,
scientist, humanitarian, explorer, or millionaire. It is the name
of the Son of God, Jesus.

Although His name has been loved and preached more than
any other name in our part of the world, it has also been ridiculed,
blasphemed, and denied. Yet, the name of Jesus still stands out
today, through the testimony of both Scripture and humanity.

Many people the world over have been attracted to the
teachings and character of Jesus. But they do not know the
most important truth about His name—that it has the power
to save and free them.

May God make us willing vessels to share this good news.
And like Peter, may we be filled with the Holy Spirit when we
share the gospel and the saving name of Jesus (Acts 4:8).

> I pray that he may grant you, according to the
> riches of his glory, to be strengthened with power in
> your inner being through his Spirit, and that Christ
> may dwell in your hearts through faith. I pray that
> you, being rooted and firmly established in love,
> may be able to comprehend with all the saints
> what is the length and width, height and depth of
> God's love, and to know Christ's love that surpasses
> knowledge, so that you may be filled with all the
> fullness of God. (Eph. 3:16–19)

*Lord Jesus, strengthen my faith to boldly proclaim the
gospel to those who have yet to call on Your saving name.*

OUR SUPREME LOYALTY

*Peter and John answered them, "Whether it's right
in the sight of God for us to listen to you rather
than to God, you decide." —Acts 4:19*

There are some experiences we never forget. As long as memory lasts, there are events that remain very vivid: a wedding ceremony, that first day of school, a certain someone who got away, a particularly special act of kindness from a friend, the passing of loved ones, and the conversion experience itself—all of these moments remain very much with us.

The disciples could not forget Jesus. They did not want to forget Him. They also could not forget that Jesus wanted them to help others to know He is the Messiah.

Jesus' command to "Go" into the world and preach the good news of the gospel was so fresh in the minds of Peter and John that the words of the scribes and elders and others who threatened them seemed unimportant. They knew that God had called them to be witnesses of Christ. What right did any man have to ask them to stop talking about Jesus? They had seen and heard things the world needed to know. Their supreme loyalty was to the call of God.

■

*Lord, please grant me a sense of loyalty to the
task of telling what I know about Jesus.*

IN THE STEPS OF JESUS

In addition, a multitude came together from the towns surrounding Jerusalem, bringing the sick and those who were tormented by unclean spirits, and they were all healed. —Acts 5:16

The ministry of the apostles in the church in Jerusalem following the day of Pentecost was much like the ministry of Jesus in several respects. Jesus Himself had taught them. The followers of Jesus were reaping a harvest from the seeds sown by the Savior during His earthly ministry.

Although people were being saved, sometimes thousands in a day, it should be remembered that great numbers of new believers probably had been present when Jesus taught. They had watched Him perform miracles and had seen His crucifixion. Now the Holy Spirit had opened their understanding, and they became convinced that Jesus was the Christ.

Miracles of healing occurred frequently. Those who had seen Jesus as He healed could see that the teachings and the deeds of the apostles were much like those of Jesus. Their healing was in His name and by His power. The success of the apostles was evidence of God's approval of their efforts, and His concern for those who were healed.

■

God, teach me to have greater concern for the sick, the broken, the needy, and the lost people around me.

WHAT IS GOD LIKE?

*Do you not know? Have you not heard? The L*ORD
*is the everlasting God, the Creator of the whole
earth. He never becomes faint or weary; there is
no limit to his understanding.* —Isaiah 40:28

The people of this world who believe in God are interested
in knowing more about Him. Although we are sure that He
has not revealed all the information to us, we do know some
things—and we like what He tells us about Himself. The information we have about God prompts us to love Him, to respect
Him, and to serve Him.

By the time Peter could say, "God doesn't show favoritism,"
he had come a long way from his former position when he
believed the gospel was for the Jews only. This change of position was due to a vision through which he came to know that
God could accept those who fear Him "in every nation."

Scripture teaches us about the character of God. We also
come to know more about Him through the experiences we
have with Him, as the Holy Spirit guides us. Wherever the
message of Jesus is preached faithfully—whether in word or in
action—there are those who will believe.

■

God, thank You for loving all people everywhere.

ENCOUNTER WITH THE LORD

"But get up and go into the city, and you will be told what you must do." —Acts 9:6

We cannot be in relationship with God and remain unchanged.

The apostle Paul had been transformed from a persecutor of Christians to one who was willing to be persecuted because he was a Christian. It all happened when he had an encounter with Jesus on the road to Damascus. The disciples, Peter and John, were also radically changed in the presence of God. They appeared to be unusually bold, though the people "realized that they were uneducated and untrained men." Those to whom they preached "were amazed and recognized that they had been with Jesus" (Acts 4:13).

This is the way it always happens. Whenever we come face-to-face with God we are different, our hearts transformed—bitterness can turn to sweetness, meanness to kindness, and hatred to love. In the presence of our God and His deep love for us, there is healing and joy (Isa. 35:5–6). That is why Paul, who knew this transformative power as well as anyone, wrote:

> Now the Lord is the Spirit, and where the Spirit of the Lord is, there is freedom. We all, with unveiled faces, are looking as in a mirror at the glory of the Lord and are being transformed into the same image from glory to glory; this is from the Lord who is the Spirit. (2 Cor. 3:17–18)

■

Lord, we ask that we would feel your presence, and that it would be reflected in our lives as a testimony to You.

WITNESSES TO CHRIST'S POWER

*This became known throughout Joppa, and
many believed in the Lord. —Acts 9:42*

How often we overlook the marvelous manifestations of God's grace and power all about us every day. We fail to recognize that the hospital, the children's home, and even public schools are the products of the Christian movement. We only need to examine the great works of art, literature, and music to find evidence of firsthand experience with the influence of Christ.

Ask a Christian who has encountered life's inevitable crises, and they will tell you how Jesus wrapped His love around them and stood beside them all the way. Let someone who knows Jesus as Savior tell you how in sorrow He wiped the tears from their eyes.

What if Christ had not died on the cross? Suppose He had not borne our sins. What could possibly give us hope for the future? It is in the intimate spiritual relationship we have with Christ Himself that we have the assurance of eternal life. He pursues us because He loves us. He came to rescue us, to reconcile us to Himself, and to give us fellowship with Him.

*Lord, give me eyes to see how You have changed
me. And whatever goodness You find in me, I
pray it will allow others to see Jesus in me.*

MAN OF MERCY

But David said to Abishai, "Don't destroy him, for who can lift a hand against the LORD's anointed and be innocent?" —1 Samuel 26:9

No one is ever justified in taking the law into their own hands. Justice may sometimes be delayed, but we must ultimately depend on God's justice being done. He still rules, and His plans will not be thwarted.

This is clearly illustrated in the story of David's mercy in sparing the life of Saul. David found Saul asleep one night, with all of his men around him. Taking Saul's life would have been easy. But David spared him and took only some of his belongings to prove he had been there and had shown himself to be merciful and forgiving.

Whatever weaknesses Saul had, he was the one chosen and anointed by the Lord. He was the king. Whatever the future might bring made no difference. David recognized that he had no right to take Saul's life. This was another fine testing of David in his preparation to become the mighty ruler of his people.

Try us, O Lord that we may receive mercy by showing mercy to others.

PROCLAIMING THE MESSIAH

"From this man's descendants, as he promised, God
brought to Israel the Savior, Jesus." —Acts 13:23

The Hebrew word for Messiah, "Mashiach," and the Greek word for Christ, "Christos," are both translated "anointed one." They are synonyms. The Jews knew many christs or messiahs but were instructed to look forward to the coming of a person superior to all other anointed ones, who would be the great deliverer of His people. Hence the title "Messiah" was ultimately attached to Jesus.

In their anticipation for a national deliverer, the Jews overlooked the fact that He was to be Savior of the people from their sins. They looked for a political Messiah of material power and splendor. Jesus fundamentally altered their conception. They were not expecting a suffering Messiah. They thought only of deliverance for Israel, and the only God they had been waiting to welcome was the God of Israel. But Jesus came for so much more.

> But he was pierced because of our rebellion,
> crushed because of our iniquities;
> punishment for our peace was on him,
> and we are healed by his wounds. (Isa. 53:5)

Thanks be to Jesus, the anointed One, our God who saves.

■

We pray that the eyes of Jewish people everywhere
may be opened to see that through Jesus Christ,
God has raised unto Israel a Savior.

PREACHING THE SAVIOR

Everyone who believes is justified through him
from everything that you could not be justified
from through the law of Moses. —Acts 13:39

Isaiah 63 opens with the question, "Who is this coming . . . ?" The reply was, "It is I, proclaiming vindication, powerful to save." Of whom does this phrase, "powerful to save" apply to better than Jesus Christ? Jesus is indeed the mighty Savior. There is no greater truth than this. John said, "We no longer believe because of what you said, since we have heard for ourselves and know that this really is the Savior of the world" (John 4:42).

Jesus is indeed the Almighty One, the great God-man. He is coequal with the Heavenly Father and the Holy Spirit. He participated with the Father in creation and now shares His Father's throne above principalities and powers. And His name is above every name that is named. He is the King of death, the Conqueror of hell, Lord of angels, Master of storms, and Savior from sin. How mighty He is we can really never tell, but Scripture tells us that He is "mighty to save."

■

Jesus, I'm so thankful for Your work on the cross. I
pray for those who are lost, and I ask that You lead me
to speak to someone this day about the Savior.

WHY AM I HERE?

What is a human being that you remember him, a son of man that you look after him? You made him little less than God and crowned him with glory and honor. —Psalm 8:4–5

As tiny and insignificant as man seems to be when compared to the solar system, Jesus teaches that God is mindful of him. Mankind is the very center and goal of all God's creation. No one has ever sunk so low or ever sinned so greatly that Jesus can no longer place infinite value upon his or her soul.

Man is subject to the minutest divine care. Prodigals and sinners that we are—all are looked upon by Jesus with eyes of compassion and in terms of eternity. Jesus sees us as the creation He intended us to be, and that's why He came to ransom us, to bring us back into relationship with Him.

For Jesus, life was a glorious adventure in doing God's will. Paul said, "For me, to live is Christ and to die is gain" (Phil. 1:21). Jesus Christ makes it possible for us to have a faith to live and die by, and a mission far greater than ourselves. He makes it possible for us to live sublimely.

Lord, I want to know You as You intended. I pray that You would make Yourself increasingly more real to me. And that I may give myself without reservation to Your service.

SALVATION BY FAITH

On the contrary, we believe that we are saved through the grace of the Lord Jesus in the same way they are. —Acts 15:11

It's surprising and incredibly unfortunate to say that there is a tendency today to divide and classify people. There are those who still weigh someone's worth based on their race, gender, education, privilege, wealth—and more. But while there are those among us determined to distinguish us by our differences, in the economy of God, there are only two classifications: those who call Jesus their Lord and their Savior, and those who do not. Or in simpler language, those who are saved and those who are not. Any other distinction does not matter one bit. "For you are saved by grace through faith, and this is not from yourselves; it is God's gift" (Eph. 2:8).

The heart of God is to see His creation—His people and image bearers—saved and reconciled to Him. Once we submit to the mercy and grace of salvation, when the gift of Christ's death and resurrection is accepted and received, and the work of the Holy Spirit can begin. A new person emerges: "Therefore, if anyone is in Christ, he is a new creation; the old has passed away, and see, the new has come!" (2 Cor. 5:17).

This is the heart of the gospel. No one comes to Christ without His grace and mercy pursuing us first. "We love because he first loved us" (1 John 4:19). As believers and students of the Christian faith, we will find no equal to this truth, the foundation of our lives.

Thank You, God, for allowing me to share the gospel with those who do not yet know Your goodness.

ACTION BY THE CHURCH

Then the apostles and the elders, with the whole church, decided to select men who were among them and to send them to Antioch with Paul and Barnabas. —Acts 15:22

We cannot read the book of Acts without being aware that, to the early believers, being a Christian and being a church member were of the first importance in their lives. It was imperative that they be careful in their conduct and preserve harmony in the stewardship of God's Word and their witness. In today's reading, we see the church sending other men with Paul and Barnabas to Antioch. These men are to be spokesmen for the church.

There are people who recognize with pride their responsibility and obligations to all types of organizations—social, civic, or educational—who are careless and indifferent in discharging their duties to the church. But ultimately, we are responsible to Christ and to His body, the Church.

> God has put the body together, giving greater honor to the less honorable, so that there would be no division in the body, but that the members would have the same concern for each other. So if one member suffers, all the members suffer with it; if one member is honored, all the members rejoice with it. Now you are the body of Christ, and individual members of it. (1 Cor. 12:24–27)

Lord, help us to be mindful of one another, acknowledging that we are all growing in faith. Link our hearts in service and fellowship, so that the church may find deep joy and peace, unified as one.

WHEN GOOD MEN DISAGREE

They had such a sharp disagreement that they parted company, and Barnabas took Mark with him and sailed off to Cyprus. —Acts 15:39

When differences arise and good people disagree, it is important that an answer to the problem be sought. No two persons see the problem in the same light. If disagreements are discussed in the Spirit of Christ, God will supply strength and wisdom to find a solution. Many disagreements have not been entrusted to the directing hand of a loving God who is adequate to help in every emergency.

After the matter has been turned over to God, it is never wise to brood over what might have been if the course of action had been different. Begin to thank Him for the good that is emerging. Look for open doors that may appear because of the new set of circumstances.

> But speaking the truth in love, let us grow in every way into him who is the head—Christ. From him the whole body, fitted and knit together by every supporting ligament, promotes the growth of the body for building up itself in love by the proper working of each individual part. (Eph. 4:15–16)

Father, we ask that we may have the grace to love those with whom we disagree and be more receptive to Your power and leadership in our daily lives.

WHAT IS THE CHURCH?

But you are a chosen race, a royal priesthood, a holy
nation, a people for his possession, so that you may
proclaim the praises of the one who called you out of
darkness into his marvelous light. —1 Peter 2:9

The Church is represented by people of all different races, nationalities, and walks of life—as it should be. We bring with us into community different life experiences and opinions, but they are of little importance when compared to the fact that we have been chosen by God and have chosen to follow Christ Jesus. The most important thing about us is our faith in Him. It is also what should unite us. "There is no Jew or Greek, slave or free, male and female; since [we] are all one in Christ Jesus. And if [we] belong to Christ, then [we] are Abraham's seed, heirs according to the promise" (Gal. 3:28–29).

Christians have different abilities and gifts but are all members of one body. We all belong to a holy priesthood. We are God's people, loved and pursued by Him. Having been called from darkness into light, we bear witness to His faithfulness and love.

Every church is or should be a community of worshipping believers, who long to see others reconciled to Christ Jesus and growing in their faith. It's in community that we discover the meaning of Christian fellowship as we worship and work together to make God's name great. There is nothing else like it. "Let the church be the church!"

Lord, thank You for allowing us to be a part of
the Church. Unite us as believers, and help
us to reflect Your glory to the world.

MOVING WITH THE MOB

The whole city was stirred up, and the people rushed together. They seized Paul, dragged him out of the temple, and at once the gates were shut. —Acts 21:30

Hearsay was the source of information. Paul had taken a Greek into the temple, an offense punishable by death. From one mouth to another the gossip flew, until a mob of Jews set out to kill him. Officials piously closed the doors of the temple so that it would not be profaned when Paul's blood was shed.

It was Romans who rescued Paul. And while they were suspicious of all new ideas, such as Christianity, they nevertheless did their duty to quell the mob.

Two forces stood ready to crush out the Way—Jews and Romans. But God took hold of both and meshed them together, using them cooperatively and serving His own purposes.

Through this event Paul got to Rome. There he preached to the highest officials of the Empire. And through his teaching, Christianity gained a foothold.

God rules! Don't forget it—whatever the news headlines seem to indicate to the contrary. He is still in control of His creation.

Lord, we pray that Your will may be done in and through the nations of the world.

GO TELL OTHERS

*You will be a witness for him to all people of what
you have seen and heard. —Acts 22:15*

The work that Jesus laid out for us as Christ followers has been laid out clearly for us. Right after the "blesseds" of the Beatitudes in the Sermon on the Mount, He instructed:

> "You are the salt of the earth. But if the salt should lose its taste, how can it be made salty? . . . You are the light of the world. A city situated on a hill cannot be hidden. . . . In the same way, let your light shine before others, so that they may see your good works and give glory to your Father in heaven." (Matt. 5:13–14, 16)

Be salt. Be light. Let your light shine.

The same command is ours: Be witnesses of the gospel. Do not boast. Do not speak of your own deeds. Instead, we are to speak of what we have seen and heard. We are to point people to Jesus.

How we fail! We're afraid of what people might think—that we're fanatics, that we're pious, that we're peculiar. And so we let our witness be weakened or wiped out by fear of public opinion. Are we convinced that, through the life, death, and resurrection of Christ, eternal life is ours? If the answer is yes, then we must say so! No, we'll never be worthy of this gift of salvation! Of course, our lives do not measure up! Yes, we may be ridiculed! But our call, nevertheless, is to share the gospel of Jesus Christ with the world.

■

*Lord, I want to know You. Open my eyes, ears, heart,
and mind to see You better, and please give me the
courage to tell others about my relationship with You.*

PAUL'S INVISIBLE ALLY

*The following night, the Lord stood by him
and said, "Have courage!"* —Acts 23:11

The Bible has various ways of saying that spiritual resources are available to those who call on the name of Jesus. Sometimes, it says an angel speaks. At other times, it says God Himself speaks. Still at other times, it says the Holy Spirit communicates. Here, in today's passage, the Lord Himself stood by Paul and said, "Have courage."

Are these not biblical ways of saying the same thing? Is this not an admission that man is more than matter, more than an animal? Is it not claiming that man has a spiritual side to his nature and that there is a spiritual force, a spiritual world, from which impressions, insights, and guidance come to a seeking heart?

It is strange, but true, that the saints of God testify that it is in crises that the Lord has stood by to reassure them. Even so, it was like that with Paul as he reflected in his night's confinement of the day's narrow escape and of the impending threat that tomorrow held. Then, the Lord stood by with encouragement that all would be well.

■

*Open my eyes, Lord, so that I will become sensitive to You,
my invisible ally, standing by me to cheer and to guide.*

THE BATTLE CRY OF FAITH

*David said to the Philistine: "You come against me with
a sword, spear, and javelin, but I come against you in
the name of the LORD of Armies, the God of the ranks
of Israel—you have defied him. —1 Samuel 17:45*

Most people have a rallying cry that calls them to action. It
may be money, prestige, or a desire to serve.

The person concerned with service to mankind asks few
questions before diving in and acting. All that person needs is
the knowledge that someone is in need, and that something
must be done to help them.

What was the difference between the people of Israel and
their enemies? God was on the Israelites' side. It's as simple
and as powerful as that. God's people were confident in Him,
and so they went forth to meet their challenges with confidence, and then enjoyed the Lord's support in their efforts.

All the shining armor of Goliath could not blind David's
simple faith. Knowing Scripture made David fully aware of
God's sovereignty, so he felt no reason to hesitate before going
to fight the man-giant. David met and defeated the powerful
Philistine solely in the strength of the Lord.

*Lord, please grant in us the kind of faith that will help
us undertake high and worthy causes for Your glory.*

FALSE ACCUSATIONS

For we have found this man to be a plague, an agitator among all the Jews throughout the Roman world, and a ringleader of the sect of the Nazarenes. —Acts 24:5

Paul was being accused periodically. He held to strong convictions and identified himself with whatever cause he espoused. This, of course, was a sure way to become unpopular with some, and to risk having trumped up charges brought against him. Specifically, he was accused of being "a perfect pest," of stirring up discontent among the Jews, of being a ringleader of an outlawed sect, and of trying to profane the temple.

If we stand for right, speak our convictions, and challenge prejudices, we, too, will face false charges. Frustrated people will seek ways to defame our character, intimidate our families, and frighten us into silence.

We must be aware of our enemy, who is a thief who "comes only to steal and kill and destroy (John 10:10). Jesus knew exactly what He was asking of His disciples, and what the circumstances would be. That's why He told them, "Look, I'm sending you out like sheep among wolves. Therefore be as shrewd as serpents and as innocent as doves" (Matt. 10:16).

He encouraged them to stand strong and confident in their faith when those trials came: "But when they hand you over, don't worry about how or what you are to speak. For you will be given what to say at that hour, because it isn't you speaking, but the Spirit of your Father is speaking through you" (vv. 19–20).

Lord God, make us bold in the face of false charges and intimidation. Thank You, Holy Spirit, for giving us words to say. Help us to stand firm and fight for what is right.

A STRONG DEFENSE

I always strive to have a clear conscience
toward God and men. —Acts 24:16

Our worldly culture teaches us to look out for ourselves, that each of us is "on our own" and responsible for our own well-being. But in the economy of God, we are called to Christian community (Rom. 12:4–5). We must look to our brothers and sisters in Christ if we are to survive.

This is why Paul's contention before the Roman authorities that he was guiltless stands out so dramatically. No one was there to defend him. It was strictly his word against others. In such a lonely stand, nothing—absolutely nothing—can supply someone with fortitude and defense like knowing that they are innocent and blameless.

Without the saving work of Jesus, we would all stand before God rightly accused and guilty of our sin. "For the wages of sin is death, but the gift of God is eternal life in Christ Jesus our Lord" (Rom. 6:23). But because of the gospel of salvation, those who trust Jesus will forever stand innocent and blameless before God, who "proves his own love for us in that while we were still sinners, Christ died for us" (Rom. 5:8).

■

Lord Jesus, thank You for Your saving work on
the cross. Thank You that I now stand pure and
secure before my God, and will forevermore.

YIELDING TO EVIL PRESSURE

*After two years had passed, Porcius Festus succeeded
Felix, and because Felix wanted to do the Jews a
favor, he left Paul in prison. —Acts 24:27*

It is commonly thought that everyone has their price, their personal breaking point. Not many can endure pressure indefinitely. It is the rare soul whose character is so rock solid and whose interests are so selfless that they are indifferent to pressure.

So Felix, the Roman governor, yielded to popular wishes and left Paul bound for his successor, Festus, to consider. By so doing, he was courting favor with the Jews.

Can you take your stand and hold it when others exert pressure? What if some of these are your friends, or even members of your family? Of course, it is wise to yield when no basic principle is involved. But what if your philosophy of life will be compromised by "selling out"? Here is character's highest test. And Felix could not pass it.

This evil thing asserts itself even in churches. The pressure to conform, for the sake of a false peace, is one of character's greatest enemies.

*Lord, keep me humble. Please give me the ability to hold
to my convictions even if everyone else abandons theirs.*

THE MEANING OF CHRISTIAN LOVE

*Dear friends, if God loved us in this way, we
also must love one another.* —1 John 4:11

As Christ followers, we talk much about the supremacy of
love. Well we ought to, for God is love. But it is far easier to
talk of love than it is to actually do the work of loving someone well. Of course, we cannot force affection. But the word
here for love is not affection. It is, rather, intentional good will
actively expressed in word and in deed. It is a choice of action.

We have good will toward all people and never consciously
do them wrong. But this is still not the Christian love we are
called to. Instead, we must actually begin to express good will
irrespective of the attitude of others. In other words, our loving
someone is not dependent upon whether or not they love us
the same way. This is no easy feat on the part of the human
heart. But we are called to love in this way because that is
precisely the way that God, who is love (1 John 4:8), chooses
to love us.

He is love. He is never anything else. Whether we are pos-
itively wonderful or completely horrible, God's character does
not change (Heb. 13:8)—God is still love. For this reason we
should love one another. In so doing we are exhibiting our
Father's character, bearing His image, and glorifying His parentage of us. We are His.

*God, help me to understand how wide and long
and high and deep Your love for me truly is. Please
grow in me the desire to love others in this way.*

COURAGE FROM GOD'S PROMISES

So take courage, men, because I believe God that it
will be just the way it was told to me. —Acts 27:25

One faithful follower of the Lord can guide a people safely through storms even, when those in authority have invited disaster through their refusal to heed the warnings of God. Our disobedience of God's Word is always costly—often in property and worldly things, yes, but even more so in relationships and even in life.

But for the faith and divinely imparted wisdom of our brother Paul, the ship with its cargo—both human and material—would have been lost. Paul could have panicked with fear. He could have welcomed death at sea as an escape from the tortures of a maritime prison. But he chose to use the storm-driven vessel as his pulpit to declare his allegiance to the One who has power over the wind and the waves. He chose to affirm his faith in God's unfailing promises, and in His abundant ability to save.

■

Father, in the midst of this lost and broken generation, may
Your sustaining promises enable us to love others well for Your
glory, even when the storms assail around us and in our hearts.

GOD'S PROMISES FULFILLED

The rest were to follow, some on planks and some
on debris from the ship. In this way, everyone
safely reached the shore. —Acts 27:44

When Paul encouraged his fellow voyagers to be of good cheer, he did more than declare his own faith. He practiced his faith in both word and in action. He continued declaring the way of salvation: "Unless these men stay in the ship, you cannot be saved" (Acts 27:31). He took food, gave thanks to God, urging them all to eat for the sake of their health. Whatever the situation, the normal processes of life need to go on. In times of peril, fasting and prayer are incredibly helpful; but a healthy body is always an imperative vehicle for bearing a convincing, contagious testimony.

Paul practiced his faith in God's promises while the storm was still raging and the ship was being driven. The hand of God was in the storm, driving the ship toward a haven. God works through the natural and the unnatural, the normal and the abnormal, in keeping His covenant with His people. "Blessed be the LORD! He has given rest to his people Israel according to all he has said. Not one of all the good promises he made through his servant Moses has failed" (1 Kings 8:56).

Father, You alone are able to fulfill Your promises. Enable and strengthen our hearts to believe them through unfailing faith.

SERVICE DESPITE HARDSHIP

After this, the rest of those on the island who had
diseases also came and were healed. —Acts 28:9

Our God often employs unusual agents and situations in
fulfilling His purposes. Barbarians are used to sustain His
messengers. The sting of a viper is turned into a convincing
testimony for Him. It was even God's will that Paul appear
before Caesar—all for the sake of pursuing the hearts of men
and women. "We know that all things work together for the
good of those who love God, who are called according to his
purpose" (Rom. 8:28).

Storms, shipwrecks, superstitions of pagan people—none
of these things could defeat God's overruling purposes for his
servant, who did not wait until he arrived in Rome to begin
sharing the gospel through service to mankind in both word
and deed. Paul saw that in whatever situation he was in, wherever he was, whomever he met, an opportunity to proclaim
the gospel and the sufficiency of the power of the living God
in mending broken bodies, redirecting misguided lives, and in
healing souls bound by sin.

Paul never was defeated by hardship. Instead, he submitted
to the Father's will and allowed himself to be used in any and
all situations to demonstrate the greatness and the goodness
of God.

Father, may our service declare Your goodness,
Your greatness, and Your glory.

THE UNFETTERED GOSPEL

Paul stayed two whole years in his own rented house.
And he welcomed all who visited him. —Acts 28:30

After having heard Paul's plea, Agrippa said: "This man could have been released if he had not appealed to Caesar" (Acts 26:32). God's messenger was in fetters, but the gospel he proclaimed could not be bound by chains. When Paul came to Rome, he boldly preached the gospel of Jesus there, bringing liberty to captives who were enslaved by a state-imposed religion—one that set a cheap price on human life; that had no regard for the dignity of personality; that placed the welfare of the state above the rights of its citizens; that cultivated and enticed the lusts of the flesh rather than sowing to the fruits of the spirit; that kept the heart, mind, soul, and body in bondage.

Paul, the prisoner, dealt a death blow at such character-crippling, soul-destroying ideologies when he taught that in Jesus Christ all men are brothers. Many who entered his hired house as slaves emerged as free men—free from the law of sin and death.

■

Father, we thank You that Your glorious gospel
penetrates prison walls of all kinds, in particular
the walls we build up around our own hearts.

WHEN WE ARE DISCIPLES

"Go, therefore, and make disciples of all nations, baptizing them in the name of the Father and of the Son and of the Holy Spirit, teaching them to observe everything I have commanded you. And remember, I am with you always, to the end of the age." —Matthew 28:19–20

The code of conduct for Christ followers in today's lesson is a mirror in which each one of us can see ourselves. It is a gauge by which to measure ourselves and the will of our hearts. No one can understand themselves until they place their weakness up against the clear character and compassion of Christ. We are to live as He lived, talk as He talked, forgive as He forgave, love as He loved.

When we fix our eyes on Him and follow His example for living, humility subdues pride; kindness outlaws injustice; selfishness is conquered by lovingkindness and service. We learn through His beautiful example in gracious living that the way of holiness is the way of peace; the way of true greatness is the way of self-denial; the way of love is the only acceptable law of life. May we live by His example, "speaking the truth in love, let us grow in every way into him who is the head—Christ" (Eph. 4:15).

Father, help us to teach by our lives those things which You have taught us to observe.

THE HABIT OF DAILY, PERSONAL PRAYER

In the morning, LORD, you hear my voice; in the morning I plead my case to you and watch expectantly. —Psalm 5:3

A camel kneels at the dawn of day so that the guide may replace its load and at the close of day that the guide may remove its load. So should we, who are professed followers of Jesus Christ, the great Guide, begin and end the day with a "bent-knee" time.

Our God is our Guide, but much more than a guide. He is our King, to whom homage, and glory, and praise belong. He is more than a king; He is our Father, to whom love and thanksgiving and adoration are due.

He knows the load we are to bear, for He planned it and proportioned it to our strength. He knows the road we are to travel, for He has walked the way before us. He knows the needs of each heart at the end of each day's journey and has promised to give rest to those who labor and are heavy laden. But to receive this gift of His love, we must accept His invitation: "Come to me, all of you who are weary and burdened, and I will give you rest" (Matt. 11:28).

◼

Father, thank You for the privilege of carrying everything to You in prayer.

OPEN THE DOOR TO JESUS

*"See! I stand at the door and knock. If anyone hears
my voice and opens the door, I will come in to him and
eat with him, and he with me." —Revelation 3:20*

Not a single word of commendation did Christ have for the
Laodicean church; only rebuke. Smug and complacent, the
church had allowed the spirit of its wealthy and worldly city to
creep in.

However, Christ still loved the church and stood patiently
waiting for it to change. If any one single member would "open
the door" of his heart, he could again enjoy fellowship with the
Savior.

Were you ever tempted to blame the church for your own
spiritual lethargy? Remember, the invitation of Christ is personal.
Regardless of the course others may take, you may live in sweet
fellowship with Christ. Only God knows the number of churches
whose turning point was the rededication of one person.

> "Do not judge, so that you won't be judged. For you
> will be judged by the same standard with which you
> judge others, and you will be measured by the same
> measure you use. Why do you look at the splinter
> in your brother's eye but don't notice the beam of
> wood in your own eye? Or how can you say to your
> brother, 'Let me take the splinter out of your eye,'
> and look, there's a beam of wood in your own eye?
> Hypocrite! First take the beam of wood out of your
> eye, and then you will see clearly to take the splin-
> ter out of your brother's eye." (Matt. 7:1–5)

*God, help me to stop being distracted by the shortcomings
of others. Search my heart and show me my sin, and then
give me the courage to turn to You and repent of it.*

MARY, THE MOTHER OF JESUS

And Mary said: My soul praises the greatness of the Lord, and my spirit rejoices in God my Savior." —Luke 1:46–47

Between the two extremes of completely ignoring the virtues of Mary, the mother of Jesus, and of deifying her, there is a biblical medium.

Mary is an example to all young mothers today, who aspire to rear their children in the nurture and admonition of the Lord. Mary probably did not always understand her unusual child, but like most mothers, she probably never truly tired of being His mother. Under her cautious and loving care, He increased in wisdom and stature, and in favor with God and man.

Above all, Mary did not allow the fact that she was His earthly mother to overshadow the fact that He was her Savior. The full meaning and significance of her spontaneous praise before His birth became evident as she continued to be His disciple following His death and resurrection.

Lord Jesus, first and foremost, You are my Savior and my God. Thank You for the gift of faith that You are growing in me. May nothing overshadow or distract me from my relationship with You.

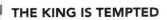

THE KING IS TEMPTED

Then Jesus told him, "Go away, Satan! For it is written: Worship the Lord your God, and serve only him." —Matthew 4:10

Temptation comes to all at one time or another. Immediately following His baptism, Jesus was "tempted by the devil" (Matt. 4:1). As Christ followers today, we can most likely attest to the constant struggle between good and evil. In fact, it is when we seek to live closer to the Lord that the enemy works against us the hardest.

In his formative work, *The Art of War*, Chinese military strategist and philosopher Sun Tzu said, "Every battle is won or lost before it's ever fought." Have you ever felt this way in the face of temptation? Does it feel like you will always struggle in the same way with certain sins? Perhaps you can't even imagine a victory in the face of temptation.

By prayer and meditation and the reading of God's Word, our hearts and minds are renewed, allowing us to feel the sense of victory before we meet with temptation. Because the temptations come at unexpected times and places, it benefits us to hide God's Word in our heart, so that we may follow the example of Christ by meeting each temptation with the Scriptures.

He has promised that, "No temptation has come upon you except what is common to humanity. But God is faithful; he will not allow you to be tempted beyond what you are able, but with the temptation he will also provide a way out so that you may be able to bear it" (1 Cor. 10:13).

Lord, help me to treasure Your Word in my heart that I may not sin against You (Ps. 119:11).

THE LAW OF FORGIVENESS

*"For if you forgive others their offenses, your heavenly
Father will forgive you as well." —Matthew 6:14*

Forgiving and asking for forgiveness are hard for most of us. Yet some of our most rewarding experiences come as a result of these. We grow in relationship with God and with others when we are forced to confront sin, to repent of it, to seek and also grant forgiveness, and then receive it.

A wrong spirit toward another person may or may not hurt him, but it is certain to hurt you. An unforgiving spirit can be dynamite to our souls. Shakespeare tells us that "the quality of mercy is not strain'd, it droppeth as the gentle rain from heaven." When we consider how great our debt is to God, it should be easy for us to forgive others. But we can allow bitterness and resentment to grow in our hearts. We can surround ourselves with an unforgiving spirit and block the abundance of God's mercy that is available to us.

When we are inclined to be unforgiving, we should remember that even while on the cross, Christ practiced what He had preached on Earth when He prayed, "Father, forgive them, because they do not know what they are doing" (Luke 23:34).

■

*Lord, please give me a heart that is eager
to forgive as I have been forgiven.*

THE LAW OF RICHES

"But store up for yourselves treasures in heaven,
where neither moth nor rust destroys, and where
thieves don't break in and steal." —Matthew 6:20

Riches can be used to serve many wonderful purposes. But how unfortunate it is that many people are robbed by their riches! Christ tells us, "No one can serve two masters, since either he will hate one and love the other, or he will be devoted to one and despise the other. You cannot serve both God and money" (Matt. 6:24). When we trust in wealth, we are certain to suffer great disappointment.

In his book, *The Secrets of Happiness*, Billy Graham shared this: "A French leader once said that if people had enough to eat, money to spend, and security from the cradle to the grave, they would ask for nothing." Only a casual understanding of human nature will show how false this statement really is.

Jesus said that security and riches do not in themselves bring happiness and contentment. It's only when we begin to realize that true treasures are spiritual and eternal, that life takes on a new dignity and the beauty God intended.

■

Lord, please grant me a stronger faith
in eternal things. I do not want to serve two
masters. May devotion to You be unwavering.

NICODEMUS, CAUTIOUS INQUIRER

*Jesus replied, "Truly I tell you, unless someone is born
again, he cannot see the kingdom of God." —John 3:3*

Nicodemus, the cautious inquirer, was earnestly seeking an
answer to his questions when he approached Jesus at night.
How? How? How? were questions that continued to bother
him.

Jesus minced no words with Nicodemus. He informed him
at once of the absolute necessity of the new birth. He told him
that the new birth was so important that without it he could
not see the kingdom of God. If physical blindness is tragic,
how much more tragic is spiritual blindness!

The new birth was essential for Nicodemus, a religious
leader, a man held in high regard by his fellow men. It is also
essential for you and for me—for everyone. With new birth
comes new sight—new vision. New thoughts, new loyalties,
new appreciations are given. Our eyes are open so that we may
see Jesus. Praise God, for this gift!

As unimaginably wonderful as this gift is, the apostle Paul
reminds us that, this side of eternity, our understanding will
always be somewhat limited: "For now we see only a reflection
as in a mirror, but then face to face. Now I know in part, but
then I will know fully, as I am fully known" (1 Cor. 13:12).

There is so much to be grateful for now, and so much to
look forward to in eternity. Thanks be to our God.

*Lord, please guide me as I seek to share with others
how the gospel has changed my heart and my life.*

THE MYSTERY OF HIS DEATH

"For as Jonah was in the belly of the huge fish three days and three nights, so the Son of Man will be in the heart of the earth three days and three nights." —Matthew 12:40

One of the most glorious experiences possible is to stand at the Garden Tomb, just outside the city gates of Jerusalem, and realize anew that it is an empty tomb. Christ died as every man must die, as every great prophet has died, but there is a mysterious difference. After three days in the heart of the earth, He arose triumphant from the grave.

The Pharisees came seeking a sign, and Christ gave them a sign that was irrefutable—resurrection from the dead. No other sign could prove His complete victory over the power of sin and Satan. Someone greater than Jonah and greater than Solomon, was in their midst, and they refused to recognize Him. The empty tomb is still giving its silent witness, even today. Only Christ's redeemed can understand the mystery of the empty tomb. The power that raised Jesus Christ from the dead, is now with those who believe.

> And if the Spirit of him who raised Jesus from the dead lives in you, then he who raised Christ from the dead will also bring your mortal bodies to life through his Spirit who lives in you. (Rom. 8:11)

Lord Jesus, help me to live daily with knowledge that the power of Your resurrection now lives inside of me.

PETER PASSES THE TEST

*"Don't you understand yet? Don't you remember
the five loaves for the five thousand and how many
baskets you collected?" —Matthew 16:9*

Did any man who ever lived provoke greater divergence of opinion about himself than Jesus?

The scribes alleged that He was in a league with Satan, and that He performed His miracles by satanic powers.

Herod the king, guilty of the murder of John the Baptist, tremblingly supposed that He was that wilderness preacher restored to life.

Among the common people it was rumored that He was Elijah, or Jeremiah, or some other prophet, resurrected from the dead.

And members of His own family declared that He was mentally unstable.

Jesus was not unconcerned about these opinions. But they mattered less to Him than the judgments of His own disciples. "'But you,'" he asked them, 'who do you say that I am?'" (Matt. 16:15). Imagine the kind of joy Jesus must have felt when "Simon Peter answered, 'You are the Messiah, the Son of the living God'" (v. 16).

What do you think of Christ? Your answer matters to Him. "For the joy that lay before him, he endured the cross, despising the shame, and sat down at the right hand of the throne of God" (Heb. 12:2).

You are Christ's joy.

*Jesus, may Your Lordship be extended through
all of our lives. May You be Lord of all.*

Jesus Faces His Great Test

As they were coming down the mountain, Jesus commanded them, "Don't tell anyone about the vision until the Son of Man is raised from the dead." —Matthew 17:9

Death! What a subject for a conversation after the glory of the Transfiguration. Yet afterward, when Jesus spoke to His disciples, He continued to talk about the subject which He had discussed on the mountaintop with Moses and Elijah.

This side of heaven, shall we ever understand the greatness of that love that caused Jesus to go to Calvary in our place? Peter, who witnessed the splendor of the transfiguration, knew something of the price that Jesus paid:

> "For you know that you were redeemed from your
> empty way of life inherited from your fathers,
> not with perishable things like silver or gold, but
> with the precious blood of Christ, like that of an
> unblemished and spotless lamb." (1 Pet. 1:18–19)

Precious to whom? Certainly to God the Father who gave His Son to die. But surely also to Jesus Himself. The prospect of death lay heavily upon His soul. But, strengthened by the experience of the transfiguration, and certainly the Father and the Holy Spirit as well, He passed the test, walked down the mountainside, and set His face toward Jerusalem.

*Lord, may my life reflect my thankfulness
for the way You love me.*

THE SIN OF UNFORGIVENESS

"So also my heavenly Father will do to you unless every one of you forgives his brother or sister from your heart." —Matthew 18:35

For Christ followers, this parable of the forgiven yet unforgiving servant has a special meaning. Becoming a Christian means that the first act of this parable, the king's forgiveness, has already taken place. As believers in Jesus, we have received, like the servant of the parable, the cancellation of a debt greater than could ever be paid. The message of the parable, however, is that while the cancellation of this debt is complete in and of itself, it is clear that the forgiven ought to become the forgiving.

Jesus made it clear that the forgiveness of God is ours and it is secure. But we are also called to forgive others—God's act of forgiveness enables our own (1 John 4:19). This is true because a genuine acceptance of divine forgiveness creates a "new spirit" in us, whereby we give what has been given unto us. It is in and through our forgiving relationships with other people, weak and broken like ourselves, that divine forgiveness becomes effectual in us. This is what the prayer of our Lord means by the petition, "Forgive us our debts, as we also have forgiven our debtors" (Matt. 6:12).

God, thank You for Your forgiveness of my sins through Jesus Christ. Help me to believe that I am truly forgiven, and please give me the grace to be forgiving to others.

THE HIGH COST OF SELFISHNESS

*When the young man heard that, he went away grieving,
because he had many possessions. —Matthew 19:22*

Few accounts from the life of Jesus speak so direct a message to our own present-day circumstances as this visit of the
rich young man who sought from the Master the way of eternal life. This young man represents the persistent possibility
that the things we own can come to own us. He came seeking
man's greatest treasure, but he went away sorrowful—not only
because he had great possessions, but because his possessions
had ownership over him.

In reality he could not follow the commands of Jesus
because he was no longer free to do so; he was subject to his
great riches, enslaved to his possessions. They had become the
idol he worshipped, and the god he served.

Even more so in today's culture, success is measured by "the
abundance of things possessed." We can seek so earnestly after
the laying up treasures on Earth—the possessions we wrongly
place our trust in, believing they will bring us safety and comfort and acceptance—that we lose our ability to respond to the
divine calling. In order to be a disciple of Jesus Christ and follow Him in the way everlasting, we must be willing, like Peter,
James, John, and Matthew, to leave all at Christ's bidding.

■

*God, we ask that You make us willing to use any and
all of our possessions as instruments and resources for
Your purposes and the growing of Your Kingdom.*

JESUS FORETELLS HIS REJECTION

"The Son of Man did not come to be served, but to serve,
and to give his life as a ransom for many" —Matthew 20:28

"Adopt the same attitude as that of Christ Jesus . . .
he humbled himself by becoming obedient to the
point of death—even to death on a cross."
(Phil. 2:5, 8)

When the mother of James and John, the Zebedee brothers,
asked for her sons to be given places of honor in the kingdom,
she did not know what she was seeking after. Greatness in the
Kingdom of God is not a station to which we are appointed
by some preferential status where some people receive more
divine favor than others.

Greatness is not something we should seek to be, but rather,
something we ought to want to give in ministry. Scripture tells
us that as Christ followers, we have the indwelling of the Holy
Spirit, giving us the mind of Christ (1 Cor. 2:16; 6:19). And
in having the mind of Christ, our greatest and highest calling
is to share the gospel with others and serve them selflessly.
As disciples, we are all called to this kind of "greatness." This
calling should cause us to humbly reflect on our own personal
standards of spiritual values.

Even as they watched Jesus die at Calvary, His closest followers still did not understand their calling in terms of service.
We have but one standard of greatness: "Whoever wants to
become great among you must be your servant" (Matt. 20:26).

May the sacrificial service of Christ be our
example of what it means to love.

JESUS PRESENTS HIMSELF AS KING

Then the crowds who went ahead of him and those
who followed shouted: Hosanna to the Son of David!
Blessed is he who comes in the name of the Lord!
Hosanna in the highest heaven! —Matthew 21:9

With what joy the people of Jerusalem and pilgrims from the whole country went out to welcome the now famous prophet of Nazareth! They greeted this figure who was humbly riding on a donkey with titles and symbols befitting royalty. Yet, there is no doubt that they were giving Him this welcome out of the mistaken notion that He was coming to be their liberator, and earthly king to free them from the yoke of Rome. Instead, He had come to die, to offer all of mankind a kingdom that is not of this world.

Even today, we can offer Him the titles of King and Lord, while still mistaking His mission and its meaning for our lives. For by His own death He taught us that the reality of the Kingdom of God comes only to those who are willing to accept the cross, the symbol of self-sacrifice and self-denial. The priceless membership Christ won for us in the family of God is ours as we take up our cross and follow Him (Matt. 16:24).

◼

Lord Jesus, help us to grasp more and more the
meaning of the cross for our own lives.

THE FRUIT OF THE KINGDOM

"Therefore I tell you, the kingdom of God will be taken away from you and given to a people producing its fruit." —Matthew 21:43

In our verse today, Jesus tells the Jews very plainly that they had failed in accomplishing the purposes for which God had chosen them. In their failure there is a sober warning. The Jews had interpreted God's call as an honor that set them above other nations. They were victims of spiritual pride, which prevented them from seeing the meaning of their election.

The call of God is to serve our fellow man by sharing the gospel of Jesus Christ, and telling others about the blessings that come from relationship with Jesus. Scripture tells us the kingdom belongs to those who are "producing its fruit," but Jesus knew that we could not do that in our own strength—nor does He want us to.

> "Remain in me, and I in you. Just as a branch is unable to produce fruit by itself unless it remains on the vine, neither can you unless you remain in me. I am the vine; you are the branches. The one who remains in me and I in him produces much fruit, because you can do nothing without me." (John 15:4–5)

Lord, forgive me of my spiritual pride, when I fail to serve others in Your name. Forgive me also when I try to bear fruit and serve in my own strength. You have called me to remain in Your presence. Help me to abide with You and to be a vessel through which You display Your love.

ENEMIES QUESTION THE KING

"Jerusalem, Jerusalem, who kills the prophets and stones those who are sent to her. How often I wanted to gather your children together, as a hen gathers her chicks under her wings, but you were not willing!" —Matthew 23:37

This is Jesus' answer to the question concerning the single greatest guide for our lives. Our lives can have but one center, one focus that has final authority and ultimate meaning for us. Jesus affirms that our commitment to God should be complete. All the energies of our lives should revolve around our concern for the Almighty. This is a needed tonic when we are all too easily distracted by the things of this world.

The same thought is found in the Sermon On the Mount: "But seek first the kingdom of God and his righteousness, and all these things will be provided for you" (Matt. 6:33). We become guilty of idolatry when we allow anything other than God to become our object of worship. The idols we worship are seldom made of stone or wood, they are rather the idols of self, ambition, and wealth.

Lord, I ask today for a deeper faith and commitment to You and Your purposes.

TRAINED AND TESTED FOLLOWERS

*"We are unable to stop speaking about what
we have seen and heard." —Acts 4:20*

One of the most common failings of Christians concerns sharing our faith. We tend to think of witnessing as an unpleasant responsibility, something that we know we are supposed to do, but also something we find so difficult that it is often neglected entirely.

Thankfully, this was not the spirit of Peter and John. Even as threats fell from the lips of the Jewish authorities, they vowed their intention to continue witnessing. Their zeal was rooted in the reality and ultimate importance of what they had "seen and heard" throughout their time with Jesus.

And so it is with us today, that an effective witness must be based upon a vital, personal, spiritual experience with Jesus Himself. As we are committed more fully to Christ, we feel compelled to share our experience with others. And as we share Him with others, we in turn come to know Him better.

Jesus, there is no greater joy than knowing You and being known by You. Increase my faith and my courage to tell others what You have come to mean to me. Make me a vital witness to the gospel, and give me an even deeper knowledge of You.

THE MEMORIAL OF HIS DEATH

*"For this is my blood of the covenant, which is poured out
for many for the forgiveness of sins." —Matthew 26:28*

Jesus spoke frequently of His eminent death, seeking to prepare His disciples for enduring the experience and understanding it. He established no memorial service for His birth,
nor for His greatest sermon or miracle—only for His death. He
wanted to make it clear that this was the event of central and
eternal significance in human redemption.

Observance of the Lord's Supper involves commitment.
Jesus, in instituting the ordinance, called it a covenant. This
would remind His disciples of the covenant made with the children of Israel after God's deliverance of them from Egyptian
bondage.

"We will do all that the LORD has spoken," said the children
of Israel, accepting the covenant (Exod. 19:8). In observing the
Lord's Supper may we remember God's covenant of grace that
provides for human redemption through the sacrifice of Christ.
"'Though the mountains move and the hills shake, [His] love
will not be removed from [us] and [His] covenant of peace will
not be shaken,' says your compassionate LORD" (Isa. 54:10).

Thanks be to God.

■

*Lord, we ask that each experience of the Lord's Supper
may be a true spiritual experience of communion
with Christ and deepening devotion to Him.*

DEATH AND BURIAL OF THE KING

When the centurion and those with him, who were keeping watch over Jesus, saw the earthquake and the things that had happened, they were terrified and said, "Truly this man was the Son of God!" —Matthew 27:54

People react in various ways to the cross of Christ, which is the meeting place of mankind's worst and God's best. The cross judges us. It demands decision, one way or the other.

Some see the death of Christ as a symbol of suffering meekness, a good man forced to death by powerful forces of this world. Others see it as the supreme manifestation of God's love and the propitiation for human sin. As for the centurion who was there when Jesus died, he too, came to conviction about Christ's crucifixion, saying, "Truly this was the Son of God!"

The apostle Paul became a radically changed man when he encountered the resurrected Christ:

> But everything that was a gain to me, I have considered to be a loss because of Christ. More than that, I also consider everything to be a loss in view of the surpassing value of knowing Christ Jesus my Lord. Because of him I have suffered the loss of all things and consider them as dung, so that I may gain Christ and be found in him, not having a righteousness of my own from the law, but one that is through faith in Christ—the righteousness from God based on faith. (Phil. 3:7–9)

The cross demands an answer. How will our hearts respond?

■

Like Paul, I pray to better know You, Jesus, and the power of Your resurrection and the fellowship of your sufferings (Phil. 3:10). Amen.

ADVENTURE IN JERICHO

They told Joshua, "The LORD has handed over the entire land to us. Everyone who lives in the land is also panicking because of us." —Joshua 2:24

Moving day is usually anticipated with mixed emotions. There are tasks to be performed and duties to be completed. If much distance is involved, there are likely to be moments of parting between loved ones. Often, however, some things brighten the experience. They may be new opportunities: a new house, an increase in income, an opportunity to make new friends, or special recreational advantages in a location. And sometimes when people move, they forget about the Lord and what He has done for them.

The people of Israel were preparing to occupy a new land. This was a new adventure for them. They had anticipated it for many years. The people were aware that the Lord had made this move possible, and they knew that they would need His help. Thus, they made their move according to the will of God, and they were victorious over obstacles.

Father God, I ask for Your leadership and blessing in all the ventures that You've called me to.

THE MAN BORN BLIND

If we walk in the light as he himself is in the light, we have fellowship with one another, and the blood of Jesus his Son cleanses us from all sin. —1 John 1:7

Light, fellowship, cleansing—how beautiful they are!

In today's text, John is an old man who recognized the danger and the fallacy of the heresy that was sweeping through the Christian churches. The gnostics were teaching that there was a higher knowledge than the gospel, and John knew this false gospel could not stand.

John was the apostle of love, but he was also a son of Zebedee—he was a son of thunder! (Mark 3:16–17). We admire and respect his moral earnestness and his integrity that made him hate evil and sternly condemn it. How his words flash and roll! With John, life seems either all black or all white.

John also knew the friendship of Jesus, as well as the fellowship of the other disciples. Fellowship with God and our community helps keep our faith strong and results in one of life's greatest joys. Indeed, we were made to be known by one another in Christian community (Heb. 10:24–25).

One of the greatest needs of our churches today—for all people, everywhere—is to belong to a community that "walks in the light." We need the warmth of Christian fellowship, of friends who will walk this life with us, speak truth to us, and sharpen us even as we sharpen them (Prov. 27:17).

◼

Lord, we pray that in all our ways and in all our relationships we will acknowledge You, and that You will direct our paths.

JESUS IN DEBATE

Jesus spoke to them, "Isn't this the reason why you're mistaken: you don't know the Scriptures or the power of God?" —Mark 12:24

The firm rebuke Jesus administered to the Sadducees in our Scripture lesson today was due to their lack of spiritual perception. Their god was too small. They were more interested in maintaining their traditional position than in receiving divine enlightenment. They were more concerned with making a point than in establishing truth. Their god was as small as their materialistic ideas.

This passage can serve us well in pointing out our own lack of understanding of God's teaching, as well as our failure to experience His power and mercies anew each day in our own lives.

How long has it been since you have taken the time to sit down with your Bible open before you and really seek the guidance of the Holy Spirit as you read? Is your experience with God's matchless power as fresh as this new day? He waits to meet with each of us now, this day.

> Finally brothers and sisters, whatever is true, whatever is honorable, whatever is just, whatever is pure, whatever is lovely, whatever is commendable—if there is any moral excellence and if there is anything praiseworthy—dwell on these things. Do what you have learned and received and heard from me, and seen in me, and the God of peace will be with you. (Phil. 4:8–9)

Lord, I ask for the wisdom to understand Your Word, and a willingness to experience Your power in new, fresh ways.

PILATE JUDGED BY JESUS

"You are a king then?" Pilate asked. "You say that I'm a king," Jesus replied. "I was born for this, and I have come into the world for this: to testify to the truth. Everyone who is of the truth listens to my voice." —John 18:37

How often we fail to bear witness for Christ even though we profess Him as Lord! We wait for the time to be "ripe" before we dare speak up for our Savior. We justify our timidity by saying we don't want to "rush" anyone on a matter so serious.

How different from Jesus' own example. As a lowly prisoner He stood before a haughty judge. In quiet yet bold terms He defined His purpose and claimed spiritual Kingship. He stood alone, deserted by His own and surrounded by those who seethed with hatred for Him. Yet He stood courageously to bear witness to the truth. He faced Pilate's unjust court and abuse at the hands of Rome's soldiers, and then died on Calvary still bearing witness to the truth. God grant us a liberal portion of His courage!

■

God, I pray that You will embolden my faith, that I may stand firm in my conviction that Jesus Christ is Lord.

DRINKING THE CUP

And he said, "Abba, Father! All things are possible for
you. Take this cup away from me. Nevertheless, not
what I will, but what you will." —Mark 14:36

No one would want to plan a funeral for a loved one. We
don't want to face sorrow. We flinch at the thought of pain.
We wince and procrastinate if the doctor suggests surgery. We
shun embarrassment and disappointment. We don't want to
bear the blame for others' misdeeds. We're only human, we say.

Jesus was human, too. He faced the condemnation of the
sins of the world. The penalty would be death on a cross. In
prayer, He asked His Father to let this cup of shame, suffering,
and death pass from Him. Jesus knew it was possible for the
Father to save Him from this experience. But there was no
other way to settle the debt of sin. Jesus was submissive, being
willing to do His Father's will at all costs.

Jesus took His problem to His Father. We have the same
privilege. Knowing and being submissive to God's will is our
privilege as His children.

> The Spirit himself testifies together with our spirit
> that we are God's children, and if children, also
> heirs—heirs of God and coheirs with Christ—if
> indeed we suffer with him so that we may also be
> glorified with him. (Rom. 8:16–17)

Your thoughts are higher, and Your ways are
better. Your will, not mine, be done, Lord.

FORETELLING THE BIRTH OF JESUS

"Now listen: You will conceive and give birth to a son, and you will name him Jesus." —Luke 1:31

Overshadowing the honor that accompanied this prediction by the angel, overlooking the miraculous nature of this amazing event, and overstepping the personal sacrifice involved—is the satisfaction and joy of reading this remarkable passage of Scripture about Mary, the mother of our Lord, and her noble, far-reaching contribution to all generations.

What greater demonstration of the truth that it is "more blessed to give than to receive" could we have than this, the story of the virgin birth? When she named her Son, Jesus (Savior), she was personally associated with God, the sovereign ruler of the universe, in providing redemption for all generations of mankind.

The greatest contribution we can make to humanity—which will also bring the greatest satisfaction to our own lives—is to be in some way pointing to Christ, and sharing the gospel. It is God who brings souls into a relationship with Jesus Christ, but He allows us to participate in the process of introducing others to His saving grace.

Lord God, I ask that You direct my steps to follow You, and to stay in Your presence. In doing so, may my relationship with You reflect Your glory and goodness, and somehow by Your power, point others to Christ Jesus.

WITNESSES TO THE RESURRECTION

Jesus said, "Because you have seen me, you have believed. Blessed are those who have not seen and yet believe." —John 20:29

"Seeing is believing" and "you've got to show me" are maxims of worldly wisdom and philosophy, but the Christian experience puts them in reverse.

Thomas needed visual evidence, and in His kindness, Jesus obliged him that—and Thomas was convinced. He may have missed the choice blessing Jesus describes for those who believe without seeing; but in the end, Thomas got what he, personally, needed most: personal interaction with the risen Christ. This is surely a picture of how intimately Jesus loves each one of His sheep, knowing exactly what each requires.

The psalmist said: "I am certain that I will see the Lord's goodness in the land of the living" (Ps. 27:13). And Jesus said to Martha: "Didn't I tell you that if you believed you would see the glory of God?" (John 11:40).

How many choice blessings have we missed because we were waiting for more evidence on our own terms? Do we have to see in order to believe that what Christ has for us is both desirable and profitable? Thomas wisely presented himself that second Sunday night, but he robbed himself for a whole week, doubting and grieving, because he would not believe without seeing. There was blessing waiting for him in the days between. It waits for us too.

■

Father, grow us up in our faith. Help us just to believe—even for the unseen—and be blessed.

THE WONDERFUL DRAUGHT OF FISHES

When they did this, they caught a great number of fish, and their nets began to tear. —Luke 5:6

We settle for so little because our expectations are so limited. Perhaps today you were feeling a little dejected because your personal inadequacy looms large in your self-perception. As a Christ follower and fisher of men, you long to make a catch for God, but you find yourself lacking in skill, and your perseverance is almost exhausted. So far you have only made a "water hole"—the net is empty. You seem to have exhausted all your resources, to say nothing of your patience.

Finally! It's just as it should be: now you will be completely dependent upon the Lord. At His direction you will make one more cast. On the right side, at the right spot, at the right moment, and that one heart that you believed too hardened, too broken, suddenly melts and seeks forgiveness from God. This starts a chain reaction, and before long a whole family is safely inside the fold.

At the moment of total despair, "a great multitude of fishes," which literally threatened the strength of the net, was the fishermen's reward. So when your hopes are sinking, and discouragement is about to scuttle your ship; when you have spoken to so many, but they don't seem to be listening—better to ask God where to cast the net this next time.

■

Lord, show us where to cast the net. Lead us to others who need to know about You.

CHRIST'S GREAT SERMON

"But I say to you who listen: Love your enemies, do what is good to those who hate you." —Luke 6:27

The words and the deeds of Jesus were always the same. He practiced what He preached, and His way was the way to God. He spoke what He knew, and it was truth. He gave what He had, and it was life. His nature is to love, and the cross is the eloquent, moving testimony of His utter faithfulness to His own nature and desire to rescue His creation.

That was the amazing gospel that the early Christians gave to the world. God—the eternal God, the God of the universe—had come and taken man's sin and death that man might have righteousness in life. Paul called it "the mystery hidden for ages and generations but now revealed to his saints" (Col. 1:26). To the Jews it was a stumbling block. Who ever heard of the just and holy God being crucified? "Cursed is everyone who is hung on a tree" (Gal. 3:13). It was absurd, they said.

Mystery of mysteries, it is true. And today, as then, wherever man is being delivered from sin and death, it is through faith in Jesus, who "loved us and gave himself for us" (Eph. 5:2).

God, please help us to practice what we preach—to be both hearers and doers of Your Word (James 1:22).

SENDING OUT THE SEVENTY

*After this, the Lord appointed seventy-two others, and
he sent them ahead of him in pairs to every town and
place where he himself was about to go. —Luke 10:1*

The first command of the great commission is to make disciples. We who have received from Christ the blessings of the spiritual life have been called to share the gospel whenever the opportunity presents itself—wherever we are.

When we obey and step into this calling, we may expect opposition. The "demons" encountered by the seventy whom Jesus sent out are still active today. Because the testimony of His followers is so essential in Christ's plan for winning the lost, Satan and his forces are diligent in seeking to keep Christians from doing Kingdom work.

Surely this must be the source of the strange reluctance that so many of us feel when we think of talking to someone about becoming a Christian. But when, with our Lord's help, we overcome our hesitance, we find that—out of all our incredible experiences as Christ followers—there is immense, incomparable joy in helping to lead a soul to Christ.

*Lord, I pray that I might have a part in helping
someone to know Christ as Savior.*

JESUS DENOUNCES SOME CRITICS

*"Take care, then, that the light in you is
not darkness." —Luke 11:35*

To use our spiritual sight—which comes with the Holy Spirit's indwelling given to us at the new birth—we must have spiritual light. We can see physically only in physical light. In the same way, we can see spiritually only in the presence of our Lord, who is the "light of the world" (John 8:12).

What is it that separates us from the awareness of Christ's presence, closing off our spiritual vision so that we lose sight of Jesus' commands, and fail to recognize and overcome temptations when they come? Perhaps it is when we knowingly refuse to yield to His will, which then leads to our sin and disobedience. When we shut Him out of our hearts and minds and then start making plans of our own, it becomes all too easy to turn from the light and toward the darkness instead.

In the Model Prayer, Jesus warned us specifically against the sin of unforgiveness, which keeps us from opening to the door of our wills, and shuts His light out of our hearts. This kind of disobedience is far more subtle, but no less corrupt, than when we turn from Him with some blatant sin of the flesh. The only way to obey His good and perfect will is to remain in the light of His presence.

*Lord, please reveal to me any unforgiven sin, which may
have closed off my heart to the light of Your presence. I
want to live my life in the light of Your presence, always.*

CHRIST'S CALL TO LOYALTY

"And I say to you, anyone who acknowledges me
before others, the Son of Man will also acknowledge
him before the angels of God." —Luke 12:8

Our Lord asked His followers to be faithful in confessing Him before man. He said, "You will receive power when the Holy Spirit has come on you, and you will be my witnesses . . . to the end of the earth" (Acts 1:8).

This is His plan for the gospel. While He does not need us to carry out His will, He is inviting us to play a part in doing so. Jesus knew that in sharing the gospel with others, our faith would only grow stronger; therefore, the work of evangelism is just as much for our hearts as it is for the person to whom we are witnessing.

The only true qualification necessary for sharing our faith is to have become a believer in the gospel of Jesus. It is also important for our testimony to be lived out in both word and action. Our testimony will be empty without the mark of Jesus in our lives.

Our Lord, who gave His life for us, asks us to "be faithful to the point of death," at which point He promises to "give [us] the crown of life" (Rev. 2:10). This means that we are to be loyal to the extent of dying, if need be, before we would do or say anything that would hurt our influence for Christ.

To love Jesus, is to be faithful to Him. But He does not leave us on our own to do so. He gives us the Holy Spirit to empower us, strengthening our faith, and encouraging our hearts to speak the truth of the gospel.

■

Holy Spirit, help me to be loyal to Christ in both my
testimony and in my life, each and every day.

THE TRUE TREASURE

Seek his kingdom and these things
will be provided for you. —Luke 12:31

As Christ followers, our truest treasure is the Kingdom of God. This is a simple yet beautiful illustration of the relationship between Jesus and His followers. In order to belong to the Kingdom of God, we must receive Jesus' gift of salvation and confess our allegiance to Christ, the King.

Jesus says that when we enter the Kingdom and become followers of the King, His guidance and strength will ensure our material necessities—the things that consume so much of our time with worry—and will bless us with spiritual blessings that are of infinitely greater value.

Our Lord likened the Kingdom to a pearl of great price, of which a man "went out and sold everything he had" in order to purchase it (Matt. 13:46). Complete dedication to the King is still the price of entering the Kingdom and enjoying its blessings.

The blessings of the Kingdom are worth their price. They include forgiveness of sin, new spiritual life, strength for victorious and abundant living, guidance, comfort, peace of mind and heart, and, when this earthly life is over, an eternal inheritance with the King of glory.

Lord Jesus, help me to completely dedicate
my life to You and to Your Kingdom.

WHOLE-HEARTED SERVICE

*"No servant can serve two masters, since either
he will hate one and love the other, or he will be
devoted to one and despise the other. You cannot
serve both God and money." —Luke 16:13*

Everyone faces the problem of dual allegiance. One part of our nature reaches up for God in righteousness. The other part grasps for the carnal and material. There between the two wills develops a continual tug-of-war until each of us settles, once and for all, who is to be Lord over our hearts. The unhappy and unfruitful Christian is the one who tries to serve both the will of God and the will of the flesh.

Paul, when writing to the Romans, said, "Don't you know that if you offer yourselves to someone as obedient slaves, you are slaves of that one you obey—either of sin leading to death or of obedience leading to righteousness?" (Rom. 6:16).

King Saul of Israel revealed his subjection to the flesh when he failed to destroy the Amalekites as God had commanded (1 Sam. 15). God called Saul to be obedient to one Master alone. And in the same way today, Christ calls us to single-minded devotion to Him.

■

*Lord Jesus, help me to give my full allegiance
to You as Master of my life.*

THE RICH MAN AND LAZARUS

"'Son,' Abraham said, 'remember that during your
life you received your good things, just as Lazarus
received bad things, but now he is comforted here,
while you are in agony.'" —Luke 16:25

The biggest mistake we can make is to order our lives in terms of time instead of eternity. The rich man's crime was not that he was rich, but that he trusted his destiny to riches, squandered his wealth upon his fleshly appetite, and refused to share his material abundance to relieve human misery. Blessed by God with unusual resources for good, he selfishly refused to concern himself with the needs of those less fortunate. To him, Lazarus represented a loathsome burden to society rather than a unique opportunity for service.

Pastor and abolitionist Henry Ward Beecher once said, "Riches are not an end of life, but an instrument of life." True living is giving as gloriously demonstrated by our Savior Jesus. "For you know the grace of our Lord Jesus Christ: Though he was rich, for your sake he became poor, so that by his poverty you might become rich" (2 Cor. 8:9).

■

Lord, please give me eyes to see and a heart
to respond to the needs of others.

THE GRACE OF GRATITUDE

But one of them, seeing that he was healed, returned and,
with a loud voice, gave glory to God. —Luke 17:15

This text reveals two striking qualities of the Samaritan leper. When he realized he was cured, he grasped the opportunity to thank Jesus, and he praised God aloud. Perhaps the other nine were just as glad to be free of the malady but gave no gratitude of glory to God.

The application is obvious to us as Christ followers. Just as the lepers, we were under the condemnation of death, sick in sin, without hope of cure. One glad day Christ became known to us as the Great Physician and we appealed to Him for mercy. His ready response gave us new life. But how often do we "turn back" to express gratitude and praise?

No doubt, many Christians grieve the Lord daily by taking for granted His provision of grace. Fear of criticism for being "overly emotional" should never stifle joyous praise, or quench the spirit of gratitude. A spirit of ambivalence reflects a heart that may have grown numb in relationship to the Lord. But by His grace, may none of these be true of us.

Author and biographer Izaak Walton once said, "God has two dwellings: one in heaven, and the other in a meek and thankful heart."

■

Lord, You have blessed me with so much. Please forgive
me when I neglect to give You praise and glory for
Your provision. I ask that You grow and develop in me
the fine art of practicing praise in Your name.

JESUS HEALS THE BLIND MAN

"Receive your sight." Jesus told him. "Your faith has saved you." —Luke 18:42

Two kinds of blindness are portrayed here. The first is evident in the disciples. When Jesus told them of His approaching death, their spiritual blindness prevented their understanding.

The second blindness was physical. The afflicted man had an unusual insight, however, which prompted the crowd's discouragement. He called out to the Master for mercy. Sensitive to the needs of all men, Jesus rewarded his simple, straightforward appeal with restored sight.

The blind man's recognition of need and call for mercy symbolizes the plight and pardon available to all of lost humanity. Blinded by sin, every man needs healing. Jesus "passes by" and healing becomes available. Will He recognize and call? Will we, His disciples, help or hinder?

The change brought about in the blind man and its effect upon the crowd were significant. He immediately received his sight and followed Christ, glorifying God. "All the people, when they saw it, gave praise to God" (v. 43). The world is still impressed when Christ's changed people demonstrate joyful fellowship.

Lord, I ask that You, "Restore the joy of your salvation to me, and sustain me by giving me a willing spirit" (Ps. 51:12).

ZACCHAEUS AND JESUS

*"For the Son of Man has come to seek
and to save the lost." —Luke 19:10*

In the fullness of time, God brought prophecy to full fruition. For many centuries, He had appeared in partial revelation in various types and signs. He had spoken through dedicated but imperfect men. Now, He reveals Himself fully in the dynamic person of His Son. This Son, Jesus, was "the radiance of God's glory and the exact expression of his nature, sustaining all things by his powerful word" (Heb. 1:3).

Jesus began His active ministry by confronting men and women with God's eternal purpose. "For the Son of Man has come to seek and to save the lost." His objective dictated His action! He walked among the poor, the needy, the despised— never neglecting the rich and the mighty—because He had come to seek and to save all men!

Zacchaeus was a hated tax collector, but Jesus responded to his curiosity and his interest. He led him to a full knowledge and acceptance of His Lordship. The change in him was dramatic and deep. His attitude changed. His work was affected. His relationship to his fellow man was made right. Zacchaeus found himself and life's purpose in Christ.

■

*God, we humbly ask for opportunities to point lost souls
to the Savior who is always seeking after their hearts.*

CHRISTIAN PRINCIPLES IN DAILY WORK

*Whatever you do, do it from the heart, as something done
for the Lord and not for people.* —Colossians 3:23

Perhaps the most difficult truth to "get over" for the average
Christian is that Christ is Lord of life. His principles are practical. Every area of life should be permeated with His presence. The laymen and laywomen of the church are on the front
lines of Christianity in their daily work. The battle for souls
wages on as the church invades the office, the classroom, and
the factory forty hours every week. The reality is that many
unbelievers judge Christ by the Church "in working clothes."

Our attitude towards work itself is important from the
beginning. God ordained labor for our good (Gen. 2:15).
Throughout biblical history, work is a dignified and rewarded
act. When our labor becomes "merely making a living," it
becomes drudgery, breeding an utter lack of gratitude and pur-
poseless living. But when our vocation fulfills God's purpose in
life, we labor with joy, satisfaction, and profit. And so we fulfill
Paul's earnest plea: "Whatever you do, do it from the heart, as
something done for the Lord and not for people" (Col. 3:23).

*Lord, thank You for the gift of work. Please grow in me a
spirit of satisfaction in the daily work You have called me to.*

THE GOD OF THE LIVING

"He is not the God of the dead but of the living,
because all are living to him." —Luke 20:38

Moses led his father-in-law's sheep to the backside of the desert one day. An encounter with God in that place was probably the last thing he expected. But he did encounter Him "in a flame of fire within a bush." When Moses removed his shoes, he was permitted to draw near the burning bush. Then God spoke: "I am the God of your father, the God of Abraham, the God of Isaac, and the God of Jacob" (Exod. 3:6).

Jesus used this event long afterward to teach that Moses showed that the dead are raised. It is not a case of God was the God of Abraham, Isaac, and Jacob, but He is their God. He is the God of the living! Jesus said, "Because I live, you will live too" (John 14:19).

What we call death should be recognized for what it is—a gateway into the presence of God. Paul was so convinced, he could say, "For me, to live is Christ and to die is gain" (Phil. 1:21). Again, "For we know that if our earthly tent we live in is destroyed, we have a building from God, an eternal dwelling in the heavens, not made with hands" (2 Cor. 5:1).

■

Thank You, God, for our eternal life, both now
and to come, through Jesus Christ.

THE LAST SUPPER

Then he said to them, "I have fervently desired to eat this Passover with you before I suffer." —Luke 22:15

Christ had come into Jerusalem to observe the Passover feast for the last time. A few days before He had used a little child as an object lesson. That had been forgotten. Now the solemnity of the evening is broken by the recurrence of a popularity contest among the twelve.

Greatness and recognition are to be reckoned in terms of service, Christ said. His disciples did not believe that. Do we? That greatness comes through service? The thing now passing under the name of service is too often a gimmick, a "three cents off the regular price" slogan that one pays for in the final analysis.

Service as taught by Christ has no price tag. It is given freely. It springs from the heart that loves God. It is an overflow of gratitude to God for all His gifts. Particularly for Christ Himself.

The table before the pulpit calls us to the sacrament: to take and eat and to "do so in remembrance" of our Savior, the Suffering Servant who served so faithfully.

■

Jesus, I ask that You show me clear opportunities to serve others for Your sake.

BETRAYAL

*"But Jesus said to him, "Judas, are you betraying
the Son of Man with a kiss?" —Luke 22:48*

Betrayed by the kiss of one of His own must have been the bitterest dreg in the cup Jesus dreaded but chose to drink. It has had a dreadful fascination for us through the centuries as it did for the writers of the Gospels. Expressions of speech in many languages and countless pages of print speculate on what really happened in the heart of Judas.

Was the desire to proclaim Jesus as Lord struggling in his soul with the determination to strike Him down? Isn't it interesting that the voice of Judas was the only one raised even in a semi-defense of the condemned Jesus?

Can we relate to a struggle here that takes place in our own souls as well? How often has the combination of a testimony for Christ and the presence of open sin in the life of the witness been the "kiss of death" to someone seeking to know Christ?

It is good to remember that Christ, who is able "to sympathize with our weaknesses" and was "tempted in every way as we are, yet without sin" (Heb. 4:15), also understands our weaknesses and is ready to make us strong.

■

*Lord Jesus, I pray that each day, my walk with You will point
others to You as Lord and Savior. But I also ask that each
day, You will draw my heart nearer and nearer to Yours.*

PRELUDE TO VICTORY

*"Lord," he told him, "I'm ready to go with you
both to prison and to death." —Luke 22:33*

History is replete with accounts of people and of nations who
have gone down in disaster while on the verge of victory. Yet
here is something new. Here is the God-man Jesus rejected;
His message discredited, boycotted, and opposed by the leaders of His own people; deserted by His trusted followers;
and crucified as a criminal along with the very dregs of society. They had expected a king who would break the noose of
mighty Rome. At first glance, it seems a rather sorry conclusion
to it all.

But no, it is not the end. It is truly the prelude to victory.
The Father "made the one who did not know sin to be sin for
us, so that in him we might become the righteousness of God"
(2 Cor. 5:21).

The earth broken and suffering, the torn veil of the temple,
and the darkened sun were not only God's cry of anguish—they
were His way of joining Jesus' claim of victory, "It is finished"
(John 19:30). Salvation was, and is, won for all mankind.

■

*Thank You, Jesus. Thank You, thank You, thank
You, for Your sacrificial and steadfast love.*

LAST SCENES ON EARTH

And while he was blessing them, he left them and
was carried up into heaven. —Luke 24:51

As Luke gives his account of the last time Jesus' disciples saw Him in His physical body, the overwhelming message is one of expectancy. This same kind of expectancy permeates the events of the next few years, as Luke relates to them.

Not expectancy in the sense of patiently enduring something. No, Luke's Gospel tells us that, "After worshiping him, they returned to Jerusalem with great joy" (v. 52). Through every trial and every victory, their lives echoed a heart of praising and blessing their God. They were on the move, empowered and strengthened by the gospel message. In fact, the apostle Paul's haste and always pushing westward, gives every indication that he was motivated by a sense of urgency.

A common criticism of Christianity has to do with this quality of looking forward. Yes, heaven is our home. But there is more, right here—eternity is now. Christ says as much with His parting promise: "Remember, I am with you always, to the end of the age" (Matt. 28:20). He wanted His disciples—and all Christ followers—to know that yes, we will see Him again in our eternal home of heaven. But He is with us here and now. And nothing can separate us from His love—not even death (Rom. 8:38–39).

Lord, I ask that You would make me more aware
of Your presence here with me today, and for the
faith that You are coming back again.

JESUS RECOGNIZED

The next day John saw Jesus coming toward him and said, "Here is the Lamb of God, who takes away the sin of the world!" —John 1:29

We are always interested in seeing outstanding people and their unusual achievements. In today's text, John the Baptist invites mankind to come and see Jesus, the most wonderful personality to ever walk the face of the earth, and to witness the most tremendous achievement in all of history: the salvation of mankind through His sacrifice.

First, John says, "Look"—come and see for yourself. Jesus repeats this invitation to "come and see" (v. 39). Just as no one can be a son or a daughter to our parents for us, no individual, church, sacrament, or other agency can step in to establish a relationship with God on our behalf. We must see and accept Jesus for ourselves.

As Christians, much of our experience may be summarized in these two commands: "come and see" and "go and tell." Today's lesson illustrates both, as the cycle of coming to Jesus, and in turn witnessing to others, proceeds from John the Baptist on to Andrew, on to Peter, and then on to the three thousand at Pentecost—even down through the centuries to us today.

■

Lord, I pray that my faith in You would become fresh again. I ask that You renew my heart and my mind to see more of Your beauty, goodness, and power.

JESUS REVEALING HIMSELF

Jesus did this, the first of his signs, in Cana of Galilee. He revealed his glory, and his disciples believed in him. —John 2:11

Our Scripture reading for today shows Jesus attending two functions: a wedding and a synagogue service. It is interesting to note that at the first, He performed a most gracious act— and His first miracle—of turning of water into wine. Yet while attending the second function, He came closer to violence than at any other time in His life.

His great power was unleashed on behalf of the first group of people, but against the second group. We ask ourselves why? Is it not that the first group displayed attitudes of faith, trust, and obedience to Him, while those of the second group where disobeying God's commands concerning His house and desecrating it for their own gain?

It is a startling thought to realize that, if we are in Christ's will, the power that turned water into wine is available to us. But we must also remember that if we are rebelling against His will, that same power will work against us, to frustrate our will, and shake us free from our flesh and sin. Both are acts of love.

■

I pray that I may be so yielded to Christ, have such an immovable faith in Him, that I may have eyes to see His miracle-working power in my life and in the lives of others.

JESUS' VITAL DOCTRINE

For God did not send his Son into the world to condemn the world, but to save the world through him. —John 3:17

In an effort to escape the criticism of his fellow Pharisees, Nicodemus came to Jesus by cover of night. Yet, in spite of this, Jesus gave to him the blessed words of salvation. How like our gracious God, to honor even the smallest mustard seed of faith, understanding the doubt that dwells within our hearts.

The heart of the gospel is here. In verse 7, Jesus says, "You must be born again." Each word is significant.

> **You:** Salvation is a personal and individual matter.
> **Must:** It is the primary imperative of life and demands a response.
> **Be:** This indicates (in a passive voice) that there is a miracle that must be performed by God in each of us; we cannot do it ourselves.
> **Born:** This is a beginning of life—eternal, spiritual life.
> **Again:** This beginning is completely new, a different life entirely from the one before.

The succeeding verses proclaim that this new life is embodied in God's Son and may be received by faith alone. The grammar used indicates that this life is received now and can never be lost.

Thank You, God, for Your gift of eternal life. I humbly ask for opportunities to share the gospel message with others.

JESUS AND THE SAMARITAN WOMAN

"But whoever drinks from the water that I will give him will never get thirsty again. In fact, the water I will give him will become a well of water springing up in him for eternal life." —John 4:14

In yesterday's reading, Nicodemus, the Pharisee of tarnished reputation, was told that all of his human qualities of excellence had to be laid aside, and he must have a supernatural life given to Him from above—he could not earn it for himself. In today's selection, we see Jesus dealing with quite a different type of person: the outcast woman of Samaria. Jesus approached them differently but the end result is the same. Both were brought to see their need of Him as their Savior from sin.

The degree of sin does not affect this need; the reality of sin is in all of our lives. We need the cleansing power of the Savior, whether we're struggling with outward "sins of the flesh," or inward sins of the heart like pride, envy, and selfishness.

Both Nicodemus and the Samaritan woman alike had a thirst for the supernatural Water, which this world cannot give, either in self-righteous good works or in sensuous pleasure. Jesus, who is the Water of life, promises to satisfy fully the thirst of our souls, if we will but come to Him.

Jesus, make me more and more aware of my own thirst that can only be satisfied in You.

JESUS' DEVOTION

"My food is to do the will of him who sent me and to finish his work," Jesus told them. —John 4:34

Jesus' disciples had gone into the city to buy food. It was as He waited at the well that He met the woman of Samaria and led her to accept His offer of the Water of life. Some time had passed, and upon the disciples' return, they marveled that Jesus was not hungry. When they pressed Him to eat, He spoke of His experience of witnessing as the "food to eat that you don't know about" (v. 32).

Jesus was saying that witnessing is to the soul of a Christian what food is to the body. And it is like food, in that it is necessary for Christian health and growth. But we do not eat food merely to stay alive, for normally healthy people desire good food, too. If we witness through duty only, we do not share Jesus' attitude and motivation of love.

Do we try to nourish our souls by merely snacking, when we should be enjoying the satisfying feast that, according to Jesus Himself, witnessing provides? Is this nourishment we know about in our own lives?

God, I pray my growing faith will develop a holy appetite for sharing the gospel, and thereby experience the deep soul-satisfaction that can only be found in eternal things.

DEMANDS OF CHRISTIAN CITIZENSHIP

"Well then," he told them, "give to Caesar the things that are Caesar's, and to God the things that are God's." —Luke 20:25

As people born into a free nation, we certainly ought to be grateful for the blessing of freedom. As citizens, we owe our country our loyalty, support, and service in thanks of this freedom. But we owe the God "from whom all blessings flow" absolutely everything we have. Jesus taught His followers to maintain their values by keeping the most important things first and foremost in their hearts.

On several occasions, Jesus taught that allegiance to God must supersede even the strongest of family, as well as national, ties. He summarized this when He said, "Seek first the kingdom of God and his righteousness, and all these things will be provided for you" (Matt. 6:33).

The political climate of our nation fluctuates, swinging like a pendulum. Our hope cannot be in the men and women who seemingly rule this land. Our hope must be in Christ alone. And what our country needs more than anything else, is for the hearts of God's people to be fully submitted to His will.

Jesus, I pray that You "might come to have first place in everything" (Col. 1:18) and especially in my heart.

JESUS MASTERING DIFFICULTIES

But he said to them, "It is I. Don't be afraid." —John 6:20

A great ship was caught in the midst of a raging storm in the North Atlantic. The howling gale that whipped up the tremendous waves played with the ship as though she were a toy. When night approached, the passengers became tense and frightened as the storm continued to threaten the groaning ship. Unable to sleep, the unnerved passengers huddled in the salon and began to weep and pray. How much longer could the ship withstand the strain of the pounding waves? What would happen to them?

Suddenly the captain stood in their midst and began to speak quietly, confidently. The strong, weathered seaman told them of storms through which the ship had passed through before. He reassured them that the engines were working perfectly and that there was no evidence of danger. With a kind face and masterful but calm voice, he said, "We will trust in God and our good ship, and He will bring us through."

His words calmed the people. They had looked into the face of their captain who trusted the Master of the sea. Their fears diminished, and they became calm again. No matter what the storm of difficulty may be in your life, look to your Captain. He will see you through.

> "God is our refuge and strength, a helper who is
> always found in times of trouble. Therefore we
> will not be afraid, though the earth trembles and
> the mountains topple into the depths of the seas,
> though its water roars and foams and the mountains
> quake with its turmoil." (Ps. 46:1–2)

Forgive me, Lord, when my faith gives way.
Strengthen me and deliver me from my fears.

THE LIGHT OF THE WORLD

Jesus spoke to them again: "I am the light of the world. Anyone who follows me will never walk in the darkness but will have the light of life." —John 8:12

The contrast of darkness and light is a theme woven all throughout God's Word. Mankind's eternal, miserable struggle of life without God is the darkest of darkness. But we do not have to stay in darkness. Those of us who follow Jesus "have the light of life." Jesus is "the true light that gives light to everyone" (John 1:9).

The "light of life," however, is not just something we receive from Jesus; it is Jesus Himself. Jesus is life, and our "light of life" is Jesus' dwelling within us through the Holy Spirit: "In him was life, and that life was the light of men" (v. 4).

Then, though all around us there may be darkness, we walk in light because the light is within. "That light shines in the darkness, and yet the darkness did not overcome it" (v. 5). Rather, if we are following Jesus, the darkness only makes the light shine brighter, just as the darkness of Calvary was brilliantly displayed by the eternal victory of the resurrection.

Thank You, Lord God, for the ever-shining "light of the world" who is our never-failing "light of life."

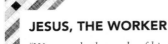

JESUS, THE WORKER

"We must do the works of him who sent me while it is day. Night is coming when no one can work." —John 9:4

How marvelous and gracious are the works of Jesus who "went about doing good" (Acts 10:38). But today's text tells us that even for the Son of God, the works are not His own works but the works of the Father, the one who sent Him. Jesus testifies later, "The Father who lives in me does his works" (John 14:10).

Jesus also testifies, "I and the Father are one" (John 10:30). This indicates a oneness beyond the fact that Jesus is divine as God is divine. It is a perfect oneness of heart and mind and purpose, a oneness so deep and strong that the Son cannot be thought of separately from the Father, or even the Holy Spirit. In this sense, Jesus' works are indeed God's works because Jesus Himself is God's, completely. Then Jesus says to us:

> "Remain in me, and I in you. Just as a branch is unable to produce fruit by itself unless it remains on the vine, neither can you unless you remain in me. I am the vine; you are the branches. The one who remains in me and I in him produces much fruit, because you can do nothing without me." (John 15:4–5)

So our works, too, must be God's own works, brought about by the indwelling Christ through the Holy Spirit. God can do marvelous things through us, these human instruments, if we are one with Christ through complete surrender to Him.

Lord, I place myself wholly in Your hands so that Jesus may fully dwell within my heart and accomplish Your works in and through me.

JESUS, THE SON OF GOD

"If this man were not from God, he wouldn't
be able to do anything." —John 9:33

Jesus has worked the works of the Father who sent Him and has liberated a man from darkness. "He has opened my eyes," declares the man born blind. This man has personally experienced a miracle of Jesus, and he knows most assuredly that Jesus must be of God because such a work could only have been done by God.

Precious is the gift of physical light, but far more precious is the gift of spiritual sight—the revelation of who Jesus is. The blind man has joyfully received both gifts and boldly testifies for Jesus before all.

How sad in contrast are the spiritually blind and arrogant Pharisees who, even in the face of such indisputable evidence, still refuse to believe that Jesus is of God. Instead, they cast the now sighted man out of the synagogue and seek even more determinedly to destroy Jesus.

And what is our stand? Have we opened our hearts to the light and life of Jesus? Do we love Him enough to testify boldly for Him?

■

God, please give me the courage to proclaim boldly that Jesus
is "the Messiah, the Son of the living God" (Matt. 16:16)

JESUS IN SECLUSION

Jesus therefore no longer walked openly among the
Jews but departed from there to the countryside near
the wilderness, to a town called Ephraim, and he
stayed there with the disciples —John 11:54

Although Jesus loved His creation, the people of the world, they did not love Him. It was by their choice that He walked among them no more. He knew of their plot to kill Him. It was as if they were saying, "We are better off without Jesus." How depraved, indeed, is the human heart. They forced Him from this earth. Do we fare any better now, centuries later?

The world today is the victim of its own choices. Somehow it has conceived of an ideal world that leaves Jesus out. By pacts and treaties and "united" nations, humanity dreams of "peace and security." But all without Jesus! We build ships and guns and missiles and bombs to prove that we believe in peace. But we do not allow Jesus to walk openly among us.

And so it is in our hearts and in our churches. Jesus is our honored guest, or He is not present. He is there by invitation, but not from His self-imposed presence. He will not force His way in. "See! I stand at the door and knock. If anyone hears my voice and opens the door, I will come in to him and eat with him, and he with me" (Rev. 3:20).

Lord Jesus, I pray that no part of my heart or life
would be separated from You and Your will.

JESUS ANOINTED

*Then Mary took a pound of perfume, pure and
expensive nard, anointed Jesus's feet, and wiped
his feet with her hair. So the house was filled with
the fragrance of the perfume. —John 12:3*

Jesus is the watershed of life. The answer to, "What do you think of Christ?" is demonstrated for us here in the lives of two primary characters: Mary and Judas. Mary could take her lovely perfume—a year's wages in value—and joyously anoint Christ as a testimonial of her love and devotion to Him. Judas, on the contrary, could only conceive of such devotion as an act of waste and extravagance. There is a law of love that he could not fathom.

> The voice common of sense said, "What waste!"
> and no doubt it was right! But there is a world of
> difference between the economics of common
> sense and the economics of love. Common sense
> obeys the dictates of prudence; but love obeys the
> dictates the heart. —William Barclay

How we love Mary for this act! How few times Jesus was honored with the dignity that was rightly due Him! In the Old Testament, anointing was the rite of inauguration into each of the three primary offices: prophet, high priest, and king. Jesus came to be the fulfillment of all of these for us. Hallelujah! What a Savior!

◼

*Lord, I long for my love for Jesus to be seen by the light
of my sacrificial gifts. May they be pleasing to You.*

JESUS DECLARES HIS DEATH

Truly I tell you, unless a grain of wheat falls to the ground and dies, it remains by itself. But if it dies, it produces much fruit. —John 12:24

Perhaps the greatest truth we learn from this passage is death's new dimension. In Christ it is a vital part of human experience but not a terminal point. Jesus saw no conflict with the charge "that the Messiah will remain forever" and His impending death (John 12:33–34). Instead of being the end of all things, it was rather the threshold to the fullness of life.

The laws of nature illustrate this spiritual truth. Small grains picture for us a fruitful harvest—some thirty, some sixty, and some a hundredfold. The lowly caterpillar becomes the beautiful butterfly, picturing the progress of life no longer bound to this earth. From science we learn of the release of nuclear energy bringing an almost perpetual power from substances once considered of low-energy value. We understand so little, really, of this physical world.

And so it is that no man can really see Jesus except in the light of His vicarious death and redemptive life. It is in our dying to self, that we find ourselves really living for Him.

God, I pray that I might die to my plans for my life and, taking up the cross, see Christ live in the multitudes.

JESUS SETS AN EXAMPLE

"For I have given you an example, that you also should do just as I have done for you." —John 13:15

As yesterday reflected a new dimension in death, so today we have a new dimension in greatness. In contrast to the world's ideas of success, Jesus set forth His Kingdom principle in terms of service. The most menial task of life—even drawing a cup of cold water—has eternal significance when it is performed in the name of Jesus.

Scripture tells us that it's not the result of the work as much as the attitude of the heart, that matters most to the Lord. "There is nothing better for a person than to eat, drink, and enjoy his work. I have seen that even this is from God's hand, because who can eat and who can enjoy life apart from him?" (Eccles. 2:24–25).

Indeed, what does life matter apart from our Creator God? Life is empty without Him. And so we do well to examine our lives and the resources of our time and talents—both given to us by Him. Apart from Him, truly, we can accomplish nothing of significance.

■

Lord, I humbly ask for a personal willingness to serve God's people.

WHAT CAN I DO FOR WORLD PEACE?

*"Blessed are the peacemakers, for they will be
called sons of God." —Matthew 5:9*

The beginning of peace is personal and Godward. It is not a feeling so much as it is a redemptive act that sets things in harmony with God. It is first inward and spiritual, the byproduct of righteousness, which is "rightness" restored with God. This is why Paul wrote that "the kingdom of God is not eating and drinking, but righteousness, peace, and joy in the Holy Spirit (Rom. 14:17).

Mankind talks about world peace, but neglects this truth: peace is only fulfilled in relationship with God. The most noble calling God gives His children is that of peacemakers. It is an important act of service to bring peace to the human heart, and to the world. And we, as Christ followers, know the only true source of peace: the Prince of Peace, Christ Jesus. Those who know Him can say with the psalmist, "I will both lie down and sleep in peace, for you alone, Lord, make me live in safety" (Ps. 4:8)—both now and forevermore.

Telling others about Jesus is not the equivalent of forcing an ideology onto them. It is literally the kindest thing one person can do for another.

■

*Lord, make me an evangelist of peace, sharing the
gospel and proclaiming redemption in Christ Jesus.*

JESUS BETRAYED

*"Jesus of Nazareth," they answered. "I am he,"
Jesus told them. Judas, who betrayed him, was
also standing with them. —John 18:5*

This is one of the saddest scenes ever recorded in human history. One of the disciples who might have stood with Jesus in the most crucial hour, chose rather to stand with those who were against Him. Judas, at the crossroads of his life, might have chosen differently. Still, by choosing to sell the Lord's life for profit, he fulfilled the Scriptures (Zech. 11:12–13; John 13:18–30).

Each of us has this choice to make at the crossroads of life. We must either stand with Christ or with those who are against Him. There is no other alternative. To stand with those who oppose Christ is to betray Him. But we also betray ourselves, and we betray those who may be influenced by our decision. No man ever betrays Christ alone.

To join those who stand with Christ means we accept Him as personal Saviour, and recognize Him as the living Lord of our lives. Judas made his decision. It cannot be changed. It is the most important decision we have to make. Where, and with whom, do we stand?

■

*God, strengthen my faith to stand with Christ
in every experience and not against Him.*

JESUS ON TRIAL

"My kingdom is not of this world," said Jesus. "If my kingdom were of this world, my servants would fight, so that I wouldn't be handed over to the Jews. But as it is, my kingdom is not from here." —John 18:36

Certain names in history are always referred to with contempt. Pilate is perhaps the prime example. For though he plainly saw his duty toward Christ, he did not have courage to fulfill it. Confronted with the fanaticism of the Jews and the possibility of his own political suicide, he yielded to their demands. Though he found no fault in Jesus, he delivered Him to be crucified—even after his own wife's plea to release Him (Matt. 27:19). As the Gospel of Matthew tells us, Pilate then washed his hands of the whole affair (Matt. 27:24).

Jesus was a righteous man who lived a righteous life—the most righteous, ever. But He is so much more. He is God incarnate, the Word made flesh, who came to set His captive creation free, far as the curse is found. In the end, He will be the righteous Judge. But long before that, He came to Earth to rescue the souls of mankind. He provided for Himself the sacrificial Lamb of God (Gen. 22:8)—all for the joy that lay before Him: for you and for me (Heb. 12:2).

■

Lord, make me a vessel of truth. May my faith and my testimony, in both word and deed, be the aroma of Christ, pointing them to the good news of the gospel.

JESUS CRUCIFIED

When Jesus had received the sour wine, he said, "It is finished." Then bowing his head, he gave up his spirit. —John 19:30

"Who really crucified Jesus?" is a question often asked and argued but seldom settled. Actually, there are several answers that may be given. The Roman soldiers took part, for this was their official duty to which they were assigned. Many Jews also joined in, but not all the Jews cried, "Let Him be crucified." Some chose to crown Him Lord of their lives rather than crucify Him.

The truth is that I crucified Him and so did you. Because of you and me Jesus went to the cross. It was for our sins that He died. But His cry, "It is finished," was not a cry of defeat but of victory. For as He died He made it possible for us, all who trust Him, to live.

Our right to salvation comes only through our faith in Christ Jesus' righteousness. "This is the message of faith that we proclaim: If you confess with your mouth, 'Jesus is Lord,' and believe in your heart that God raised him from the dead, you will be saved" (Rom. 10:8–9).

Thanks be to our Savior God.

■

God help us never to take for granted the great gift of your Son. In our lives and in our hearts, may we crown Him Lord of all.

THE RESURRECTION

"The other disciple, who had reached the tomb first, then also went in, saw, and believed." —John 20:8

Have we ever stopped to consider what the news of Christ's resurrection meant to the disciples? It is hard to imagine their sorrow, disappointment, and despair when they saw Him taken down from the cross and laid in a borrowed tomb. Surely this was the end of their fondest hopes.

But the resurrection morning changed their gloomy night into the dawn of their most brilliant day. Their sorrow changed to singing, their despair into hope, and their defeat into victory.

The resurrection is also the guarantee of victory for everyone who receives Christ. It guarantees victory over sin. It is our guarantee of victory over death. It changes our fear to faith, and our doubt to assurance of eternal life.

May our hearts echo that of the psalmist's: "God, create a clean heart for me and renew a steadfast spirit within me. . . . Restore the joy of your salvation to me, and sustain me by giving me a willing spirit" (Ps. 51:10, 12).

Lord, we ask that the story of the resurrection of Jesus will stir anew in us the joy of serving a living Christ.

JESUS APPEALS TO PETER

*He asked him the third time, "Simon, son of John,
do you love me?" Peter was grieved that he asked
him the third time, "Do you love me?" He said,
"Lord, you know everything; you know that I love
you." "Feed my sheep," Jesus said. —John 21:17*

We live in a world of hunger. Many of the people who live in it will go to bed hungry tonight. The shortage of food, at least the distribution of it, continues to be a major problem of our day.

But even so, the world's greatest hunger is not for physical food, however, but for the Word of God. Jesus underscored this in His command to Peter. Out of all the ways Peter might have proved his love for Jesus, the best was by feeding the sheep.

It is not enough to say that we love Christ. We do not really love Him as we should until we become involved in helping others find and follow Him.

> "If a brother or sister is without clothes and lacks
> daily food and one of you says to them, 'Go in
> peace, stay warm, and be well fed,' but you don't
> give them what the body needs, what good is it? In
> the same way faith, if it doesn't have works, is dead
> by itself." (James 2:15–17)

*God, we pray for opportunities to be used in a
personal way to help ease the spiritual hunger
of those who have yet to know Jesus.*

THE WHOLE FAMILY OF GOD

So then you are no longer foreigners and strangers,
but fellow citizens with the saints, and members
of God's household. —Ephesians 2:19

Paul was well acquainted with the loneliness that so many experienced in foreign lands in his day. There were two types of these foreigners: the "strangers," who were people belonging to another land, and the "sojourners," who were foreigners dwelling in a land without the privileges and rights of citizens. This had also been the condition of the Gentiles in relation to the Christian faith.

Because of redemption and adoption, the Gentiles could also become a part of the body of Christ. Now, all the blessings of Christian fellowship were theirs, potentially making loneliness a thing of the past.

As Christians, we are also a part of the family of God. We need not be strangers on the fringe, when we have access to all the benefits and blessings of Christian community available to us. We do not have to live in loneliness. Because of Jesus, there is a place for every one of us at the table. Through Him, one day, we will all be at home with God the Father.

Lord, I do not want to live a life of loneliness and isolation.
Please give me a fresh sense of belonging in Your family. Show
me ways to better connect with other Christ followers.

A PARTING AND A PROMISE

They said, "Men of Galilee, why do you stand looking up into heaven? This same Jesus, who has been taken from you into heaven, will come in the same way that you have seen him going into heaven." —Acts 1:11

Luke is the only writer who tells us about the ascension of Jesus. He also tells us that after watching Jesus be carried up into heaven, the disciples began "worshiping him." Then "they returned to Jerusalem with great joy. And they were continually in the temple praising God" (Luke 24:52–53).

How could the disciples be happy after seeing their Lord go from them? The answer is found in the promise that He would come again. With this hope they could go back to their task of sharing the good news of the gospel with the whole world.

We also have this promise. God has a plan for each one of us and for the world. The second coming of Christ is the divine event that all of creation has forever been moving toward, groaning for eternity (Rom. 8:22). Like the disciples, all Christians have reason for joy in their hearts. Our concern must be to accept the challenge of that promise and to make ourselves ready for His return when it comes to pass.

Lord, I pray that the promise of Christ's coming again may become more and more real to me.

A POWER THAT PERPLEXED

They were all astounded and perplexed, saying to one another, "What does this mean?" —Acts 2:12

We do not really know what happened at Pentecost. Of one thing we can be certain. The disciples experienced unusual power from the Holy Spirit, and afterward, they were emboldened to share the gospel with people as they never had before. They were effective in their witness because they were willing to be used of the Holy Spirit in proclaiming the gospel of Christ. While others argued and doubted, they were busy about their task. No wonder the people were amazed at what they saw and heard.

We, too, may receive power and courage from the Holy Spirit when we tell others about Jesus. He helps us overcome the tendency to be casual or careless about our call. As we work at the job of sharing Christ with others, we must remember that the results are left to Him alone. Only He can work in the hearts of unbelievers. Even now, the power of the Holy Spirit is ready to amaze us.

Lord, make me willing for the Holy Spirit to rise up in me in an unusual way to accomplish the work You've called me to do.

FIRST FRUITS OF THE HARVEST

"So those who accepted his message were
baptized, and that day about three thousand
people were added to them." —Acts 2:41

A marvelous change had come into the lives of the disciples. At Jesus' trial and crucifixion they were cowardly and fell away; the flock scattered when the Shepherd was struck (Matt. 26:31). Peter, as fervent a follower and friend as he was, even went so far as to deny that he ever knew Jesus (Luke 22:54–62).

But at Pentecost they were no longer afraid and witnessed with unusual courage and power. Their witnessing was accompanied by the Holy Spirit's power, resulting in three thousand people's turning to the truth, and receiving Christ as Savior.

What made the difference in these men? They were the same men, but they were no longer relying upon their own strength and sufficiency. Their reliance was now where it ought to be: squarely upon God and the power of the Holy Spirit.

Are you willing to be used by God and for His purposes of spreading the gospel message? Or are you intimidated by the task at hand? It's good to recognize that sharing your faith with another, witnessing to them, is an act of eternal significance— at least God's part in it is. God alone whispers to our hearts and causes them to turn back to Him. Our part is to relate to others how He has pursued our own hearts, individually, relentless.

May our words be true, but may God's voice be louder than all the rest—including ours.

Lord, I ask for the courage to tell the truth
about all You've done for me.

BETTER THAN MONEY

*But Peter said, "I don't have silver or gold, but what
I do have, I give you: In the name of Jesus Christ
of Nazareth, get up and walk!"* —Acts 3:6

To the crippled man it was obvious why the gift from Peter
was better than money. Money could not heal him but through
Jesus Christ, Peter could heal him.

Money is impersonal. It changes hands quickly, passively.
At one time it may be in the pocket of a crook and at another
in that of a righteous, God-fearing man. Unlike money, Peter's
gift was personal. It came from Jesus Christ through Peter,
who was merely a vessel of healing. His time with Jesus, the
prayers, confessions, temptations, tears, and joys had brought
Peter to the point where he could say, "But what I do have, I
give you."

What Peter had, he gave. God gave His only begotten Son.
The Son gave His life as a ransom for many. And "whoever loses
his life because of [Jesus] will find it" (Matt. 16:25). Christ's
way is that of those who have received the gift and therefore,
want to share that gift, the goodness of the gospel.

*Lord, cleanse and empower us so that we
may be the vessels of Your gifts.*

A LESSON FOR PETER

Again, a second time, the voice said to him, "What God has made clean, do not call impure." —Acts 10:15

An angel told Cornelius to send to nearby Joppa for Peter, "who would tell him what he must do." About the time Cornelius' servants arrived in Joppa, Peter went up on the housetop to pray. He was very hungry and while dinner was being prepared he fell asleep. He had a threefold vision of a great sheet, tied at each corner and let down to earth. It contained all kinds of tame and wild animals, creeping things, and birds. And then a voice said to him, "Get up, Peter; kill and eat" (Acts 10:13).

Peter learned one of the most important lessons of his life on the housetop. The next day, when Cornelius fell upon his knees at Peter's feet, Peter practiced what he had learned. He said to Cornelius, "Stand up. I myself am also a man. . . . God has shown me that I must not call any person impure or unclean" (vv. 26, 28).

What about us? Have we been on the housetop? Has God been revealing new truths to us that we have yet to share or walk out? It is not for us to decide whose hearts will be changed by Jesus' finished work on the cross. Our part is to "Go into all the world and preach the gospel to all creation" (Mark 16:15).

■

I ask, Lord, for a heart that will not judge but will instead be willing to share the gospel with anyone You would put in my path.

GOD'S INDISCRIMINATE GRACE

Peter began to speak: "Now I truly understand that God doesn't show favoritism, but in every nation the person who fears him and does what is right is acceptable to him. —Acts 10:34–35

This was probably the best news Cornelius had ever heard. Though a Gentile, he was a man of excellent character who gave to the poor, feared God, and prayed daily. Peter was a Jewish Christian who found it difficult to believe that the gospel could also be for the Gentiles. But on the housetop of Simon the tanner, in Joppa, God made it clear to him that the gospel is for all people.

Cornelius said, "So now we are all in the presence of God to hear everything you have been commanded by the Lord." To which Peter said, "Now I truly understand that God doesn't show favoritism" (Acts 10:33–34). And Peter went on "proclaiming the good news of peace through Jesus Christ" (v. 36).

Immediately they believed, and the Holy Spirit came upon them with power. That very day, new converts were baptized in the name of the Lord Jesus Christ. Jewish believers were astonished that God's grace included Gentiles as well as Jews, but they, too, joined all the rest of the Christ followers in praising the Lord.

Lord, Your Word is clear: the gospel is for everyone.
I humbly ask for the privilege of proclaiming
Your gospel to all who would hear it.

GOD'S MIGHTY DELIVERANCE

*"Therefore tell the Israelites: I am the LORD, and I will
bring you out from the forced labor of the Egyptians and
rescue you from slavery to them. I will redeem you with an
outstretched arm and great acts of judgment. I will take you
as my people, and I will be your God. You will know that I
am the LORD your God, who brought you out from the forced
labor of the Egyptians. I will bring you to the land that I
swore to give to Abraham, Isaac, and Jacob, and I will give
it to you as a possession. I am the LORD."* —Exodus 6:6–8

The Christian way will always be the way of belief and faith in
Almighty God's absolute power and desire to come to the aid
of His followers.

But to live in faith involves absolute submission and
patience, letting the Lord choose His method and way of
procedure. The Lord led them by a devious way that they
knew not, but the destination was sure. I have seen it and
experienced it in my own life and can say, with Solomon, "In
all thy ways acknowledge him, and he shall direct thy paths"
(Prov. 3:6 KJV).

■

*Lord, I ask for the fortitude, endurance, and greater faith
to strengthen me for hours of stress and hardship.*

THE SONG OF THE SAVED

About midnight Paul and Silas were praying and singing hymns to God, and the prisoners were listening to them. —Acts 16:25

All too often, even we, as Christ followers, can look at the future and find that it seems rather bleak. Paul and Silas had come into Macedonia out of obedience, following a vision from the Lord. At first they had success; however, Philippi was the devil's territory. He would not give it up without a terrible fight. Surely, the situation would have looked distressing to mere human eyes. But praise God! He has already won the battle (John 16:33).

Bleeding backs and broken hearts at midnight are not conducive to optimism. And so Paul and Silas did the only natural thing for Christians to do. They prayed. God heard their prayers and healed their hearts, encouraging them so much that they forgot that their backs were bloody.

"Praise God from whom all blessings flow!" He does not abandon His own. He does not leave His beloved destitute in the dust of despair. That night the song of victory burst forth from the mouths of the saved. God shook the shackles loose and splintered the stocks!

Have you come to the midnight hour of your Christian experience? Do not give up now! This is the time to pray.

Lord, thank You for Your saving love. May the "song of the saved" bring refreshment and renewal to my weary heart.

MOB VIOLENCE IN EPHESUS

*Some were shouting one thing and some another, because
the assembly was in confusion, and most of them did
not know why they had come together.* —Acts 19:32

John Wesley writes: "As I returned home in the evening, I had
no sooner stepped out of the coach than the mob quite closed
me in. I rejoiced and blessed God, knowing this was the time I
had long been looking for; and immediately spake to those that
were next to me of 'righteousness and judgment to come.' At
first not many heard, the noise round about us being exceedingly great. But the silence spread farther and farther till I had
a quiet, attentive congregation; and when I left them they all
showed much love, and dismissed me with many blessings."

The moving multitudes of today's cities seem to be hostile
to the gospel. But they do not know where they are going. They
have no one to point out the way. They are driven by the materialism and moralism of this world. Perhaps if we are faithful
to speak of "righteousness and the judgment to come," the mob
may be turned into a receptive congregation of the eternally
blessed.

*God, help me to live in such a way that some
of the "mob" may see Jesus through me.*

SHARED LEADERSHIP

According to the grace given to us, we have different gifts: If prophecy, use it according to the proportion of one's faith; if service, use it in service; if teaching, in teaching; if exhorting, in exhortation; giving, with generosity; leading, with diligence; showing mercy, with cheerfulness. —Romans 12:6–8

Moses was about to be bogged down by the hundreds of requests for counseling that came to him every day. He was the absolute ruler of Israel, and he tried to attend to every little detail and problem the people brought his way. Not only was this situation unbearable for Moses, but the people sometimes stood in line for days awaiting their turn to consult him. This was a situation that could not last forever.

God is wise, and He is kind. In His wisdom, He led Moses to delegate authority and distribute responsibility so that his great teaching talent would not be lost in the crowd. There were plenty of people who could take care of the details. Their talents could be used of God, too. Some of them were even better suited for administrative duties than the great prophet.

God, in His Church, has distributed talents and "gifts" of all kinds to the many people He has redeemed and brought into Christian community. Together, we must share the leadership of the kingdom of heaven "according to the grace that is given to us."

God, I ask that You would mercifully reveal to me the place in which You've called me to serve You.

THE RIGHT OF APPEAL

*If then I did anything wrong and am deserving of death,
I am not trying to escape death; but if there is nothing
to what these men accuse me of, no one can give me
up to them. I appeal to Caesar!" —Acts 25:11*

The law and order of the Roman Empire enabled the growth of movements that proved to be of detriment to the advancement of the gospel. It is ironic that the same governmental system also guaranteed the protection of and the right of appeal to one of its citizens, the apostle Paul, the itinerant missionary. This proved to be God's way of sparing Paul's life for greater things. In answering Paul's prayer, the servant's hope was renewed, giving him the needed encouragement to preach the gospel to those who were at Rome also.

In the first chapter of his Philippian letter, most likely written from Rome, the apostle Paul was careful to point out that, despite his incarceration, the gospel was being preached by the boldness of those who succeeded him in leadership among the churches, through his writing ministry, and through his preaching to the soldiers who guarded him in Rome. What may have felt like a tragedy proved to be a great blessing.

*Lord, help me to see through the unavoidable delays
and distractions of the day. Please give me eyes to see
that You are always at work in every circumstance.*

A QUESTION FOR THE JUDGE

*"Why do any of you consider it incredible
that God raises the dead?" —Acts 26:8*

A man on trial is usually expected to answer questions pertaining to his own guilt or innocence. Before King Agrippa we find Paul so concerned with the judge's own heart and sins that for a time it almost seems that Agrippa is on trial.

The question Paul asks is pointed. A person's answer to that question may well determine whether or not they are ready to consider the teachings of Christianity. If God cannot raise the dead, then we have no Savior. For Jesus was slain on the cross, and today we would have to regard Him simply as a good man who died a fool's death.

Was it possible for the king to believe that God could raise the dead? Paul clearly thought he could believe, and he did not want to miss the chance to engage the king's heart with gospel truth.

Trusting God to fulfill His promises is essential to our faith in Him. People today have the capacity for faith, too. If they believe there is a Creator God who brought everything around us to life, then they have the capacity to believe that same God is able to raise the dead to eternal life. And so He can, and so He will.

■

*Lord, we pray that more people around the
world will come to believe that God can raise
the dead to eternal life in Christ Jesus.*

GOD'S COVENANT WITH HIS PEOPLE

"And to love him with all your heart, with all your understanding, and with all your strength, and to love your neighbor as yourself, is far more important than all the burnt offerings and sacrifices." —Mark 12:33

God Himself is the author of the covenant. This means, ultimately, that the response of each individual heart to spiritual matters is first and foremost an act of God. And being a covenant-keeping God, He often takes miraculous and even extreme measures in the pursuit and preservation of His people.

Those who believed and entered into a covenant relationship with Him assumed the grave responsibility of obeying Him with righteous living—all out of thankfulness and reverence for His saving grace. Once they learned to obey Him, the Lord challenged His people to be vessels through which His spiritual blessings would pour forth to a needy world.

As Christ followers, we know firsthand that we are unable to keep our promises to God without His help through the Holy Spirit. We can do nothing in our own strength. "But God proves his own love for us in that while we were still sinners, Christ died for us... For if, while we were enemies, we were reconciled to God through the death of his Son, then how much more, having been reconciled, will we be saved by his life" (Rom. 5:8, 10).

When we learn to rest in His presence, abiding in sure relationship with Him, only then will we be able to begin living the life He's called us to as His redeemed (John 15:4).

■

Lord, I want to love You supremely, before all else in my heart. Help me to become more and more aware of your goodness around me, and help me to trust You with every fiber of my being.

THE OPTIMISM OF FAITH

*So take courage; men, because I believe God that it
will be just the way it was told to me.* —Acts 27:25

Paul had just learned that the ship in which he was sailing was
soon to be wrecked. An angel of the Lord had told him. Long
before that he wrote that he had already suffered shipwreck
three times, and that he had spent a day and a night in the
deep.

But according to the angel, no lives would be lost. And Paul
believed it. He had trusted the Lord before, and his faith had
become strong as a result of such experiences.

Like a muscle, faith grows stronger with exercise. Strong
faith encourages optimism. In times of peril the person whose
faith is in the Lord is likely to be at their best. They are likely
to be considerate of others who share in their peril and circumstances. A word of encouragement from such a person is
likely to be of deep encouragement to someone struggling with
fear and doubt, even to those who pretend to believe there is
no God.

*Lord, I ask for greater faith, and for the ability
to encourage others to have faith also.*

THE FAVORS OF FRIENDSHIP

Now the brothers and sisters from there had heard the news about us and had come to meet us as far as the Forum of Appius and the Three Taverns. When Paul saw them, he thanked God and took courage. —Acts 28:15

The fact that some Christians from Rome came a good distance to meet Paul as he approached the city was an encouragement to him. Many of us are willing to go to great lengths to show kindness to a friend. Lives have been greatly enriched, and friendships deepened, by the thoughtful consideration of Christian people for other servants of the Lord.

Encouragement from friends so often spurs someone on to do better than they would have done otherwise. We can never do our best without our friends. We were built and designed to be in relationship and community.

In a strange land or experience, the appearance of Christian friends is a cause for thankfulness. Their presence in our new circumstances is also a cause for rejoicing. We have so much in common with other Christians, that enduring friendships often grow out of experiences we share as we serve the Lord.

Lord, help me to do and say those things that would encourage others. You know what their hearts need to hear. I pray You'll use me to help encourage them in some small or big way.

GOD'S PEOPLE LEARN TO WORSHIP

Come, let us worship and bow down; let us kneel
before the LORD our Maker. —Psalm 95:6

God wants His people to worship Him. And as God's people, we need to worship our Creator. Worship is an essential part of our relationship with God.

It can be difficult to remain consistent in worship. There are so many distractions and so many heartaches in this world. There are scores of other things that claim the attention of God's people. For centuries and generations, material possessions and addictions have caused the people of God to forget their Maker.

Still, God calls His people unto Himself. He calls us into relationship, and worship helps us to reconnect to Him. We must learn to put God first if we are to please Him. Just as Jesus taught His disciples while preaching the Sermon on the Mount, when we put God first, everything else in heaven and on Earth will fall into its rightful place (Matt. 6:33).

When we are communing with the Lord, constantly speaking with Him, His voice begins to drown out the other voices of fear and doubt that can so easily distract us. As our Creator, God knows the nature of our hearts is to wander, and so He calls us to continually seek after Him and remain in His presence.

Lord, there have been times when my heart has
grown cold toward You. Please forgive my fleshly
indifference. I pray that through worship, You would
renew my fervor for relationship with You.

A SALUTE TO THE SAINTS

To all who are in Rome, loved by God, called as
saints. Grace to you and peace from God our Father
and the Lord Jesus Christ. —Romans 1:7

In Paul's salutation to the Roman Christians, he describes the glories of those who are called to be saints—the living servants of the living Savior. As the beloved of God, they are assured and strengthened by His grace, sustained by His peace, and empowered by the presence of God the Father and God the Son and God the Holy Spirit.

One of the most comforting and reassuring thoughts that can possess the heart of a Christian is that we love and serve a living Lord. He proved His power and His perfect holiness by His own bodily resurrection and the redemption of His creation. He turns the world of His followers upside down, showing them firsthand that those who lead must serve; indeed, if we are in Christ then we are fellow servants with Him. And like Paul, we are also fellow sufferers for the gospel of salvation (1 Pet. 4:13).

Jesus knew that, as His followers, we would face great trouble in this world. But He assures us that He has already overcome this world (John 16:33). And we are not left alone to suffer. Jesus Himself lives to make intercession for His saints.

■

As saints of our Lord, may we be faithful
to the high calling of Christ Jesus.

THE SINFULNESS OF SIN

For his invisible attributes, that is, his eternal power and divine nature, have been clearly seen since the creation of the world, being understood through what he has made. As a result, people are without excuse. —Romans 1:20

God spoke the universe into existence in answer to a need of His great love. As often as He reviewed His work, we read, "God saw that it was good." It was a perfect, harmonious creation. It moved in response to God's perfect will. But, in the sixth period, even after He had placed animal life on the earth, the Father heart of God was not satisfied. His work could declare His glory, but it could not adore Him; it could reveal the majesty of His might, but it could not worship Him. It was a soulless creation.

God said, "Let us"—the Father, the Son, and the Holy Spirit—"make man in our image, according to our likeness" (Gen. 1:26). God yearned for an object of affection that could return His affection; a creature that could bear the image of the Creator; one that could reason, will, and love. The sinfulness of man's sin, in willfully separating Himself from God, can be measured only by the love against which He sinned.

Lord, I pray today to bear more perfectly the likeness of You who loved me even before the foundation of the world.

JUSTICE IN JUDGMENT

We know that God's judgment on those who do such things is based on the truth. —Romans 2:2

At the last judgment, those who must hear the condemnation, "Depart from me," will stand without excuse. The light of truth preceded man on the earth. God revealed it to Adam, that man might dwell forever in perfect harmony with Him. God identified Himself with a whole race in an effort to identify Himself with the whole world. He dictated His law to Moses as a design to bring man into a saving knowledge of "the way, the truth, and the life" (John 14:6).

He made visible and audible manifestations of His presence to His chosen people. He sent His prophets to teach and warn them in order that man might look and live. In the fullness of time, the types and shadows that had so eloquently pointed to the Redeemer became the best authenticated reality in world history and in human experience. "Why would you choose to die?" is the cry from the Father's heart.

We do not have to die. Infinite Mercy has devised a plan for our salvation from sin and death. Infinite Love offers it: "But as I told you, you've seen me, and yet you do not believe" (John 6:36).

> "The time is fulfilled, and the kingdom of God has come near. Repent and believe the good news!" (Mark 1:15)

■

Lord God, I pray that all may be justified through faith in Christ.

THE LIMITATIONS OF THE LAW

For no one will be justified in his sight by the works of the law, because the knowledge of sin comes through the law. —Romans 3:20

We do not know how divinity became clothed with humanity in order that the plan for our redemption might be consummated, but John says, "The Word became flesh and dwelt among us. We observed his glory, the glory as the one and only Son from the Father, full of grace and truth" (John 1:14).

When Adam transgressed God's law and passed sin and death on himself and his race, divine law was broken and divine blood had to be shed. For "without the shedding of blood there is no forgiveness" of sin (Heb. 9:22). If Adam had broken a civil law, he could have met the penalty with his own life; but the law is limited. It cannot save us from sin, "For whoever keeps the entire law, and yet stumbles at one point, is guilty of breaking it all" (James 2:10).

But like a teacher, the law can inform us about sin, and point us to a sin bearer, a Savior. God "made the one who did not know sin to be sin for us, so that in him we might be become the righteousness of God" (2 Cor. 5:21). "A person is not justified by the works of the law but by faith in Jesus Christ" (Gal. 2:16).

Lord, we pray to be faithful in declaring the one and only way through which the lost and broken may be saved.

BLESSINGS OF THE BELIEVER

*Therefore, since we have been declared righteous
by faith, we have peace with God through
our Lord Jesus Christ. —Romans 5:1*

The believer who is justified before God is satisfied with the justice of God. They have peace with God and access to His comfort. They can rejoice in the hope of sharing in the glory of God. They walk with poise in the presence of accusers because of the indwelling of the Holy Spirit, who is the controlling and motivating power in the hearts of believers—a power that transcends all earthly trials.

Instead of fearing the doom awaiting sinners who fall into the hands of a righteous God, believers in Christ can rejoice in the assurance that they are justified by the blood of Christ and will be saved from the wrath to come. They are reconciled to God through the death of His Son and will be saved through His Son's life, which is our pattern in holiness, because He "has been tempted in every way as we are, yet without sin" (Heb. 4:15). As we grow in His likeness, we partake more abundantly in the blessings designed for believers.

*Because of the blessings that are ours as believers, Lord,
we ask that You help us to be faithful in declaring the love
of God, through every expression of our daily lives.*

FAITH ON TRIAL

Be strong, and let your heart be courageous, all you who put your hope in the LORD. —Psalm 31:24

Believers in Christ can hope in the Lord because of the two-fold purpose that brought Him into the world: to seek and to save the lost, and to deliver us from the limitations of bondage of sin into the beauties of abundant living. God's purposes are upheld by His power, His wisdom, and His presence. They are fortified by His love, which is without end or beginning. His purposes cannot fail.

Believers can hope in the Lord because His promises are supported by His character. He who is able to save us is able to keep us. In sunshine and shadow; in waiting and wandering; in delays, denials, and disappointments; in trials and triumphs—God's promises are being fulfilled, and He is keeping faith with His own. In testing times we can be of good courage. Our God will supply our strength. As He was with His people in the wilderness, so will He be with us. "He who promised is faithful" (Heb. 10:23).

Lord, we ask that even in times of testing we may hold fast to the profession of our faith without wavering.

SALVATION BY FAITH

For what does the Scripture say? "Abraham believed God, and it was credited to him for righteousness." —Romans 4:3

How good of God not to set up a plan of salvation that would make it difficult or impossible for any seeking soul to come to Him!

A thief on a Roman cross was assured of his salvation in his dying hours. It was too late for him to do any good work or to be baptized. With his strength ebbing low, his tongue swelling with fever and pain, he could hardly confess his long list of sins, or bear testimony for Jesus who hung on the center cross.

But the repenting sinner could lift his eyes in faith towards Him. He could yield his heart in love to Him as he humbly prayed, "Jesus, remember me when you come into your kingdom," and then pass through the portals of death in peace.

He who serves in an effort to earn his own salvation, serves through fear, not love; through selfishness, not through gratitude for the full and free salvation purchased for us on Calvary. "For you are saved by grace through faith, and this is not from yourselves; it is God's gift" (Eph. 2:8).

Lord, we humbly ask that our lives may magnify the name of Him who is our Light and our salvation.

HOPE FOR THE TEMPTED

No temptation has come upon you except what is common to humanity. But God is faithful; he will not allow you to be tempted beyond what you are able, but with the temptation he will also provide a way out so that you may be able to bear it. —1 Corinthians 10:13

Being tempted is no sin. But deliberately placing ourselves in a position to be tempted is sinful. Temptation comes in many forms. And as Christ followers, we sometimes face temptation even—and sometimes especially—when we are in the midst of dedicated service to our Lord.

We are tempted at many points, but perhaps one of the most common to Christians is the matter of service. We become distracted and half-hearted in our love of Jesus and are tempted to slow our pace in service to the Kingdom. Life here on the earth has a way of making us feel weary of it all.

In this kind of temptation—and in all kinds—we must remember Jesus. He was tempted in every way just as we are, yet without sin. How will God make a way of escape? By His Holy Spirit to be sure. But, in remembering Jesus' faithfulness in His temptation, we find hope and encouragement, keeping our eyes fixed on Him.

> How happy are those whose way is blameless,
> who walk according to the LORD's instruction!
> Happy are those who keep his decrees
> and seek him with all their heart. (Ps. 119:1–2, 5–8)

Lord, make us strong when temptation comes.

THE SPLENDOR OF LOVE

Love never ends. But as for prophecies, they will come to an end; as for tongues, they will cease; as for knowledge, it will come to an end. —1 Corinthians 13:8

It may seem that love sits alone on the throne of virtues. But crowded around that throne are many others of the "queen's" court. Jealousy is not permitted in the same room. Neither is hate nor pride nor fear. Love treats these impostors like the light treats darkness, expelling it from the room.

The love mentioned here is not a quality or possession of the natural man, but only of a redeemed man. Jealousy, pride, hate, envy, greed—all deter us in the race. Love drops these shackles from us to permit better race-running.

Love has an element of faith in it, for no one could possibly love God supremely without faith in Him. Love in Him also begets hope, that we are secure in our relationship with God, both now or forevermore.

It is good to take inventory of what we love, which is what Paul has done for us in 1 Corinthians 13. Read the full chapter and take an honest look at how you love. With Christ as our perfect example of love, we will forever have inspiration and reason to love one another better.

May the love described by Paul possess my heart as well.

THIS IS VICTORY

But thanks be to God, who gives us the victory through our Lord Jesus Christ! —1 Corinthians 15:57

The promise of the resurrection is victory indeed! The reality of the resurrection will be joy incomparable!

The Christ followers' resilient faith is in stark contrast to the doubt and confusion that plagues our modern culture. Today, mankind seems far more interested in moralism than it does the Messiah. But imagine the peace to be found if only they would confess with their mouths and believe in their hearts that Jesus is Lord—then they would be saved (Rom. 10:9).

The Lord invites everyone to come to Him. But to do so, they must, "Enter through the narrow gate. For the gate is wide and the road broad that leads to destruction, and there are many who go through it. How narrow is the gate and difficult the road that leads to life, and few find it." (Matt. 7:13–14).

Oh, to see and receive the blessing of assurance by entering through the narrow gate! The road to destruction is wide, plagued by doubt and confusion and the futility of self-sufficiency. But in truth, it is the Lord who leads His sheep through the narrow gate out into wide open, spacious places. He comes to rescue them and leads them out to freedom, under His watchful and protective care. He does so because He delights in us (Ps. 18:19).

This is the victory: eternal salvation and freedom with Christ Jesus.

■

Thank You, God, for the victory You give us through our Lord Jesus Christ.

THE PEOPLE DEMAND A KING

Happy is the nation whose God is the LORD—the people
he has chosen to be his own possession! —Psalm 33:12

This is a hard day for kings. Few of them remain in power, and that power can sometimes be easily shifted. But rulers appear under other names, too. Today, we have presidents and prime ministers and politicians elected by the people, as well as military dictators and terrorist extremists, who force their way into power through fear, manipulation, and brute force. In Samuel's day, the children of Israel wanted a king like the nations surrounding them. They liked the splendor that went with such a ruler. It seemed to bring a dignity and power—albeit by the world's standard—to the people.

But in choosing Saul, son of Kish, as their first earthly king, they forsook their Creator God as their King. This new king craze was, in short, an effort to rid themselves of obedience to Jehovah.

In our day, freedom of religion is protected mostly by the separation of church and state—not so much in the hearts of the citizens. God has become a myth to many, and as a culture, we are far more prone to choose other gods.

Affection for our true God and King gets replaced by our pride in believing the lie that we don't need God—perhaps the enemy's most convincing work to date. In sprawling suburbia and bustling cities, mankind escapes from God into the tyranny of leisure, laxity, and worldly pleasure.

May we as a people and nation come to honor God.
And though we are free today, may we not exchange
our freedom of faith for the things of this world.

GLORYING IN INFIRMITIES

If boasting is necessary, I will boast about my weaknesses. —2 Corinthians 11:30

What do you boast about? Did becoming a Christian make a difference in the things you are proud of?

When Paul became a Christian, his set of values was reversed completely. What once would have been cause for shame became what he boasted of most. He was willing to lose his reputation, to be ridiculed, abused, and persecuted because of his love for Christ. He learned to glory in the things that made him appear weak and contemptible in the eyes of his critics.

Yet, in Paul's life as in ours, what appears to be weakness may prove to be strength. The death of Jesus on the cross may have marked Him as a failure in the eyes of some, but we know that it was one of God's greatest victories: the redemption and rescue of creation, for all who would believe in Christ Jesus.

Suppose we, like Paul, should make out a list of the things for which we are suffering for the gospel. Is there any area of our lives where we have been willing to forego some of our earthly comforts in exchange for the furthering of God's eternal Kingdom?

■

Lord, I want to value what You value. Give me a new sense of what matters most. Teach me to boast in what honors Christ rather than in what exalts me.

GOSPEL FROM ABOVE

For I want you to know, brothers and sisters, that the gospel preached by me is not of human origin. —Galatians 1:11

The gospel Paul preached was divine both in its origin and its nature. He did not earn it; he did not learn it. It was given to him by the risen, reigning Lord.

A study of the history of religions reveals man's continuing effort to make a god for himself. Some, like Roman Caesars and the Egyptian Pharaohs, proclaimed themselves as gods. At the close of World War II, the emperor of Japan proclaimed publicly that he was not divine, as his nation had previously claimed him to be.

A faith whose King suffers and dies for His people is quite different from the man-made religions we are often offered as a substitute for Christianity. Our God "so loved the world that he gave" himself to us and for us. This is the gospel, the "good news" that we can share with others today. What God did for Paul, what He has done for us, He longs to do for all of mankind.

> Therefore the LORD is waiting to show you mercy,
> and is rising up to show you compassion,
> for the LORD is a just God.
> All who wait patiently for him are happy. (Isa. 30:18)

■

Lord, I ask that You would grow my faith that I may boldly proclaim Your gospel plan of salvation.

THROUGH DEATH TO LIFE

I have been crucified with Christ, and I no longer live, but Christ lives in me. The life I now live in the body, I live by faith in the Son of God, who loved me and gave himself for me. —Galatians 2:19–20

Our Christ was a suffering Christ. To provide eternal life for us, He went to the cross, to Joseph's tomb. He died! But then He arose from the dead, victorious forever over the power of death.

We, too, must die. We must die to sin. The old ways of self-will must be crucified in order that the new life in Christ can come into being. This new life is one bound intimately with Christ. Like our Lord, we must suffer for others. We must love as He loved, forgive as He forgave, serve as He served. We are still responsible beings, but we are now moved by a mightier power than our sinful natures. This new life and power are ours by faith in the Son of God who loved us and gave Himself for us.

Thanks be to God.

Thank You, Jesus, that I can say, "Christ lives in me." You are my one true hope and joy. May my life reflect my love for You.

JUSTIFICATION BY FAITH

Now it is clear that no one is justified before God by the law,
because the righteous will live by faith. —Galatians 3:11

The law and faith are like two keys. The law condemns and convicts and proves all of mankind fall under condemnation. Faith is the key that opens the door and leads us out to freedom. Each of us is given the capacity for faith and the opportunity to choose either to have faith in God or to reject God's divine purpose for our life. We can live this new life only by faith. Not only are we saved by faith, we live by faith.

The Galatians were reminded, as we need to be, that having begun a new life by faith they cannot hope to reach perfection by depending on the works of the flesh.

Will this day bring suffering, sorrow, personal worries, or concerns? Then you may triumph over them by praying for a faith that is greater than your problems. There is no surer, safer way than the way of faith in Christ Jesus.

Lord, You alone know what's best for me. You know
how to best comfort and encourage me. Help me to
turn to You first—not some worldly distraction—and
ask for the power of the only One who can save.

HEIRS OF GOD

For through faith you are all sons of God in Christ Jesus. —Galatians 3:26

What a glorious inheritance! What joy it inspires! Think of it; we unworthy, sinful creatures are heirs of God and joint heirs along with Jesus Christ of all that heaven affords.

Occasionally we read of someone receiving an unexpected inheritance or winning the lottery sweepstakes, lifting them overnight from poverty to great wealth. But in truth, this is what has happened to every believer who has called on the name of Jesus.

It does not matter where we come from or what we have or have not accomplished in this life. We do not have to get ourselves cleaned up and together. One's social status is no barrier. It is no longer a question of who is my neighbor, who is my brother. For, by faith in Christ Jesus, we are the children of God, and together we will inherit His Kingdom. His invitation is to all.

> "Come to me, all of you who are weary and bur-
> dened, and I will give you rest. Take up my yoke
> and learn from me, because I am lowly and humble
> in heart, and you will find rest for your souls. For
> my yoke is easy and my burden is light." (Matt.
> 11:28–30)

■

Lord, I pray Your Kingdom come, and that Your will be done.

SET FREE

*For you were called to be free, brothers and sisters; only
don't use this freedom as an opportunity for the flesh,
but serve one another through love. —Galatians 5:13*

Freedom in Christ is an experience unlike any other. It can open our hearts in ways we never dreamed before. When we begin to comprehend the depth of Jesus' love for us and receive His gift of salvation, it exposes in each of us an inexplicable kind of vulnerability. It is as if being loved and accepted by Jesus makes it possible for us to love and accept ourselves— sinful, though we are, but still bearing the image of God.

And from this sense of love and acceptance comes a new kind of freedom. What do we care what the world thinks of us, when the Creator God of the universe loves us so? This is the kind of freedom that ought to motivate us to serve our brothers and sisters, looking for opportunities to display the goodness of God and point others to Jesus.

"What then? Should we sin because we are not under the law but under grace? Absolutely not!" (Rom. 6:15). With hearts submitted to our Savior, our lives are no longer our own, for we were bought at a very great price (1 Cor. 6:19–20). We cannot ignore the claims of Christ upon our lives.

We must be sensitive and obedient to the will of Christ Jesus in our lives—not out of legal requirement but out of overflowing love and gratitude. It is for freedom that Christ has set us free. Therefore, we must stand firm in that freedom, and no longer live like slaves of our flesh (Gal. 5:1).

*Lord, help me to remember that I have been bought with
a price and that I am a new creation in Christ Jesus.*

ALL OF GRACE

For you are saved by grace through faith, and this is not from yourselves; it is God's gift. —Ephesians 2:8

Man's part is to trust; God's part is to work. We are to be delivered from the power of sin. A real work is to be brought about in us and through us. The Lord Jesus has come to do what we cannot do for ourselves (Rom. 8:3). What can be said about our part except that we must continually surrender ourselves and continually trust? All we can claim is that by an act of faith we put ourselves into the hands of the Lord. Faith is both the beginning and the continuing foundation. When we trust, the Lord works.

The Lord does mighty work in and through us, but He will not force Himself on us. Jesus stands at the door and knocks, waiting for us to open up our hearts to Him (Rev. 3:20). Through faith in Him, all things are possible. God's works in us are perfect in every stage of our growth and faith. God works. We trust.

Lord, forgive me when my faith wanes and weakens under the pressures of this world. I ask for renewed and unwavering trust in You, Lord, my good and gracious God.

FOOD FOR THOUGHT

*Finally brothers and sisters, whatever is true, whatever
is honorable, whatever is just, whatever is pure,
whatever is lovely, whatever is commendable—if
there is any moral excellence and if there is anything
praiseworthy—dwell on these things. —Philippians 4:8*

The peace of God that fills the heart and mind is often regarded as a rare, exalted moment—a mountaintop experience. Somehow there is the notion that each mountaintop experience must be followed inevitably by a descent into a valley of harsh, faith-shaking reality. It is true that as we follow Jesus and His companions down from the mount of transfiguration, we meet the milling crowd: the afflicted boy, the distraught father, and the unsuccessful disciples. But there is more. Into this scene of confusion and defeat comes the incomparable Christ, giving peace to a tortured soul. This is reality, too.

Paul regards God's peace as more than transitory; it is the way of life. The God of peace abides with those who trust and abide in Him (John 15:4). One tried and true way of doing so is to return again and again to God's Word. If we want to know the mind of God and be reminded of His love for us, there can be nothing better than to feast on Scripture, to meditate on it day and night (Josh. 1:8). Then "the peace of God, which surpasses all understanding, will guard [our] hearts and minds in Christ Jesus (Phil. 4:7).

■

*Lord, may my life bear witness to a heart
and mind that knows Your peace.*

THE HOPE OF HIS COMING

On that day when he comes to be glorified by his saints and to be marveled at by all those who have believed, because our testimony among you was believed. —2 Thessalonians 1:10

There are dangers in developing extreme views on the subject of the second coming of Christ. One extreme is that the second coming is in the future, and we have limited information about it; therefore, we should pay little attention to it and give our time to other doctrines about which there is little difference of opinion.

The other extreme view tends to neglect and ignore all other teachings of the Bible, giving attention only to references of the Lord's return. A person who holds this view may feel that a pastor is not preaching the gospel unless he talks about the second corning. There are some who believe God has revealed to them the time of His return. But they have forgotten the Scripture passage that assures us that the time of Jesus' return is kept secret from all, even Jesus Himself: "Now concerning that day or hour no one knows—neither the angels in heaven nor the Son—but only the Father" (Mark 13:32).

Surely there is a way to find balance between these extremes. May we remember that the second coming of Jesus means nothing to those who do not know about His first coming. Let us watch and pray and labor till Jesus returns, but let us continue to share the good news of His life, death, and resurrection. When He does return, may we be found in Him.

With the help of the Holy Spirit, Lord,
make us ready for Your return.

UNPROFITABLE MADE PROFITABLE

I became his father while I was in chains. Once
he was useless to you, but now he is useful both
to you and to me. —Philemon 10–11

This is the difference Christ makes: from darkness to light, from death to life, from unprofitable to profitable. What would have happened to Onesimus but for Christ? The Savior changed this slave, put grace in Paul's heart to intercede for him, and doubtless caused Philemon to be forgiving.

We can as well ask where and what we would be apart from Christ. It is nearly as easy to think of the world with the sun gone out as it is to think of our lives without the Son of God to light us on our way. Many are the accomplishments of mankind, but under all is this truth that we must remember: "Acknowledge that the LORD is God. He made us, and we are his—his people, the sheep of his pasture" (Ps. 100:3).

Thanks be to God for the land of beginning again. And what will we be because of Christ? "Dear friends, we are God's children now, and what we will be has not yet been revealed. We know that when he appears, we will be like him because we will see him as he is" (1 John 3:2).

■

Lord, make me a vessel through which You do
Your eternal work and grow Your glory.

THE SUPREMACY OF THE GOSPEL

For this reason, we must pay attention all the more to what we have heard, so that we will not drift away. —Hebrews 2:1

In the first chapter of Hebrews the author explains the exalted Christ. And then suddenly, chapter two begins with, "For this reason, we must pay attention all the more . . ." Therefore, because of Christ, we must listen.

It is plain that in Christ, God has spoken. God's message is not a theory to be tested. We are confronted by this truth. The decision to hear or not to hear is ours. Since Christian knowledge is always personal, each individual must choose to hear what God has said in the sending of Christ. Hearing the message of God in Christ involves more than our ears. Receiving divine truth includes will, intellect, emotion, and behavior. What we hear depends upon the kind of person we are and what we are ready to receive. Scripture tells us only the pure in heart shall see God (Matt. 5:8). Being pure in heart is not necessarily moral perfection. It is a heart that is right with God (James 4:8). We must hold tight to God, so that we will not drift away with the influence of this world.

Holy Spirit, quiet my heart that I might hear Your voice and give attention to what God is saying to me.

A SOLEMN WARNING

Watch out, brothers and sisters, so that there won't be in any of you an evil, unbelieving heart that turns away from the living God. —Hebrews 3:12

What is unbelief? Is it the refusal to accept certain doctrines? Is it merely the rejection of semantics, a form of words?

To the author of Hebrews, unbelief was not so much a rejection of the words spoken, as separation of our hearts from the one speaking to us—in this case, the living God. The words *turn away* literally mean to fall away from, to break the relationship.

It is often easier to accept words rather than to receive the person. We hear God's commandments given to Moses with our ears but fail to see the person of God revealed in Christ's character.

A child at play may follow the command of the parent, but fail to love the parent. Is it not the same with us? It is possible to hear God's words without finding God, the person, in them. And whether we realize it or not, our unbelief speaks to a relationship. It is not merely the rejection of words or doctrine, but of God Himself. Our God is not an ideology or the means to an end. What He offers us through the gospel is a reconciled relationship with Him.

■

God, I want to know You better. Please teach me something new about You today that my faith may grow in strength and wonder.

THE SYMPATHETIC SAVIOR

For we do not have a high priest who is unable to sympathize with our weaknesses, but one who has been tempted in every way as we are, yet without sin. —Hebrews 4:15

At times, every person feels that they are experiencing life alone. A successful businessman might say, "No one really understands life's pressures and temptations as I experience them."

A mother could say, "I am the only person who really understands the burden of responsibility for my children." A teenager might say, "No one really understands me." A young child might say, "Nobody loves me."

But do we truly face life alone, left in our own weakness? Do we have to live alone, or is that our choice? What if there were just one person who truly understands? Glibly, we might concede that God knows our circumstances. Yet how could Jesus, One who has all of the divine resources available to Him, truly understand me?

We must remember that Jesus was both fully God and yet fully man (Phil. 2:6–8). The full scope of the nature of Christ is understood when we grasp that He also experienced a full human life. This means that He was tempted in every way imaginable, as we are. He knows firsthand what our lives are like, the struggles we war with.

Therefore, "Who is the one who condemns? Christ Jesus is the one who died, but even more, has been raised; he also is at the right hand of God and intercedes for us" (Rom. 8:34).

Jesus, I believe You understand my internal struggle here on this earth. I pray that I would turn to You for comfort instead of some worldly distraction.

BY GOD'S APPOINTMENT

In the same way, Christ did not exalt himself to become
a high priest, but God who said to him, "You are my Son;
today I have become your Father." —Hebrews 5:5

Jesus said, "For everyone who exalts himself will be humbled, and the one who humbles himself will be exalted" (Luke 14:11). Although Jesus often claimed much for His mission and work, He rarely talked of His inner self. He had a respect for self, but He had freedom from the preoccupation of self. He did not seek His own security. He had no home or bank account (Matt. 8:20). He came not "to be served, but to serve, and to give his life as a ransom for many" (Matt. 20:28). How did He come to attain this freedom?

Jesus knew and trusted the Father. To know God is to be free from the need to attain man's acceptance, man's honor, man's possessions, and man's security. Real freedom is found in God's authority. Scripture warns us that, "The fear of mankind is a snare, but the one who trusts in the LORD is protected" (Prov. 29:25). But Scripture also encourages us that, "The fear of the LORD is the beginning of wisdom, and the knowledge of the Holy One is understanding" (Prov. 9:10).

Who and what our hearts meditate on and revere determines how we live our lives. Jesus trusted and was always about the business of His Father (John 5:19). When our eyes are fixed on Him, we are freed from the distractions and snares of this world.

◼

Lord, teach me to find my identity in You each and every day,
so that I won't be distracted by the false messages of this world.

THE IMPERATIVE OF DEATH

Now without faith it is impossible to please God, since the one who draws near to him must believe that he exists and that he rewards those who seek him. —Hebrews 11:6

When we say someone is "a person of great faith," what do we mean, exactly?

A person of great faith is one who believes in something or someone. They have confidence in what they believe. They trust in that something or someone. They have no serious doubts their faith cannot answer.

As Christ followers, our faith is in God, and in His Son Jesus Christ, our Lord and Savior. We believe in God and in so many ways express our confidence in Him. We depend on our faith to give us the answers to life's questions.

Believing that God is real and good, and that He is indeed our God, we can in faith know His presence and experience His companionship.

> "I do not call you servants anymore, because a servant doesn't know what his master is doing. I have called you friends, because I have made known to you everything I have heard from my Father." (John 15:15)

Lord Jesus, thank You that You are always near, even when I don't perceive of it or acknowledge You. Forgive me for that. Turn my face toward You at all times, I humbly ask. Amen.

THE UNTAMED TONGUE

But no one can tame the tongue. It is a restless evil, full of deadly poison. —James 3:8

Being a Christ follower, and living in this world but not of it, takes a great deal of discipline. There are so many things ready to pull us away from good. There are so many people who would divert us from a life of faith. There must be determination that life's stresses and worries will not make us say and do things that would contradict our faith in God.

The Lord endows His people with all kinds of talents. We may perhaps be called to build houses, care for the sick, paint art, operate machines, teach children, write books, cook meals, sell merchandise, practice law—any number of things. We can serve the Lord in so many different ways, once we've submitted our hearts, minds, and bodies to His sovereign will.

But the tongue—that is different, James wrote. It needs the added power of righteousness to keep it under control, to say the right things at the right time, to help and not to injure others. "No foul language should come from [our] mouth, but only what is good for building up someone in need, so that it gives grace to those who hear" (Eph. 4:29).

Lord, I pray that You will be God over my tongue, that only pleasing, edifying things would come from lips—words that build up, not tear down.

WHAT IS THE GOSPEL?

He saved us—not by works of righteousness that we had done, but according to his mercy—through the washing of regeneration and renewal by the Holy Spirit. —Titus 3:5

Perhaps one of the more common sins of the flesh is that of pride, or conceit. It is good to be proud of what we have been able to do, but it is wrong to allow this pride to shut out our sense of gratitude to God for His goodness to us.

Too often we come to think that what we have accomplished is because of our ability or cleverness. But the truth is that "it is God who is working in [us] both to will and to work according to his good purpose" (Phil. 2:13).

Every one of us is indebted to others for what they have taught and shared with us, resulting in what we have, what we have done, and what we can do. It is in sharing these gifts to bless others that we will find our greatest satisfaction.

And so it is with the spiritual world as well. Our salvation is not attained by the works of our own hands, however great, or our service to God, however faithful. These things are useless in trying to reconcile ourselves to God. Only faith in Jesus Christ will bring us fully into fellowship with Him.

■

Lord, today I echo the words of the psalmist: "You do not want a sacrifice, or I would give it; you are not pleased with a burnt offering. The sacrifice pleasing to God is a broken spirit. You will not despise a broken and humbled heart, God" (Ps. 51:16–17).

RIGHTEOUS LIVING

All those who are with me send you greetings.
Greet those who love us in the faith. Grace
be with all of you. —Titus 3:15

In all three chapters of this small book, Paul seems to be telling young Titus not to be so full of high-sounding philosophies that he forgets the practical application of the Christian gospel.

In the first chapter Paul mentions those who "claim to know God, but they deny him by their works" (Titus 1:16). In the second chapter he reiterates this same theme when he admonishes Titus to "make [himself] an example of good works with integrity and dignity in [his] teaching" (Titus 2:7). Finally, Paul comes to chapter three, where he says, "Let our people learn to devote themselves to good works for pressing needs, so that they will not be unfruitful" (Titus 3:14).

One of the bitter criticisms of Christ followers is that we attend church on Sunday, but we do not really act like the Church body we're called to be (Acts 2:42–47)—we fail to be "doers of the word" and are instead "hearers only, deceiving [ourselves]" (James 1:22).

May those descriptions not be true of us. Let us be unified in action, glorifying Christ Jesus, and meeting the urgent needs of our time.

■

Lord, help us to make our daily lives and deeds reflect the gospel message You have given to us to share with others.

BROTHERS IN CHRIST

There is no Jew or Greek, slave or free, male and female;
since you are all one in Christ Jesus. —Galatians 3:28

This verse in Galatians 3 has been called the Magna Carta of
the Christian faith. Indeed, salvation has come to all of God's
children. Thanks be to God!

This message is in stark contrast to "The Three Blessings"
liturgy from the Jewish prayer book known as the "siddur":
"Blessed are you, O God, King of the Universe, who has not
made me a Gentile, a slave, or a woman." Imagine how radical
the teachings of Jesus must have been to the culture of His
day! (Mark 16:15).

We know that we are all brothers and sisters in Christ
Jesus, and yet we often fall short of loving one another as we
are called to do. We know that Jesus stepped across dividing
barriers in His day, as witnessed by His attitude toward the
Samaritans. We, too, have made progress, moving toward unity
in Christ, but we still have so much more work to do.

How can we begin to deal with prejudice in our own lives?
Let us meditate on the truth of today's verse from God's Word.
Let us ask God to help us think of all of God's children, truly,
as our brothers and sisters. Let us move toward one another in
the grace and peace extended to each of us by our Lord and
Savior, Jesus Christ.

Lord, help us to follow Christ's leadership in all things.

GROUNDS FOR ASSURANCE

*I have written these things to you who believe in
the name of the Son of God so that you may know
that you have eternal life. —1 John 5:13*

Can a Christian ever be lost again? This question that enters
the minds of many Christians today also plagued the Christians
to whom John wrote. His letter gave them the grounds for
assurance that the God who saves them, also keeps them. It
is impossible to fall back into the former state of existence.
The Spirit has "moved" into our hearts to dwell permanently.
Eternal life has already begun.

When we realize this, we can serve God more effectively
because our doubts are gone, our deepest fears assuaged. Not
having to work to maintain our salvation, we can serve God
simply because He is good, and because we love Him. This is
by far a purer, more enduring devotion.

Saved—completely and eternally. This is the state of those
who trust Jesus as Savior. May we rest in His perfect and finished work on the cross.

*Lord Jesus, there are not words enough to thank You
for the gift of my salvation. But I pray the attitude
of my heart will reflect my gratefulness and draw
others to such a gracious and loving God.*

REASONS FOR WATCHFULNESS

Watch yourselves so you don't lose what we have worked for, but that you may receive a full reward. —2 John 8

Just because we, as believers in Christ Jesus, have assurance of eternal life does not mean we have license to sin. Paul warned us against such teaching in his letter to the Romans:

> What should we say then? Should we continue
> in sin so that grace may multiply? Absolutely not!
> How can we who died to sin still live in it? Or are
> you unaware that all of us who were baptized into
> Christ Jesus were baptized into his death? (Rom.
> 6:1–3)

Instead we ought to say, "Search me, God, and know my heart; test me and know my concerns. See if there is any offensive way in me; lead me in the everlasting way" (Ps. 139:23–24). We must constantly examine our motives, our actions, and our influence to be certain that they are Christlike. And while every Christ follower has been called to tell people about what Jesus has done for us, we are also responsible for our own actions and the guarding of our hearts.

■

God, help me to guard my heart above all else, for it is the source of true life in that it connects me to You (Prov. 4:23). God will enable us to live consistently for him.

SECURITY IN CHRIST

Now to him who is able to protect you from stumbling and to make you stand in the presence of his glory, without blemish and with great joy, to the only God our Savior, through Jesus Christ our Lord, be glory, majesty, power, and authority before all time, now and forever. Amen. —Jude 24–25

What parents are not thrilled at the opportunity to teach their child to walk? At first the child is afraid (in truth, the parents are plenty nervous, too). Then comes the day when she lets go of her fear and her parents' hands, placing her faith in them instead. They have proven trustworthy, and so she believes they will hold her up and keep her from falling.

The "blessed benediction" of Jude assures us that God is more than able to steady His children as well. We trip and stumble countless times as we walk our Christian pilgrimage, but God is ever present, holding us up. He is our Maker and our Keeper. He goes before us to make the rough, uneven places level and plain (Isa. 45:2). To Him alone belongs "glory and majesty, dominion and power."

Thank You, God, for Your abiding presence that gives us strength and confidence come what may.

THE LOYALTY OF LOVE

But Ruth replied: Don't plead with me to abandon you or to return and not follow you. For wherever you go, I will go, and wherever you live, I will live; your people will be my people, and your God will be my God. —Ruth 1:16

Ruth proved the loyalty of her love for Naomi through her commitment to her. She gave her heart and life to those things that Naomi loved. She gave up her way of life, her friends, family, native land, and religion to follow her mother-in-law into a strange country and to embrace a new faith.

For ten years Ruth watched Naomi practice her faith and love in everyday living. Through observations and experience, Ruth, a Moabitess, had been drawn through the constraint of love to confess that Naomi's way of life was the best way, and her God the only God.

Ruth's loyalty and love for Naomi caused her to be in the ancestral line of our Lord. This gave Him a human identification and relationship with the two major divisions of mankind—Jews and Gentiles. When Christ offered His blood for one, He offered it for all. For all had sinned, and all were forgiven by His shed blood.

By Your Spirit, Lord, may I be loyal to the redeeming love so freely offered to me and all of mankind.

WHO WILL OPEN THE DOOR?

*Be alert and strengthen what remains, which
is about to die, for I have not found your works
complete before my God. —Revelation 3:2*

It makes a person feel strange, but also unwanted, to knock on a door when there is every reason to believe there are people inside to answer, though they are unwilling to come open the door. Of course, sometimes there is so much noise and unrest within that those inside genuinely cannot hear the knock. But it's disappointing to realize those on the inside hear but choose not to answer—either because they don't know the person outside, or simply because they do not care.

Imagine how our Savior must feel when He knows that His call has definitely been loud enough, but the individual who needs redemption refuses to respond to Him because of the iron grip sin has over their life. Whatever their reason, they do not heed the call of Christ and will not let the Savior inside. Still, He waits, longing for them to answer, to be saved, and redeemed, and healed.

Our desire to reach someone must be so utterly mild by comparison with the desperation of a compassionate Savior who longs to rescue His children. But we all have a choice to come to Him or reject His invitation of redemption.

Lord, please give a heart and compassionate for the lost.

THE TRIUMPH OF THE KING

And he has a name written on his robe and on his thigh:
KING OF KINGS AND LORD OF LORDS. —Revelation 19:16

Jesus Christ, born of the lineage of kings, is perhaps the best known person in the world today. Centuries before the birth of Christ, King David, one of the best-known men of the Old Testament, ruled upon the throne of Israel. He reigned with great majesty, yet he was once a mere shepherd boy and musician.

Jesus Christ, the Messiah, born of humble parentage, came from the same lineage as King David. Unlike David, who received acclaim and glory while he was alive, Jesus received little acclaim. He invested His life in others and died for the sins of all mankind. He chose not to be an earthly king but taught mankind how to be saved. He prepared hearts for heaven, where one day they could then acclaim and proclaim Him "KING OF KINGS, AND LORD OF LORDS."

Before Pilate, Jesus made His true identity, intention, and destination known:

> "My kingdom is not of this world," said Jesus. "If my kingdom were of this world, my servants would fight, so that I wouldn't be handed over to the Jews. But as it is, my kingdom is not from here. . . . You say that I'm a king. . . . I was born for this, and I have come into the world for this: to testify to the truth." (John 18:36–37)

Lord Jesus, please give us the courage in this life to acknowledge You as King of kings and Lord of lords.

FROM THANKS TO THANKSGIVING

Ascribe to the LORD the glory of his name; bring an offering and enter his courts. —Psalm 96:8

True thanksgiving is never alone. If we are truly thankful for Christ's great sacrifice upon the cross, we find ourselves unable to sit back and do nothing. Christ has given so much for us, we can never repay the debt—that is why He came to redeem us. As Paul tells us, "Therefore, brothers and sisters, in view of the mercies of God, I urge you to present your bodies as a living sacrifice, holy and pleasing to God; this is your true worship" (Rom. 12:1).

True thanksgiving never measures the cost. It is an act of worship. Saint Ignatius Loyola once prayed, "Teach us, good Lord, to serve you as you deserve, to give and not to count the cost, to fight and not to heed the wounds, to toil and not to seek for rest, to labour and not to ask for any reward, save that of knowing that we do your will. Amen."

If we are truly thankful for God's goodness, there will be an outpouring of gratitude; we will give thanks because we cannot help ourselves. Because we are thankful, we will give to others out of our heart's abundance. God does not require what we have or what we do, but what we are—who we are. God wants our presence with Him far more than our presents.

■

God, teach me to give thanks without thought of counting the cost.

SUSTAINER OF ALL LIFE

*How countless are your works, LORD! In
wisdom you have made them all; the earth is
full of your creatures. —Psalm 104:24*

The more closely we see the components of the atom or the elements that comprise living cells, and the further we see into that space that surrounds our earth, the more we are humbled by the majesty of our world. The more we are humbled by the majesty of our God and His Son, who "is the radiance of God's glory and the exact expression of his nature, sustaining all things by his powerful word" (Heb. 1:3).

Though our size may appear insignificant in the universe, our value as individual creatures, as children of God who are made in His image, is made known to us through our Christian heritage and made manifest in our faith in Christ Jesus. And while we have not been given to possess a full knowledge of God's universe, we have the greater gift of God's love for us.

Let us combine our faith in God's love with increasing knowledge of His ways and of His world in order to serve Him better. "For in him we live and move and have our being, as even some of your own poets have said, 'For we are also his offspring'" (Acts 17:28).

*Lord, may we give full response to what
You have called each of us to do.*

A CALL TO THANKFULNESS

*Let them give thanks to the LORD for his faithful love and
his wondrous works for all humanity.* —Psalm 107:8

Job taught us that it is not just the evil, but also the good and righteous people, who suffer. God's children all share in His material abundance as He bestows His blessings on them. But those of us who are Christ followers also have the privilege of sharing in His suffering (Phil. 1:29). However, like the psalmist who composed our reading for today, we often slip into a common human misconception—seeing ill fortune as punishment, and good fortune as reward.

God has promised us no easy life in return for our love of Him (John 16:33), nor special favor to the measure of our good works. Rather, He has promised us His continuing love and faithfulness. He has given us the gift of redemption and forgiveness—what blessing can be greater than this?

In the end, "We know that all things work together for the good of those who love God, who are called according to his purpose" (Rom. 8:28). It is from this understanding that we praise our God and Savior.

■

*Lord, please grant us a continuing awareness of Your
love and presence in the midst of all situations.*

THE BEGINNING OF WISDOM

The fear of the LORD is the beginning of wisdom;
all who follow his instructions have good insight.
His praise endures forever. —Psalm 111:10

To think on the omnipotence of God and His handiwork in our world leads us to that reverential awe, the fear of the Lord. In His omnipotence, God has chosen to be aware of man, and to provide the divine spark that makes man aware of Him. And so, from the beginning, our wisdom and understanding has come from the Lord.

This awareness of Him should give us fuller knowledge of His nature and lead us directly to the path that we should follow. It is not always so easy. We must work and study His Word in order to follow Him and His ways better.

For Descartes, the first truth was "I think, therefore I exist." For the Christian, the first truth must be, "He has made me aware of Him; therefore, I must not be apart from Him." When we begin to seek God first, we will no doubt be left in awe of His greatness. This will rightly lead us to ask, along with the psalmist, "What is a human being that you remember him, a son of man that you look after him?" (Ps. 8:4).

Lord, we humbly ask for the wisdom
that can come from You alone.

WHEN GOD GUIDES

"May the LORD reward you for what you have done, and may you receive a full reward from the LORD God of Israel, under whose wings you have come for refuge." —Ruth 2:12

Our heavenly Father never withdraws or withholds anything from one of His children unless He intends to protect them from things they cannot perceive, or to give them a better blessing.

Having lost her husband, Ruth left her family, friends, gods, and country to follow Naomi to Bethlehem. But she brought with her two priceless treasures: her love for Naomi and her faith in Naomi's God. Ruth did not have to linger long in the valley of waiting. As her faith grew, her command of the situation also grew.

In His providence, the Lord directed her immediately to the man with whom she was to share the rest of her life. Her husband Boaz was a righteous man who acknowledged the Lord God of Israel as the source of every blessing. He knew God as the rewarder of good and faithful service and as the protector of those who trust in Him.

Ruth learned that it is better to walk with God by faith than to walk alone by sight. No person is ever left so desolate and no life remains so barren and incomplete when God is allowed to be the guide.

■

Lord God, I surrender my heart and will to You. Please be Lord over my choices and decisions.

THE ROYAL LINE

The neighbor women said, "A son has been born
to Naomi," and they named him Obed. He was the
father of Jesse, the father of David. —Ruth 4:17

Verses of Scripture taken in isolation may appear like a jigsaw puzzle unassembled. But when the verses are properly related, they produce a fuller, more complete picture, and reveal a wonderful meaning, as do the words of our text today.

The Lord promised Abraham that in him all families of the earth would be blessed (Gen. 12:3). "Then a shoot [would] grow from the stump of Jesse, and a branch from his roots [would come to] bear fruit" (Isa. 11:1). Centuries later, Paul wrote, "When the time came to completion, God sent his Son, born of a woman, born under the law, to redeem those under the law, so that we might receive adoption as sons" (Gal. 4:4–5). And then we come to Matthew 1, which shows how Ruth appeared in the royal line as the mother of Obed and the great-grandmother of David (vv. 1–16).

In Ruth's life and in our own as well, it is clear that "What no eye has seen, no ear has heard, and no human heart has conceived—God has prepared these things for those who love him" (1 Cor. 2:9).

Thanks be to God.

Lord, today we ask for wisdom and understanding
from both Your Word and Your Spirit.

THE SECRET OF SECURITY

He will not fear bad news; his heart is confident,
trusting in the Lord. —*Psalm 112:7*

In Old Testament times, some Israelites wrongly believed Jehovah to be more of a tribal god than we understand Him to be today. Rewards to Jehovah's followers were believed to be physical, worldly ones, in the form of great wealth and power. But the Israelites also believed that the faithful possessed great inward strength and security just as we believe today.

As Christ followers, we have come to know the inner strength that comes from the Holy Spirit. We know that riches and control over others do not guarantee either happiness or a worthwhile existence. Rather, it is belief in the one true God, and action based on our understanding of His will, which makes for a good and abundant life.

Assurance is present in many places in the Scriptures to the effect that God's presence and concern are always upon us. With Him, we can face all things. Without Him, we risk failure, futility, and loneliness in everything. Jehovah God is our source of strength in everything.

Lord, forgive me when I attempt to seek safety and security
from anyone or anything other than You. Today, I ask
for the inner security that can only come from You.

PROTECTION AGAINST SIN

How can a young man keep his way pure? By keeping your word. I have sought you with all my heart; don't let me wander from your commands. I have treasured your word in my heart so that I may not sin against you. —Psalm 119:9–11

Life is like the Bible. Both are filled with experiences of tragedy caused by sin. Sin has much of its judgment built-in. Any act of our sin leaves its scars, and in most cases, its tragic results are felt in the lives of those around us. And inevitably, sin results in a broken, strained relationship with God.

John reminds us, "If we confess our sins, he is faithful and righteous to forgive us our sins and to cleanse us from all unrighteousness" (1 John 1:9). It is good to know that sin can be forgiven through Christ, but it is good to remember that sin can also be avoided through Christ.

> Hear now, how Christ has already prayed for you and delights to provide for you victory over the enemy's lies: "I pray for them. I am not praying for the world but for those you have given me, because they are yours. . . . I am no longer in the world, but they are in the world, and I am coming to you. Holy Father, protect them by your name that you have given me, so that they may be one as we are one. . . . Sanctify them by the truth; your word is truth." (John 17:9, 11, 17)

Heavenly Father, as I remember my Lord's death on the cross and as I recall His prayer for me, I find strength to face the temptations of this day.

GOD IS THE FATHER

*Yet L*ORD*, you are our Father; we are the clay, and you are our potter; we all are the work of your hands.* —Isaiah 64:8

Only the right kind of home can give us the right picture of God as our heavenly Father. The right kind of father provides for the child what the child cannot provide for himself. He also guides toward what is best for the child when the child does not know what is best for himself.

Father was the favorite term of Jesus in His reference to God. Jesus claimed to be His Father's Son, and He repeatedly taught His disciples to recognize God as their Father as well.

As in the human family, *father* is a term of confidence, love, and respect. Those who are fortunate enough to have a father worthy of confidence, love, and respect find it easier to look upon God in the same way. The earthly fathers who fully submit to the holy, yet joyous, call of fatherhood have the blessing of giving their children a glimpse of their heavenly Father.

> "Blessed be the God and Father of our Lord Jesus Christ, the Father of mercies and the God of all comfort. He comforts us in all our affliction, so that we may be able to comfort those who are in any kind of affliction, through the comfort we ourselves receive from God." (2 Cor. 1:3–4)

Heavenly Father, help me to believe that I am a child worthy of Your love.

NOTHING IS HIDDEN FROM GOD

Search me, God, and know my heart; test me and know
my concerns. See if there is any offensive way in me;
lead me in the everlasting way. —Psalm 139:23–24

David marveled at God's personal knowledge of all that concerned his life. Elijah had an experience that fully illustrates God's watchful eye. This experience of the "downsitting and uprising" of Elijah came when he ran away into the wilderness because of the fear of danger, disappointment, and despair that filled his heart. In utter exhaustion, he lay down and slept. Though the circumstances are different, many of our hearts know that same kind of despair, do they not?

The concern and tender care of God for His overwrought prophet is manifested by an angel with a jug of water and a freshly baked cake. "The angel of the Lord . . . touched him. He said, 'Get up and eat, or the journey will be too much for you.' So he got up, ate, and drank. Then on the strength from that food, he walked forty days and forty nights to Horeb, the mountain of God" (1 Kings 19:7–8).

We cannot name or number the ways the Heavenly Father watches over His children day and night. But we can trust that He is always present and at work on both our behalf and on the furthering of His Kingdom. He tells us:

> "Do not fear, for I am with you;
> do not be afraid, for I am your God.
> I will strengthen you; I will help you;
> I will hold on to you with my righteous right hand."
> (Isa. 41:10)

Lord, help us to be more aware of all the
ways You love and care for us.

GUIDANCE FOR THE DAY

*Let me experience your faithful love in the morning,
for I trust in you. Reveal to me the way I should
go because I appeal to you. —Psalm 143:8*

Our world can be explained only by the existence of a personal devil with a stubborn will. Since he has made our world a veritable wilderness, man's journey in it leads to certain ways.

A man's will is a man in action; it needs direction in a world of uncertainty. In God's will there is safety, truth that He can be trusted, and a life fulfilled in Christ. There are also three wills that give directions in our world—though certainly, not all of it good: God's will, man's will, and Satan's will. Only God's will can be trusted to guide us safely.

We have all taken trips facing an intersection of two unmarked roads: God's way, or our way. There are times when the Lord will lead us into the wilderness, to remove other distractions from our hearts (Hos. 2:14). There are times when choosing our own path might seems easier. But in truth, the only certain way forward is in the presence of the Father. No matter what the terrain may look like, there are no wrong turns when we are with Him.

Lord, I want to see Your name made known throughout the earth in the hearts and minds of all creation. Like Moses, I ask, "Please, let me see your glory" (Exod. 33:18).

WHEN GOD DRAWS NEAR

The Lord is near all who call out to him, all who call out to him with integrity. —Psalm 145:18

Since Satan gained his power and possession of our world through man's will, he must be defeated through man's will. Man turned away from God and by that act broke the divine relationship. Consequently, a marred man now lives in a marred world where there is much to fear and much to bear. Daily he finds himself in bitter bondage to his personal fears.

How, then, can we, mankind, live in a troubled world and yet possess an untroubled heart? The Bible gives the answer: "Draw near to God, and he will draw near to you" (James 4:8). This is the meaning of prayer. To neglect the daily drawing near to God does not affect or change our salvation, but it does, for a time, dim our vision of Him. Soon He seems a blur far off in the distance, and then we question Him, doubting that He truly cares for us—when really, we were the ones to fall away.

When He is near, our dread turns to delights, His peace dispels our fear, faith overcomes doubt, despair turns to hope, sadness to gladness, and tragedies becomes triumphs. "Therefore we do not give up. Even though our outer person is being destroyed, our inner person is being renewed day by day" (2 Cor. 4:16).

Father, be near to us and show us which way You are leading us.

IN GOD WE TRUST

Happy is the one whose help is the God of Jacob,
whose hope is in the LORD his God. —Psalm 146:5

The greatest sin and the greatest harm is trying to live independently of God. There is no way to do this so long as life is sustained by God's air, sun, and sod. A tiny raspberry in the garden needs the whole planetary heaven to ripen and sweeten it.

Satan gained possession of our world when Adam turned his will away from God. Then, man had to earn his living the hard way. During man's short history, his economy has demanded a medium of exchange: money. Money has power, and so it has become a god known as mammon. There is a form of security in money so long as man does not ignore the true God in his ways of earning a living.

Every coin that is made or spent this day, from the copper penny to the silver dollar, speaks powerfully to every person in our nation of a security greater than a thriving economic security. Spread the coins you have on the table before you and read aloud the message "In God We Trust."

> "Instruct those who are rich in the present age not to be arrogant or to set their hope on the uncertainty of wealth, but on God, who richly provides us with all things to enjoy." (1 Tim. 6:17)

Lord, may our trust be solely in You, Your
provision, and Your plan for us.

GOD'S GOOD PLEASURE

The LORD values those who fear him, those who put their hope in his faithful love. —Psalm 147:11

In the beginning, God prepared a wonderful habitation for man in His own Kingdom where there was only love, life, light, and God's holy law. Love is the nature of God; life is the breath of God's own being, light is the radiance of His presence, and the law is His righteous will and way. Yet man turned away from all this glory to live in Satan's kingdom where there is hate, death, darkness, and lawlessness.

God longed to have His lost man, His creation and image-bearer, back in His Kingdom. His great love has never abandoned them. "For God loved the world in this way: He gave his one and only Son, so that everyone who believes in him will not perish but have eternal life" (John 3:16).

God did all that could be done for the salvation of man when Christ died on the cruel cross. As Christ's work of redemption went on, the Father's voice spoke approval, "This is my beloved Son, with whom I am well-pleased" (Matt. 3:17). The conflict between the strongest love and the hottest hate continued until God had made a way back home for us.

As one by one sinners are translated from the kingdom of darkness into the Kingdom of light, God is pleased and all heaven rejoices. For your personal joy and encouragement, read Luke 15:7–10.

*Lord, we pray that the world might know
that You are a good Father.*

A UNIVERSAL CHOIR

*Praise the LORD from the earth. . . . young men as well as
young women, old and young together. Let them praise
the name of the LORD, for his name alone is exalted. His
majesty covers heaven and earth.* —Psalm 148:7, 12–13

Music is a part of all God's creative acts. The songs of angels
fill His holy temple. One of their heavenly anthems was heard
when Christ was born. Laws of nature in unobstructed opera-
tion produce a harmony. God made the human soul for music
and music for the human soul. He also created the human
voice to speak and to sing songs of love, hope, faith, peace, joy,
gladness, praise, and thanksgiving. These eight words might
well form a heavenly octave or the major scale providing notes
whereby we could set ourselves to music.

Paul exhorted all Christians to sing: "Speaking to one
another in psalms, hymns, and spiritual songs, singing and
making music with your heart to the Lord, giving thanks always
for everything to God the Father in the name of our Lord Jesus
Christ" (Eph. 5:19–20). And in his psalm, David calls for a
universal choir to rise in anthem of praise to our God:

Hallelujah!
Praise God in his sanctuary.
Praise him in his mighty expanse. . . .
Let everything that breathes praise the LORD.
Hallelujah! (Ps. 150:1, 6)

Tune our hearts to sing Your praise, O Lord.

GOD IS A LIVING SPIRIT

This is how we know that we remain in him and he in us: He has given us of his Spirit. —1 John 4:13

"The LORD God formed the man out of the dust from the ground and breathed the breath of life into his nostrils, and the man became a living being" (Gen. 2:7). Man came from dust to deity, and God's breath made the change! Then followed a tragedy in Eden—disobedience and its awful consequence: "For you are dust, and you will return to dust" (Gen. 3:19). Alienated from the life of God, the story of man now reads: From dust to deity back to dust, as in Adam, all die.

How may the life of God be restored in man? Only through Christ! "So it is written, The first man Adam became a living being; the last Adam became a life-giving spirit" (1 Cor. 15:45). His Spirit is life and only as we accept Him will the eternal life of God be in us. In Christ, the story of man may now read: From dust, to deity, to dust again, and again to deity. Though man's life was humiliated by sin, it will again be glorified by Him. Other words tell this same story: generation, degeneration, and regeneration.

We thank You, Lord, that by Your "divine power you have given us everything required for life and godliness" (2 Pet. 1:3).

TRUST AND OBEY

Trust in the LORD with all your heart, and do not rely on your own understanding; in all your ways know him, and he will make your paths straight. —Proverbs 3:5–6

The trust of which today's text speaks involves "all your heart." It cannot hold back anything for safety's sake. This is what Jesus meant when He spoke of loving God with all of our heart, mind, and soul.

We make plans for the future, but God's Word says, "Don't boast about tomorrow, for you don't know what a day might bring" (Prov. 27:1). We worry about the future, but Jesus says, "Don't worry about tomorrow, because tomorrow will worry about itself. Each day has enough trouble of its own" (Matt. 6:34).

As we learn to lean less on ourselves and more on Him, we find our path ahead has already been illuminated. We may not see all the way, but we can see one step at a time.

In the paradox of the gospel, we lose ourselves in order lo find ourselves; we are humbled before we are exalted. Promises are made that turn true as we launch out in faith. We must honestly and sincerely seek the Lord. Then we find that all these things are added, and our true needs are supplied.

◼

Lord, I ask that You search my heart and reveal to me all the areas of my life where I have yet to trust Your sovereignty.

LIFE'S TWO WAYS

The path of the righteous is like the light of dawn, shining brighter and brighter until midday. —Proverbs 4:18

Two ways face us: the way of the flesh and the way of the spirit; the path of the wicked and the path of the just; the broad road and the narrow road; the way of money and the way of God.

There is a choice available to each of us. We do not have to take the wrong road. We can live in the sunshine instead of the darkness. We are not imprisoned by circumstances such as our heredity or environment. We are conditioned, not determined, by them. Our life is determined basically by our own choices. Who and what do you choose today? "As for me and my family, we will worship the LORD" (Josh. 24:15).

But how can we choose what is best? The answer is found in Scripture, which cautions us, "Guard your heart above all else, for it is the source of life" (Prov. 4:23).

We must ask ourselves, Is my heart right with God? If it is, it will be easier to choose His will. We ought to evaluate everything in light of the will of God, and in the end to Him, saying, "Nevertheless, not my will, but yours, be done" (Luke 22:42).

O God, may our hearts be right with You so that we may choose the things that really matter.

WHAT GOD CONDEMNS

The LORD hates six things; in fact, seven are detestable to him: arrogant eyes, a lying tongue, hands that shed innocent blood, a heart that plots wicked schemes, feet eager to run to evil, a lying witness who gives false testimony, and one who stirs up trouble among brothers. —Proverbs 6:16–19

We can learn a little from everyone and from everything. The ant, for example, works hard day by day when it can, so that it will have something to eat when it cannot work. You may remember the story of the grasshopper who played all summer, while the ant worked. He had to beg the ant for food in the winter. If we use each moment wisely as it comes to us, we will have prepared well for the future.

Our God gives us the wisdom to do just that. And while He is a God of love, there are some things He cannot abide, and among them, pride is the worst. This is the primal sin. The ego wants to be its own god, and by doing so it becomes the enemy of God. This sin attacks all of us—especially those in the church-related vocations. It becomes the sin of the Pharisee, who said: "God, I thank you that I'm not like other people— greedy, unrighteous, adulterers, or even like this tax collector" (Luke 18:11). Pride is so insidious that it can even cause us to be proud of our humility!

The tree of pride then bears the other sins listed here: lies, murder and hate, evil thoughts, mischief, falseness, and discord. May the wisdom of the Holy Spirit keep us humble that we may not stray from His presence, and in doing so, better serve Him.

■

Lord, deliver us from pride and all the evils it gives rise to.

IN THE IMAGE OF GOD

So God created man in his own image; he created him in the image of God; he created them male and female. —Genesis 1:27

In the midst of so much current pessimism and discouragement about the future of our country, we are encouraged by the biblical view of the worth of mankind. We are worthwhile because of our original relation to God—we are made in God's image.

We are worth more than any other earthly creature. Although we may not agree that we are "the measure of all things," Scripture tells us God "made [us] lower than the angels for a short time; [He] crowned [us] with glory and honor" (Heb. 2:7). The Bible also says that we are worth more than the material world about us, "For what will it benefit someone if [we gain] the whole world yet [lose our] life? Or what will [we] give in exchange for [our] life?" (Matt. 16:26).

Humanity is composed of male and female, who become one in marriage. We are composed of divinity and dust, body and soul, strange and contradictory elements that can be harmonized only in a relation with Christ. And Christ Himself, in His own person, brought together God and man. We, likewise, may be made one with God through Christ Jesus.

Lord, help us to see the value of ourselves and others as being made by You and in Your image.

GUARD YOUR TONGUE!

*The tongue that heals is a tree of life, but a devious
tongue breaks the spirit.* —Proverbs 15:4

Your tongue is the most powerful muscle in your body. It can
be used either for good or for evil. It can become an unruly
tool, set on fire by sin and then blight and destroy everything
within its reach. Or it can become a benevolent instrument,
bathed in the dews of heaven to bless and build for the glory
of God.

If the potential of our tongue is so great, how much more
carefully should we guard it from evil and dedicate it to good!
And the best protection against the former is to consecrate it
to the latter. For while we are speaking words of comfort, we
cannot also be speaking profanely. We cannot encourage and
cast down at the same time. Nor can we gossip about another
person while we are also praising God.

The greatest use to which we can put our tongue is to tell
others about the love and grace of God through Jesus Christ.
In a world that hears so much negativity, we can show our
gratitude to God for the gift of speech by telling others the
beautiful and meaningful message of the gospel.

*Lord, may the words of my mouth be
acceptable and pleasing to You.*

MAN IS A SINNER

LORD, if you kept an account of iniquities, Lord,
who could stand? But with you there is forgiveness,
so that you may be revered. —Psalm 130:3–4

One of the most wonderful truths in the Bible is that God loves us. He loves us, not because of what we are, but in spite of it. The Bible teaches that we are sinners, both by nature and practice. However, even if the Bible did not teach this, it would be evident from our deeds and in the testimony of our hearts. As a sinner, we live in rebellion against the basic moral principles in the universe.

Suppose that God should make a complete list of all of our sins, and call on us to justify them. How could we stand justified before Him? The truth is that our sins are on record. And we stand before Him condemned. However, another truth is that with God there is forgiveness for all of our sins. He offers His forgiveness, not because of our merit, but by His grace through Jesus Christ. God loves all men. But He can bestow His mercy only on those who receive His Son as Savior. Therefore, in reverent awe let us open our heart to Him this very moment.

Lord, we ask that Your love may find its full fruition in
our hearts and lives through our faith in Jesus Christ.

BLESSING FOR THE BOUNTIFUL

"A generous person will be blessed, for he shares his food with the poor." —Proverbs 22:9

Of all the vital organs of the body, the eye is the most important. Through the eye one sees the glory of the heavens, the wonders of nature, the beauty of the earth, and the greatness and folly of man.

Fish, which live in sunless caves, lose their sight, and moles living underground are almost blind. Likewise, men who fail to see with their eyes soon lose the capacity to react sensitively to the beauty or unsightliness around them. But those of us with sensitive sight react to the opportunities of service about them and are, in return, blessed.

Jesus spoke in parables to the multitudes because "looking they do not see, and hearing they do not listen or understand" (Matt. 13:13). But to His disciples, He said, "Blessed are your eyes because they do see, and your ears because they do hear" (Matt. 13:16). And to Christ followers who have been born again, the Lord gives the power and privilege of the bountiful eye. The bountiful eye sees in the Spirit of Christ—freely, heartily, and self-sacrificially.

Jesus, please give me eyes to see what You see,
and a heart to respond with compassion—
to myself and to others—as You would.

A DAY OF THANKSGIVING

*Let the heavens be glad and the earth rejoice,
and let them say among the nations, "The
LORD reigns!" —1 Chronicles 16:31*

It was a glorious day for David and the nation of Israel when the ark of the Lord was safely placed in the tent David had provided. This was a memorial day of sacrifices and national rejoicing. For this occasion, an appropriate psalm of thanksgiving was composed (1 Chron.16:8–36), and David and his people expressed their gratitude and thankfulness to God.

It once was a common practice of churches to have what they called "testimony meetings." One member after another of the congregation rose and expressed his thankfulness to God for his blessings. Today, this means of expressing gratitude to God has been lost to most churches. The neglect of such testimony may cause us to lose much of the joy and vitality of our public worship.

The attitude of thankfulness should be cultivated by all Christians. It is a part of our Christian testimony to express that gratitude publicly, as well as privately.

> Give thanks to the LORD; call on his name;
> proclaim his deeds among the peoples.
> Sing to him; sing praise to him;
> tell about all his wondrous works!
> Honor his holy name;
> let the hearts of those who seek the LORD rejoice.
> (1 Chron. 16:8–10)

◼

*O Lord, we give thanks to You for Your blessings
on us, our loved ones, and our church.*

ROYAL REJOICING

*He and the whole house of Israel were bringing
up the ark of the LORD with shouts and the
sound of the ram's horn.* —2 Samuel 6:15

The ark of the Lord symbolized God's presence. The ark had been neglected for many years. But now, David sought to establish the ark in the center of Jerusalem.

As the procession with the ark moved toward Jerusalem, an accident took place. The cart holding the ark threatened to overturn. A man named Uzzah reached his hands to steady the cart, and he fell dead on the spot. The fatality affected David so strongly that he refused to proceed further. The ark was left for three months in the house of a farmer named Obed-edom.

When David finally brought the ark into Jerusalem, there was great rejoicing among the people. Singing, dancing, and shouting characterized their expression of happiness for God's presence.

How much more reason we have to rejoice than King David and his people. Throughout the centuries, God had sought to reveal Himself in history, literature, prophecy, poetry, and the lives of people. Then in the fullness of time, God was made flesh, and we beheld His glory.

■

*We glory, O Father, in the cross of our Savior
and rejoice in Your great gift of salvation.*

GOD HAS A PLAN

I know that everything God does will last forever; there is no adding to it or taking from it. God works so that people will be in awe of him. —Ecclesiastes 3:14

Who would have thought it possible? In this age in which we have finally begun to comprehend the true complexity and order of the universe, much of mankind has lost sight of God the Creator.

This age will be known for its explosion of knowledge, among other things. Today, we take for granted that a child will know things about the universe that would have baffled a university student fifty years ago. The mysteries of viruses and the pioneering breakthroughs of medicine, the geography of oceans, and the way the Internet has opened up the world's way of communicating—all are common knowledge to us today, though relatively new in the grand scheme of things.

One would have thought that such growing insight into the wonders of our world would have brought a corresponding growth in the wonder at the plan of the Creator God. This was certainly God's intention—that in beholding the heavens and earth, we would praise Him out of gratitude. This is no less true in our age of rapidly advancing knowledge and technology than it was in biblical days. But even if mankind will not praise God for His wondrous works, even if we were to stay silent, surely the stones of the earth would cry out to declare His glory (Luke 19:40).

Father, we thank You for all the ways You graciously provide for us. Help us to be more mindful of the complexities and details of Your creation, stopping in the moment to praise You for all Your mighty works.

MANKIND MISSES THE MARK

*For though they knew God, they did not glorify him as God
or show gratitude. Instead, their thinking became worthless,
and their senseless hearts were darkened. —Romans 1:21*

Do you believe there is a God? Of course I do, you might answer—doesn't everyone know there is a God? The truth of the matter is that almost everyone acknowledges the existence of God. This knowledge of His existence is realized in nature, in creation, and in the order of things in this life. The scholars of Rome to whom the apostle Paul refers believed in the existence of God. Yet their futile attempts to worship God caused them to miss the real joy of knowing how very real He is.

We are conscious of God in every part of our day. The rising sun, the rose petal, the beating heart, and the redeemed sinner cause us to want to worship Him in humility and gratitude. As we worship God in this attitude, our souls become aglow with His presence.

> I am at rest in God alone;
> my salvation comes from him.
> He alone is my rock and my salvation,
> my stronghold; I will never be shaken. (Ps. 62:1–2)

*Lord, I ask that I would never, ever lose
the meaning of true worship.*

THE PRICE OF THE PRIZE

For I consider that the sufferings of this present time are not worth comparing with the glory that is going to be revealed to us. —Romans 8:18

The trials of this life can become burdensome. Nights can grow long. Tears of disappointment and heartbreak may flow down our cheeks. We may feel as if we truly cannot go on another day.

But let us stop for a moment. Paul points out here an important truth, and it is this: regardless of what we as Christians go through now, it is less than nothing compared to our future. God has planned for us an eternity in which we will be done with this earthly body that is weakened by disease and suffering. We are to look forward with eagerness to the moment when we will take the crown of righteousness and receive our eternal reward. Do not lose faith in this present life. These trials and afflictions are a small price to pay for such a glorious prize.

> Therefore we do not give up. Even though our outer person is being destroyed, our inner person is being renewed day by day. For our momentary light affliction is producing for us an absolutely incomparable eternal weight of glory. So we do not focus on what is seen, but on what is unseen. For what is seen is temporary, but what is unseen is eternal. (2 Cor. 4:16–18)

Lord Jesus, help me to keep my eyes fixed on You. Remind me that, while I may not see You, You are always with me by Your Spirit, and You have gone ahead to prepare a place for me (John 14:1–3).

MAKE WORSHIP MEANINGFUL

*If, therefore, the whole church assembles together and
all are speaking in other tongues and people who are
outsiders or unbelievers come in, will they not say that
you are out of your minds? —1 Corinthians 14:23*

For some of the members of the church at Corinth, love was
not as important as Paul had taught them it was. They were
intrigued with a more dramatic gift of the Spirit—speaking in
tongues. Unfortunately, their unintelligible words had begun
to interfere with the worship of other believers. Therefore,
Paul strongly cautioned them that worship must make sense,
not just to the individual but to the entire congregation as well.

Unless you are responsible for planning or leading a worship
service, you may wonder how you can help make worship meaningful. Surely, the service is not something just to "go through"—
that would be nothing more than hollow ritualism. No, every
part of worship should have a purpose, one that you can understand and help to fulfill. Hymns are to be sung; prayers are to be
prayed; minds are to be opened to the Word of God. Our lively
participation will help worship make sense for the church community as a whole—perhaps even to the unbeliever. We all have
gifts to offer up in praise and worship of our great God.

> I will bless the LORD at all times;
> his praise will always be on my lips.
> I will boast in the LORD;
> the humble will hear and be glad.
> Proclaim the LORD's greatness with me;
> let us exalt his name together. (Ps. 34:1–3)

*Holy Father, please rekindle my life by Your Spirit,
whether I worship alone or with others.*

THE HIGH CALLING

I pursue as my goal the prize promised by God's heavenly call in Christ Jesus. —Philippians 3:14

In order to climb a mountain, climbers must look ahead. They must see the outcropping rock, how precarious the hand-hold. They must watch the narrow ledge and move cautiously with feet seeking the weight-supporting crevice. And they must always be looking up, not back, not down, not to the right or to the left. They must not look at the vast blur far below that speaks of danger; it will only create doubt and despair. What is behind cannot help them now, but can only serve as a distraction and endanger the present.

Life is a mountain, and we are all climbers. Each of us has our own peculiar way of walking, of grabbing, of driving pitons into rock. But we share the urge to look back and down, and around—anywhere but straight ahead. And in looking, we become paralyzed with fear.

Paul knew of these fears. But he tried to forget what was behind, and to press forward to the prize that was before him, the prize of the high calling of God.

Faithful Christians are mountain climbers like everyone else. But one thing distinguishes them from the rest of the world—they always look ahead, led by the Lord. They have their eyes fixed on a goal and they witness, work, and serve God. Nothing swerves them from pressing on.

Lord, help me to be always looking ahead to You, moving forward with vision that frees me from doubt and fear.

WHAT IS THE CHURCH'S MISSION?

*"Go, therefore, and make disciples of all nations, baptizing
them in the name of the Father and of the Son and of
the Holy Spirit, teaching them to observe everything I
have commanded you. And remember, I am with you
always, to the end of the age." —Matthew 28:19–20*

The Church's mission is to bear witness to Jesus Christ in
every realm of life. We do not make up the gospel; it is God's
plan for salvation for His lost and broken creation. But God
would have us use His power and His purposes in our daily
lives. We are not to imitate some Christians who have gone out
in the desert caves to shut themselves completely from others.

The Church is to identify itself with people to witness
to them even as Jesus witnessed to them. We must identify
ourselves with the world and its stubborn life and must work
with the world by contagion, even though it is difficult. We are
doing this by what we say and do and give. And so we are in the
world, but not of it; our home is with God.

Most of our witness is through who we are to those surrounding us. It is how we live our lives that will first bear witness to our Lord. The words come afterward. Therefore, let
us proclaim Him in deed and also in word; and always with a
heart dedicated to sharing the good news of the gospel for all.

*Lord, I pray that I may be useful to You in
fulfilling the mission of Your Church.*

THE PLEADING OF GOD

"Come, let us settle this," says the LORD. "Though your sins are scarlet, they will be as white as snow; though they are crimson red, they will be like wool." —Isaiah 1:18

The Bible is the story of God's quest for man's heart. He is always searching, pleading, and yearning for fellowship with His creation, His children who bear His image.

All sin is against God; we offend Him first and foremost (Ps. 51:4). When we become aware of this, we feel the weight of guilt and want to be rid of it. The pleading and wooing of the Holy Spirit brings a strong sense of the possibility of forgiveness and cleansing. All day and all night, He cries out "Abba, Father," to help us believe and remember who we really are (Rom. 8:15–17).

When we walk among others and say, "I trust Christ and believe He loves and forgives me," joy fills our soul. The relief of the forgiveness of sins floods our heart. There is no joy like the joy of answering God's pleading call to repent and trust Him.

█

Lord, please bring to mind for me those with whom I need to share the gospel. I humbly ask that You would give me true words to say, sweet words, that will help lead them back to You.

PROSPECT OF PEACE

He will settle disputes among the nations and provide arbitration for many peoples. They will beat their swords into plows and their spears into pruning knives. Nation will not take up the sword against nation, and they will never again train for war. —Isaiah 2:4

What is peace? To know Christ is peace. When a person has peace, the prospect of world peace becomes greater. Peace is not merely the cessation of violence or the maintenance of physical comfort. At the very time men were slaughtering each other all over the world, Jesus Christ said, "Peace I leave with you. My peace I give to you. I do not give to you as the world gives. Don't let your heart be troubled or fearful" (John 14:27).

He gave not as this world gives. He was speaking of that inner peace based on conviction and faith. This kind of peace arms us against the dangers of the world and makes us able to stand wholeheartedly in the midst of famine, war, sickness, relational turmoil, and even death itself. "And the peace of God, which surpasses all understanding, will guard [our] hearts and minds in Christ Jesus" (Phil. 4:7).

■

Lord, I ask for peace in this present disturbed world. Help me to fix my eyes on You, so that I will have the strength of faith to continue living for You. I also ask that You use me in some way to help bring comfort to others in these times of strife, tumult, and confusion.

CLEANSED AND CALLED

Then I heard the voice of the Lord asking:
Who should I send? Who will go for us? I
said: Here I am. Send me. —Isaiah 6:8

The Bible deals with all of life because it comes to cleanse and heal the whole heart. The Bible knows nothing about partial religion or a Christian calling that involves only a self-selected portion of our lives. Every believer is both cleansed and called according to God's purposes.

Take a long look at the nature of your life. Can you divide it and be Christlike in one part and not in another? Is cleansing partial? Is your submission to Christ's will and call for your life only acknowledged and revered on certain days of the week? Are there some sins you aren't willing to hand over to Him until you clean yourself up, and others you refuse to let go of at all? If so, then know this: That is not what God has planned for you. That is not a life lived fully alive in Him.

When we are cleansed and called to serve Christ, we must hold nothing back. We must give ourselves to Christ wholeheartedly.

Lord Jesus, I ask for a divine sense of cleansing and a renewed awareness of having been called to witness for You. I pray that You will awaken every part of my heart to You.

THE COMING KINGDOM

For a child will be born for us, a son will be given to us, and the government will be on his shoulders. He will be named Wonderful Counselor, Mighty God, Eternal Father, Prince of Peace. —Isaiah 9:6

Jesus was wonderful in His birth, life, and death. He constantly radiated compassion, humility, and power. And in the Kingdom He came to establish, the government will be upon His shoulders. The coming Kingdom asks a new birth of everyone who desires to enter it.

The world presses against us, asking that we bury every notion of holiness in our lives, that we relinquish every drop of true love within us, that we rename every type of sin as "love of self" and "taking responsibility for our own happiness"—and declare it to be a hangover of a primitive, backward age.

We have a chance today, as we contemplate Christ and His coming Kingdom, to see the results of those who have followed the world. Vast numbers of lives have been cut from hope and paralyzed because they lived only for the present. But the coming Kingdom is to be found in Christ, and only Him.

■

Lord, I pray that Your kingdom will come in my own heart, as it is in heaven. I ask that others will see in me a life and a heart submitted to Your good and perfect will, and that in some mysterious way, the aroma of Christ might emanate from my hope in You.

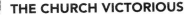

THE CHURCH VICTORIOUS

The seventh angel blew his trumpet, and there were loud voices in heaven saying, The kingdom of the world has become the kingdom of our Lord and of his Christ, and he will reign forever and ever. —Revelation 11:15

To the believer, Christ is the Alpha and the Omega—the first and the last, the beginning and the end. He shall reign forever and ever. Our Lord's redemptive forces penetrate every area of our lives and bring about permanent changes in our hearts and character. The awareness of His presence grows our faith in Him and His purposes and enables us to use our gifts and talents to glorify Him, for He is the Author of all.

As Christ followers, we love and worship Him, the One whose name is love. His response to us in turn is always one of love—even if we do not perceive it as such in the moment. "For the LORD disciplines the one he loves, just as a father disciplines the son in whom he delights" (Prov. 3:12).

God is love and His kingdom is forever. So let us approach our God with the awe and adoration He so deserves. Let us delight in the One who delights in us.

◼

God, I thank You that for committing so faithfully to me and to the gospel transformation of my heart. May my hope in You grow into deep assurance.

THE PRINCE OF PEACE

They will not harm or destroy each other on my entire holy mountain, for the land will be as full of the knowledge of the LORD as the sea is filled with water. —Isaiah 11:9

World-renowned author, John Milton, once remarked, "Peace hath its victories more renowned than war." And indeed, the victories of peace are harder to win than the victories of war. We live in an age that seems to say by the monuments in cemeteries and national parks, "Blessed are the war-makers." However, our age has placed no greater emphasis on war heroes than the age when Christ uttered, "Blessed are the peacemakers, for they will be called sons of God" (Matt. 5:9).

Jesus wanted His contemporaries, as He wants us, to catch up with the true meaning of His words. He came to be the Prince of peace—not of war. He did not come to force Himself on anyone. The prophet Isaiah knew that such a Prince would come to conquer the hearts of men and give them peace (Isa. 9:6). No true peace is accomplished but in the hearts of those reconciled to Christ Jesus. Therefore, the Prince of Peace is far greater than any victorious general of war. For His coming Kingdom and "dominion will be vast, and its prosperity will never end" (Isa. 9:7).

■

Lord Jesus, Prince of Peace, please make me a peacemaker in a world of hate and tension.

THE LORD CALLS US TO REMEMBER

Jerusalem, I have appointed watchmen on your walls;
they will never be silent, day or night. There is no
rest for you, who remind the LORD. —Isaiah 62:6

In the tabernacle of Israel, the altar of incense and the seven golden candlesticks with the seven lamps symbolized the functions of God's people to be intercessors with God, and lights in the world.

God's people still have the same responsibilities. These duties are not just for a single nation or a privileged class, but for all of God's children.

As our text for today implies, our voices should be heard in heaven. We who trust God, through the prayer of faith, remind Him of His promises. Yet we do not need to help God remember so much as we need to remember God. We do not have to beg and to coerce God. In prayer we lay hold of His highest willingness to bless all of His creation.

Our prayers must be unceasing. Perseverance is nowhere more necessary than in our pleading with God. May we learn to be intercessors for others, even as Jesus Christ Himself intercedes for each of us even now, right this very moment.

> "Therefore, he is able to save completely those who come to God through him, since he always lives to intercede for them." (Heb. 7:25)

■

Lord, make me to be faithful in prayer and to be one who
will stand to fill the gap of intercession (Ezek. 22:30).

MIGHTY TO SAVE

*In all their suffering, he suffered, and the angel of
his presence saved them. He redeemed them because
of his love and compassion; he lifted them up and
carried them all the days of the past.* —Isaiah 63:9

There are times in our lives when our trouble may be so great
that we cannot bear the burden of our grief alone. To try to
bear the weight of sorrow alone may be too much for our spirit
and may overpower our resources.

The text says clearly that God sends no substitute to deliver
His people. His own presence is "mighty to save." He is never
far from us; He shares our experiences with us. He shares our
pain. And in showing His concern for us, His children, He
discloses His true nature as a God of ceaseless love.

But faith, however, is far more than a matter of God's mission of locating our burdens. Our relationship with Him and
the condition of our hearts are of far greater importance to
Him. In truth, no experience in life can be classified good or
bad until God is finished with it. Life linked with God may not
always cancel out life's burdens, but life will become purposeful rather than merely confusing when we trust in God and His
sovereignty over all.

> We know that all things work together for the good
> of those who love God, who are called according to
> his purpose. (Rom. 8:28)

*Lord, I ask that, even when trouble comes,
I may learn something more about You, and
in doing so, come to love You more.*

A PRAYER FOR HELP

Yet LORD, you are our Father; we are the clay, and you are our potter; we all are the work of your hands. —Isaiah 64:8

Our gravest mistake is to believe we need no help in this life. Independence and self-sufficiency are luxuries Christ followers can simply not afford to be deluded by. The temptation and sinful attempt to live apart from God is what broke our relationship with God in the first place (see Gen. 2–4).

A false pride convinces us that we are self-sufficient. And so repentance loses its meaning for many of us when we cannot admit our total dependence upon God. False pride is the great deceiver, for repentance remains as basic a need as breathing for Christ followers. Asking forgiveness of God is prerequisite to our becoming Christians, but it is also a continuous part of our lives. It is a daily need in our ongoing relationship with Him. Repentance breaks our pride and wakes us up to our sin. It ushers us back into the loving arms of our Redeemer God.

Spiritual strength can come from recognizing that we are the work of God's hand. We are God's craftsmanship and yet, we remain imperfect, and so we are in need of God's daily help.

■

God, I pray that You will help me to know and remember that I need help from You and from my community.

I WILL BE WITH YOU

Do not be afraid of anyone, for I will be with you to rescue you. This is the LORD's declaration. —Jeremiah 1:8

The unknown terrifies us. The automobile, a horseless carriage, was once a demon on wheels because people did not understand it. The dark, a new country, a new job, an affliction, and death are but a few of the unknowns that terrify us. Take away the element of the unknown, however, and fear vanishes.

Even at night as we rest in sleep, the Lord abides with us. The psalmist reminds us of this truth: "I will both lie down and sleep in peace, for you alone, LORD, make me live in safety" (Ps. 4:8).

As Christ followers, this knowledge should also be enough to satisfy us and quell our fears. "Do not fear!" is a recurring and comforting theme in the Bible. It is God who delivers us from the element of the unknown. Fear is not of the Lord, but knowledge of truth removes fear. Christ replaces fear with the knowledge and presence of Himself. Thanks be to God.

Lord, we ask Your presence may be more real to us than our fears of the unknowns of life. Please grow us up in our faith.

BLESSINGS BEYOND EXPECTATION

*Even before they call, I will answer; while they
are still speaking, I will hear.* —Isaiah 65:24

This verse from Isaiah 65 is one of our most treasured hopes
and one of God's grandest promises. The fact that God already
has a rescue plan in place before we even know we need to cry
out to Him—well, that speaks to the heart and character of our
God. He is good.

Parents may anticipate most of their children's needs and
even supply them before the child must ask. With God, this
knowledge is on the grandest scale of all. But instead of simply
providing for us, our Father is leading us to make known our
desires in wisdom and faith.

God knows our needs before we ask and often gives much
more than we could ever ask or think (Eph. 3:20). Yet we
must open our eyes anew each day to the blessings that God
has given. A good place for us to begin is to find pleasure
in the simplest, most obvious blessings of life. Let us "enter
his gates with thanksgiving and his courts with praise. Give
thanks to him and bless his name" (Ps. 100:4).

*Lord, give us eyes to see Your blessings
and provision surrounding us.*

JUDGMENT AGAINST INSINCERITY

*"'This is what the LORD of Armies, the God of Israel, says:
Correct your ways and your actions, and I will allow
you to live in this place. Do not trust deceitful words,
chanting, "This is the temple of the LORD, the temple of
the LORD, the temple of the LORD."' —Jeremiah 7:3–4*

The Latin word for *sincere*, meaning "without wax," came from the insincere practices of the ancient Roman statuary dealers who used wax to conceal blemishes and cracks on pieces they were selling. So good were they at this deception that even experts were often fooled. Only when a wax-filled piece had been exposed to the summer sun in a rose garden or courtyard did the deception become known. The wax would melt revealing the ugly blemishes. Prospective buyers soon came to ask dealers, "Is this piece sine cera (without wax)?"

We hurt ourselves by our insincerity, whether we are dealing with God or people. The heat of life's experiences will sooner or later melt the wax of our insincerity and expose us for what we really are.

Today's text is just as timely for us as it was for the people of Jeremiah's day, or for the ancient Roman statuary dealers. And so, "let [our] "'yes' mean 'yes,' and [our] 'no' mean 'no.' Anything more than this is from the evil one" (Matt. 5:37).

> For we do not market the word of God for profit like so many. On the contrary, we speak with sincerity in Christ, as from God and before God. (2 Cor. 2:17)

*Lord, with Your help, may we be sincere in all our ways
and doings whether before God or our fellow man.*

THE BURDEN OF SOULS

If my head were a flowing spring, my eyes a fountain of tears, I would weep day and night over the slain of my dear people. —Jeremiah 9:1

One of the most noticeable characteristics of great men of God is their concern for souls. The greater their concern, the greater their own souls become. This was true in the case of Jeremiah. One cannot read the words of this great prophet without sensing his burden for the souls of his people. He has been called the "weeping prophet" mainly because of his outburst in today's text. But we must not overlook the many other evidences of his concern for souls. Not only did he weep for his people, but he also gave himself for them in a way that speaks to the coming Lord Jesus, and the way He gave Himself for us.

Imagine what would happen if we were to become as burdened for souls in our day as Jeremiah was in his! May our prayer for today then be an echo of this anonymous hymn writer who wrote:

> Lord, lay some soul upon my heart,
> And love that soul through me;
> And may I bravely do my part
> To win that soul for thee.

■

O Lord, make me burdened for the souls of others.

IN THE POTTER'S HOUSE

But the jar that he was making from the clay became
flawed in the potter's hand, so he made it into another
jar, as it seemed right for him to do. —Jeremiah 18:4

The attempt to harmonize human freedom and divine sovereignty is a problem as old as man. It began in the garden of Eden and reached its climax in the garden of Gethsemane.

Jeremiah had no little difficulty with the problem, but help came to him by way of a simple illustration from life. God sent him to visit a potter's house one day. As he watched this artist shaping a vessel from common clay the answer came:

> "House of Israel, can I not treat you as this potter
> treats his clay?"—this is the LORD's declaration.
> "Just like clay in the potter's hand, so are you in my
> hand, house of Israel." (Jer. 18:6)

The potter's only limitation, as Jeremiah came to see it, is the condition of his clay. As long as it cooperates and submits to his will, the potter can make lovely vessels. If it does not cooperate, then he must take steps to recondition it until it does. A fit vessel and one that will bring him honor is what the potter desires.

Lord, Your ways are better and higher than mine.
And so with faith, I can confidently say, "Nevertheless,
not my will, but yours, be done" (Luke 22:42).

PROSPEROUS BUT PERISHING

*Pride comes before destruction, and an arrogant
spirit before a fall. —Proverbs 16:18*

Had we visited Israel in the days of Amos, we would have been
most impressed by the prosperity that was evident all around.
The hit tune of the day no doubt would have been something
like "Happy Days Are Here Again!" Jeroboam was on the
throne, and Israel was enjoying an unprecedented period of
peace and plenty.

But Israel's prosperity proved to be her own undoing.
She became cool and careless toward the loving God of her
forefathers. The people, like their king, "did what was evil in
the LORD's sight" (2 Kings 14:24). When Amos, the country
preacher from Tekoa, dared to speak out against the sins of
his people, he was met by unashamed pride and haughtiness.
Even the clergy of that day were not without blemish, as is
indicated in the Amos-Amaziah affair.

Alas, Israel's heyday came to an end as she paid for all her
sins of destruction, as do all nations and individuals, whose
foundations are the sands of selfishness and ungodliness.
While "all a person's ways seem right to him," it is the Lord
who weighs the motives of our hearts (Prov.16:2). May our
hearts instead learn to love the Lord's plans for us, so that we
might submit to the path He has laid before us (v. 9).

■

*In repentance and with humility, we
thank You for Your grace, Lord.*

GOD DEMANDS SOCIAL JUSTICE

*"This is what the LORD says: Administer justice and
righteousness. Rescue the victim of robbery from
his oppressor. Don't exploit or brutalize the resident
alien, the fatherless, or the widow. Don't shed
innocent blood in this place." —Jeremiah 22:3*

Many of us find it hard at times to decide what is right and
what is wrong. We know that we cannot let social customs or
popular notions influence our decisions. But in the Bible we
find clear standards for right conduct.

What is good, pure, right, and just is rooted in the nature
of God. God is holy, God is righteous, and God is love. His
will must be the law of our hearts. If we begin with our own
desires, we go astray. If we conform to this world, we become
as tasteless as salt that has lost its savor. But if we seek first the
kingdom of God and His righteousness, we have the promise
of God's blessing.

Our world is filled with exploitation, oppression, violence,
suffering, and bloodshed. In this world, the commandment
of God comes to us as it did through Jeremiah long ago:
"Administer justice and righteousness."

> "Mankind, he has told each of you what is good and
> what it is the LORD requires of you: to act justly,
> to love faithfulness, and to walk humbly with your
> God." (Mic. 6:8)

*Lord, by the power of the Holy Spirit,
strengthen my faith to do Your will.*

A NEW COVENANT

"Instead, this is the covenant I will make with the house of Israel after those days"—the LORD's declaration. "I will put my teaching within them and write it on their hearts. I will be their God, and they will be my people." —Jeremiah 31:33

For the Jewish people, a covenant meant a binding agreement and a form of law (Exod. 31:16; Jer. 50:5.) But a covenant also meant communion with God. This was reflected in the sacrificial rites and in the covenant of salt (Num. 18:19.) The covenant was to be a relationship of the heart, not merely obedience to a legal code for fear of punishment.

Jeremiah emphasizes this feature of the covenant between God and His people, and thereby points to the new covenant established by Christ. Through the grace and forgiveness of Christ, we receive new incentive for keeping God's commandments. The new covenant does not cancel the demands of the moral law, but seeks its fulfillment in love.

The new covenant written in the heart of the individual demands both personal and collective responsibility. God's law in our hearts binds us to God and to each other. This is the meaning of the covenant promise in today's text.

Lord, help us to live as one bound to Christ in a covenant of righteousness and love.

STEADFAST UNDER TESTING

But they replied, "We do not drink wine, for Jonadab, son of our ancestor Rechab, commanded: 'You and your descendants must never drink wine.'" —Jeremiah 35:6

The story of the Rechabites reveals a people with strong convictions. These nomadic people had pledged to their ancestral father that they would abstain from wine and not build houses or cultivate the soil. The prophet Jeremiah was tasked to invite them to the temple, set wine before them, and ask them to drink. They refused.

How easily they could have found excuses. They had been invited to drink by the prophet of God. They were in the temple. It was discourteous to refuse hospitality. They also knew that their refusal would make them appear narrow and odd.

The followers of Christ in our day are being tempted, not only to conform to social customs, but to adopt the motivations of the world. Whenever they are moved by pride, lust, jealousy, or hatred, they have failed the test. But to trust in God is to remain steadfast in love and faithfulness.

> But as for me, God's presence is my good.
> I have made the Lord GOD my refuge,
> so I can tell about all you do. (Ps. 73:28)

◼

Lord, may we be steadfast, immovable, and always about the work and mission You have called us to.

AN EXAMPLE OF OBEDIENCE

*"The words of Jonadab, son of Rechab, have been carried out.
He commanded his descendants not to drink wine, and they
have not drunk to this day because they have obeyed their
ancestor's command. But I have spoken to you time and time
again, and you have not obeyed me!" —Jeremiah 35:14*

The episode of the Rechabites gave the prophet Jeremiah opportunity to dramatize to the people of Judah their need for obedience. These rough, out-of-doors people literally obeyed the command which Jonadab had given two hundred years before.

With telling force, Jeremiah drives home the lesson:

> Time and time again I have sent you all my servants
> the prophets, proclaiming, "Turn, each one from his
> evil way, and correct your actions. Stop following
> other gods to serve them. Live in the land that I
> gave you and your ancestors." But you did not pay
> attention or obey me." (Jer. 35:15)

We must not think of obedience in terms of perfunctory compliance to a command. It is rather the deep commitment at faith, an act of the heart, a submission of will. Obedience takes on new meaning after we have stood in awe before the person of Christ: "Although he was the Son, he learned obedience from what he suffered" (Heb.5:8).

*Lord, may I never grow tired of asking for a deeper
faith and greater obedience to grow in me.*

WORDS OF WARNING

So Jeremiah summoned Baruch son of Neriah.
At Jeremiah's dictation, Baruch wrote on a scroll all the
words the LORD had spoken to Jeremiah. —Jeremiah 36:4

Warning signs on the highways are common to us. We believe them to be for our safety and that of others. When a sign warns us of a sharp turn in the road, we know that the road turns. The road does not turn because the sign says so; the sign alerts us to reality that the road up ahead turns.

King Jehoiakim was enraged over the warning by Jeremiah. He thought he could get rid of God's truth by cutting shreds and burning the book the prophet had dictated. He ordered the arrest of Jeremiah and his scribe. But Jeremiah went into hiding and dictated another roll, and the events of which he had warned the king did, indeed, come to pass.

King Josiah, Jehoiakim's father, had reacted in quite another way when the book found in the temple was read to him: "When the king [Josiah] heard the words of the book of the law, he tore his clothes" (2 Kings 22:11). Josiah repented and instituted reforms. His son Jehoiakim did the opposite.

Every day we are called upon to obey the will of God revealed to us in Scripture. Disregarding them does not cancel them out or make them not true. The Lord lovingly tells us how best to live, but only we can choose to obey Him.

■

Holy Spirit, please illuminate for me the will of the Father,
and give me greater insight into the Word of God.

SOLD OUT TO EVIL

Let whoever is wise understand these things, and whoever is insightful recognize them. For the ways of the LORD are right, and the righteous walk in them, but the rebellious stumble in them. —Hosea 14:9

One who bargains with evil is a fool, for the wages of sin is death (Rom. 6:23). Such a person is not afraid of sinning, but of getting caught. The crudest way of playing the fool is to hold God's moral law to be merely writings rather than reality. Recall how Jesus exposed the Pharisees on this point (Matt. 23).

Another well-traveled way of fools is to use evil means, even in the defense of what is right. History records that thousands have been put to death by "defenders of the faith." If people are to be won from sin and reconciled to God, how can it be by killing them? Or, how can we further the gospel by stirring up strife and condemning those who disagree with us? Christianity is a way of life—not a tournament of arguments.

One of the most subtle temptations of the enemy is the believer's switch of motives. The enemy is delighted when we "fight the good fight" with his weapons. In doing so, we confuse a watching world about the true character of our loving God. How can we possibly further the cause of Christ by jealousy, vindictiveness, pride, and hate. We lose the battle, not for lack of courage, but because we let the enemy choose our weapons.

Lord, move in my heart in a fresh way, and reawaken me to Your redeeming love.

FOLLOWING FALSE LEADERS

Instead, you should say, "If the Lord wills, we will live and do this or that." But as it is, you boast in your arrogance. All such boasting is evil. So it is sin to know the good and yet not do it. —James 4:15–17

It is sometimes very difficult to find the right leader to follow. Joshua and Caleb were once rejected as leaders. The children of Israel had been freed from their bondage in Egypt. They had been led across the desert and now stood on the very border of the promised land.

What they did next is almost unbelievable—if it were not so true today. They appointed a committee to go in and take a survey to see if they really ought to go and enter into the land. The committee brought back a majority and a minority report. The chairman said that it was indeed a land flowing with milk and honey, but there were also giants there.

Joshua acknowledged that there were giants, but reminded them that is how they got to be where they were, by conquering giants—like Pharaoh's army in the desert. He reminded them that they had the same God now, and that because of Him, they were more than able to take the land. But instead, they voted not to go and marched back out into the wilderness to wander for more than thirty-five years.

Lord, may I have the faith to follow Your leadership in any and all situations.

STANDARDS FOR SHEPHERDS

As an overseer of God's household, he must be blameless:
not arrogant, not hot-tempered, not an excessive drinker,
not a bully, not greedy for money, but hospitable, loving
what is good, sensible, righteous, holy, self-controlled,
holding to the faithful message as taught, so that he
will be able both to encourage with sound teaching
and to refute those who contradict it. —Titus 1:7–9

The life of a pastor should be a magnet to draw men to Christ. But this is no easy call; ministers of Christ must be beyond reproach in their own character.

Human character is more persuasive than human speech. Pastors, who shepherd the hearts of God's children, must emphasize personal character above appearance, personal faith above speech. Pastors, like all Christians, are constantly tempted to lower their standards of Christian morality.

A pastor may have a temper, but it must ever be controlled. A pastor has the right to self-assertion, but he can never let self interfere with God's message through him.

Yet God has called all to be witnesses and ministers unto His grace. What is true for the pastor, is true for us—for all of God's children.

■

God, only You truly know what our pastors and their
families go through in order to shepherd your flock. I pray
that You would strengthen them, making them impervious
to the slings and arrows of the enemy (Eph. 6:16).

PATTERN OF GOOD WORKS

In the same way, encourage the young men to be self-controlled in everything. Make yourself an example of good works with integrity and dignity in your teaching. Your message is to be sound beyond reproach, so that any opponent will be ashamed, because he doesn't have anything bad to say about us. —Titus 2:6–8

There is an old proverb that says, "One watch set right will do for the setting of many." So it is with the minister of God. He is the church clock; many set their lives by his. People have a way of testing the sincerity, truthfulness, and sound living of their minister. Perhaps children are first-class judges of a man. Their innocence and sincerity demand the same of others. The pastor who is able to gain the love and appreciation of children often has the qualities for adult leadership also.

The queen of Sheba once sought to put the wisdom of Solomon to a test. The queen brought some artificial flowers with her, beautifully made and delicately scented. She then asked Solomon which flowers were artificial and which were real. The wise man made his servants open the window, and, when the bees came in, they flew at once to the natural flowers. It is the same with sincere leadership; many people can sense the difference between the true and the false character.

Jesus, I pray that my life will always be genuine and a reflection of You.

THE FALL OF JERUSALEM

For the Lord will not reject us forever. Even if he causes suffering, he will show compassion according to the abundance of his faithful love. —Lamentations 3:31–32

In Israel, not far from the prison that once held the infamous Eichmann, the black ribbon of road that leads to Galilee crosses a bridge of stones. It is said that the stones belonged to a church built centuries ago by the Crusaders, which the Arabs had completely demolished.

Men fall, like the city of Jerusalem. The enemies of God take lives as well as churches and cities. Life's sacred places are desecrated by our own or another's sin.

God is just. He passes judgment on our sin—it is part of His pattern in dealing with the hearts of His children. But let us never forget that in His wrath He remembers mercy, and even though He "causes suffering, he will show compassion according to the abundance of his faithful love" (Lam. 3:32). What sin destroys, God is able to use again.

Another Jerusalem was built on the ruins of the first. Then Jesus Himself came to that city. The church that the Arabs rejected has become the bridge of stones on the highway to blue Galilee, where today the vows of many are renewed in Him.

Perhaps you sense the ruin of the sacred places of your life. But take heart in the true nature and character of our God: He will not cast off for ever those who turn to Him (Lam. 3:31).

Lord, there is no such thing as a ruined life to You. No one is beyond Your grasp. I praise You for Your redeeming love, and ask that You would give me eyes to see others the way that You do.

A CHARGE TO KEEP

But as for you, exercise self-control in everything,
endure hardship, do the work of an evangelist,
fulfill your ministry. —2 Timothy 4:5

People tend to listen to a person who has done their job well. The voice of a Christian, who has been successful in this life, rings loud and clear to those surrounding them. Indeed, God can use the work of our hands to draw the attention and curiosity of others. It is clear when someone has fought the good fight, finished the course, and kept the faith.

We need to rely more upon the wise counsel of others whose work has been successful. Our usual reply to the sage advice of someone older is, "Times have changed." While the face of life changes, the needs of people remain essentially the same—though perhaps a little more pronounced in our culture's day and age.

Let us learn from the mistakes and victories of other Christ followers who have gone before us. May we watch, endure, and live out our calling with the promise that we shall receive from our Lord a "crown of righteousness" (2 Tim. 4:8).

"Let a wise person listen and increase learning, and let a discerning person obtain guidance" (Prov. 1:5).

God grant us the wisdom to grow in faith by watching
and learning from others who follow after You.

THE MISSING MAN

I searched for a man among them who would repair the wall and stand in the gap before me on behalf of the land so that I might not destroy it, but I found no one. —Ezekiel 22:30

The difference between failure and success, or disaster and victory, may rest upon one person or many. In a crowded world of people, the individual may seem insignificant and forgotten— but not so with God, who sees and values each one of us.

However, God has often relied upon one person to fill the gap. His call of Abraham demonstrated how important one man can be. Also, the strategic arrival of Moses in Egypt filled a gap in God's plan for Israel. The judges and prophets were leaders called for a purpose. In our own day, many churches have been rescued from drifting by the coming of a single man or family.

In every city, town, and congregation, there is a situation today that calls for strong leadership. If God should choose to send us, may we be ready to faithfully step in faith and fill in the gap.

> For you were called to be free, brothers and sisters;
> only don't use this freedom as an opportunity for
> the flesh, but serve one another through love.
> (Gal. 5:13)

*Lord, I ask for a willingness in my own heart to
be used in any way that You may choose.*

THE LORD'S WATCHMEN

"As for you, son of man, I have made you a watchman for the house of Israel. When you hear a word from my mouth, give them a warning from me." —Ezekiel 33:7

A prophet of doom is seldom regarded in our affluent culture today. When we imagine a prophet of today, we think of a man wearing a large sign that predicts the end of the world and coming judgment. Because of the stereotyped behavior of some persons, people tend to forget that the warning may be true.

God has long used His messengers to act as His spokesmen to warn His people, calling them back to Him in repentance and relationship. Because of man's forgetfulness, a watchman must call us back to faithfulness and watchfulness, though he need not carry a sign of judgment. We ourselves may be the watchmen if we are alert to God's leading. Each of us is called to witness to our faith, and so we must warn others of the danger of refusing God's love.

> Tear your hearts, not just your clothes,
> and return to the LORD your God.
> For he is gracious and compassionate,
> slow to anger, abounding in faithful love,
> and he relents from sending disaster. (Joel 2:13)

Lord, I ask that You would lead me to bear a faithful testimony, sharing the truth of the gospel in love.

THE SHEEP OF HIS PASTURE

*"You are my flock, the human flock of my pasture,
and I am your God. This is the declaration
of the Lord GOD." —Ezekiel 34:31*

The biblical picture of the Good Shepherd has lost some of its meaning for us. It would profit us greatly to try to understand how tenderly the shepherd of old on the bleak hillsides of Israel regarded the sheep of his pasture. Their safety and well-being were in his hands. In such a profession, he truly would go so far as to give his life for them if necessary.

The hope of Israel was constantly nurtured by the manner in which God acted as Shepherd, and by His promise of the Shepherd-King to come. Jesus fulfilled all of these expectations when He said: "I am the good shepherd. The good shepherd lays down his life for the sheep. . . . But I have other sheep that are not from this sheep pen; I must bring them also, and they will listen to my voice. Then there will be one flock, one shepherd" (John 10:11, 16).

This figure of speech should remind us vividly of the love and faithfulness of God who promised to send a Shepherd, and then kept His Word, and sent Him to save us. "For even the Son of Man did not come to be served, but to serve, and to give his life as a ransom for many" (Mark 10:45). As members of God's flock, may we follow in trust and confidence of the Good Shepherd.

*Jesus, help me to both realize the tender compassion of You,
my Shepherd, and accept Your leadership over my life.*

A NEW HEART

"I will give you a new heart and put a new spirit within you; I will remove your heart of stone and give you a heart of flesh." —Ezekiel 36:26

The message of the gospel is revolutionary. God asks not for mere change of outward behavior. He has sought through the ages to recreate the inner life and heart of His people. He has always reached down within us to accomplish what Jesus described as being born again. In the place of the cold heart of unbelief, God plants a warm and vibrant heart that is sensitive and responsive to His love.

Conversion involves the transformation of a person's mind as well as His heart. There is even a change in judgment and understanding when the eyes of our hearts are enlightened. Indeed, conversion involves the transformation of the whole person.

We acknowledge that our new birth is in God, not in ourselves. Our new life in Christ is not won by good works. It the gift of a loving God.

> "I will give them a heart to know me, that I am the Lord. They will be my people, and I will be their God because they will return to me with all their heart." (Jer. 24:7)

God, I ask for the ability to realize more clearly the meaning of your gift to me in Christ Jesus.

MAKING THE DEAD ALIVE

Then he said to me, "Son of man, can these bones live?"
I replied, "Lord GOD, only you know." —Ezekiel 37:3

Many times in history, a nation has found itself ruled and controlled by cruel conquerors. Each of these groups has had in common a sense of despondency and defeat. Their common cry has always been, "Is there any hope for our nation?"

Such was the lot of Israel when they were carried into exile in Babylonia after the fall of Jerusalem. In the midst of despair, God spoke a message of hope that gave assurance for a brighter day. Ezekiel was led to understand that God would bring these scattered bones of the nation together, breathe life into them again, and reestablish His people in their land.

We as individuals have shared this feeling of defeat when our personal hopes and ambitions have been dashed to the ground. Even as God was ready to accomplish the impossible for His people, Israel, He will bring order out of the chaos of our misfortunes. We must faithfully seek His will and wait patiently for the working out of His purposes.

> "This is what the Lord God says to these bones: I will cause breath to enter you, and you will live. I will put tendons on you, make flesh grow on you, and cover you with skin. I will put breath in you so that you come to life. Then you will know that I am the Lord." (Ezek. 37:5–6)

Lord, we ask for Your blessing upon our nation so that we may become a light unto the nations of the world.

GOD FIRST

He said to him, "Love the Lord your God with all your heart, with all your soul, and with all your mind. This is the greatest and most important command. The second is like it: Love your neighbor as yourself. All the Law and the Prophets depend on these two commands." —Matthew 22:37–40

It is impossible to sum up our history and heritage in a few words. Volumes have been written to interpret the teachings of Jesus from the Scriptures. But nowhere is the tendency to interpret more evident than in religious writings.

The Law of the Lord would certainly qualify as a rich heritage for Christ followers. And while some would try to explain away the need for the Law in light of the gospel, Jesus stressed that the gospel of grace did not make the Law null and void. In fact, He said to them, "I did not come to abolish but to fulfill. For truly I tell you, until heaven and earth pass away, not the smallest letter or one stroke of a letter will pass away from the law until all things are accomplished" (Matt. 5:17–18).

In His Sermon on the Mount, Jesus reduced the Ten Commandments, already a summary of the Law, to two basic commandments. Clearly, He sought to focus on the core of the Law as love—one's wholehearted love for God and his love for his neighbor. But love for God should always come first. As John said, "We love because he first loved us" (1 John 4:19). When we love God with all of our being, our love for others will naturally come.

■

Lord, I ask that You continue to grow me toward that all-inclusive love for You that Jesus placed as first of all commandments.

THE EVERLASTING KINGDOM

*"In the days of those kings, the God of the heavens
will set up a kingdom that will never be destroyed,
and this kingdom will not be left to another people.
It will crush all these kingdoms and bring them to an
end, but will itself endure forever." —Daniel 2:44*

One thought stands out in Daniel's startling interpretation of
the king's dream. The God of heaven would set up a Kingdom
that would never, ever perish. This is a glorious truth that we
can remember and treasure. Many of us have experienced
hours when we were discouraged and impatient with the slow
progress of the growth of the Kingdom. There are times when
we can be tempted to believe we know a better way. But the
will of the Lord will not be thwarted, ever. And in the end,
Scripture tells us this truth remains: "Every knee will bow to
me, every tongue will swear allegiance" (Isa. 45:23).

We live in a world where everything passes away— nothing
at all lasts forever here, in our earthly home. But our true citi-
zenship is in heaven (Phil. 3:20). Therefore, we can stand with
the apostle Paul and declare that,

> "we do not give up. Even though our outer person is
> being destroyed, our inner person is being renewed
> day by day. For our momentary light affliction
> is producing for us an absolutely incomparable
> eternal weight of glory. So we do not focus on what
> is seen, but on what is unseen. For what is seen is
> temporary, but what is unseen is eternal." (2 Cor.
> 4:16–18)

■

*Lord, help me to appreciate the truth of Revelation 19:6:
"Hallelujah, because our Lord God, the Almighty, reigns!"*

A MAGNIFICENT REFUSAL

"If the God we serve exists, then he can rescue us from the furnace of blazing fire, and he can rescue us from the power of you, the king. But even if he does not rescue us, we want you as king to know that we will not serve your gods or worship the gold statue you set up." —Daniel 3:17–18

For more than two thousand years, the story of the three Hebrew captives who said "no" to a king has been a monumental object lesson of one thing: the difficulty of turning away from temptation.

One of the hardest words in the English language to say is the little two-letter word "no." But what are we afraid of in giving this answer? Who is it that we most want to please: God or man? Because the truth is that whenever we say "no" to something, we are actually saying "yes" to something else, in this case, our God. Every time we choose Him—even in the midst of walking through a fiery furnace of our own—we bring Him glory. Every time.

We do not have to walk alone any more than did Shadrach, Meshach, and Abednego. Their experience reminds us of the divine assurance expressed in Isaiah:

"I will be with you when you pass through the waters, and when you pass through the rivers, they will not overwhelm you. You will not be scorched when you walk through the fire, and the flame will not burn you." (Isa. 43:2)

■

Lord, give me the courage to believe and trust in You—even in the hours of temptation.

A KING'S SUBMISSION

"Now I, Nebuchadnezzar, praise, exalt, and glorify the King of the heavens, because all his works are true and his ways are just. He is able to humble those who walk in pride." —Daniel 4:37

Many people have worked hard and honestly for many years and, after much frugality and perseverance, have not acquired much of this world's material goods. Others have become wealthy and influential with what seems like ease. But regardless of what we earn in this lifetime, we ought to acknowledge that our provision comes from God.

Christ said a person should choose their soul's welfare above all that this world offers. We must submit ourselves to God and walk in His way regardless of our circumstances. Many pray to God, "Your will be done," but they do not really mean it. Yet when we submit to the will of the Father, we will find peace and comfort in knowing He is sovereign. The One who spoke the universe into being loves us.

> The LORD your God is among you,
> a warrior who saves.
> He will rejoice over you with gladness.
> He will be quiet in his love.
> He will delight in you with singing. (Zeph. 3:17)

Thank You, God, for Your grace, Your gifts, and Your generous provision.

WEIGHED AND WANTING

"'Tekel' means that you have been weighed on the
balance and found deficient." —Daniel 5:27

Every honest person knows that when we are weighed in God's balances, we are found wanting. Even those Christ followers whom we deem to be particularly fruitful, seem to find that the closer they get to God, the more aware of their sins and shortcomings they become.

Although we cannot be perfect, we must lean into the perfection of our Lord Jesus, who said, "Be perfect, therefore, as your heavenly Father is perfect" (Matt. 5:48). Our heart's greatest desire must always be to know our God better and to grow our faith in Him. And so it is not perfection but our relationship with our Savior that should always be our focus. The apostle Paul put it this way: "Not that I have already reached the goal or am already perfect, but I make every effort to take hold of it because I also have been taken hold of by Christ Jesus" (Phil. 3:12).

We must be repentant of our sins and have our faith fixed firmly in Christ alone for our salvation. With this assurance, we should seek each day to live closer to God, leaning more and more into the person of Christ for comfort and direction. He has already made us clean, and if we remain close to Him, He will grow in us the fruit we are meant to produce (John 15:4–5).

Lord, please forgive me when I try to do the work
of making myself clean and perfect—You have
already done that for me. Teach me to abide in You,
and to seek to do Your will, one day at a time.

THE REBUKE OF PRIDE

Though you seem to soar like an eagle and make your nest among the stars, even from there I will bring you down. This is the LORD's declaration. —Obadiah 4

Until rather recently, we were taught that what goes up must come down. This is no longer true. It seems likely that at some point, our exploration of space will enable us to journey to another planet, overcoming the magnetic pull of the earth.

Yet, God's laws are immutable. He can raise men up, or bring men down. Our pride is the very essence of the sin that caused our downfall in the Garden, as it still is today. It's our lofty estimation of ourselves that leads us to believe—even subconsciously—that we can live out of our own self-sufficiency, and independent of God.

But it is still God who raises up and brings down according to His perfect will and plan. He "resists the proud, but gives grace to the humble. Therefore, submit to God. Resist the devil, and he will flee from you. Draw near to God, and he will draw near to you" (James 4:6–8).

Lord, please grant me humility in the knowledge that all I have and am comes from You and is to be used for Your glory.

GOD OF ALL NATIONS

*Many nations will come and say, "Come, let us go
up to the mountain of the LORD, to the house of
the God of Jacob. He will teach us about his ways
so we may walk in his paths." —Micah 4:2*

God's ways are not our ways. Because of our flesh, this can
be one of our greatest frustrations and, at the same time, one
of our highest hopes. But the thought that even one of the
nations of this world today would say, "Let us go up to the
mountain of the Lord," is difficult to fathom. Many nations
and their leaders today reject our God, and if not the nation as
a whole, then certainly many of the individuals.

But those who put their hope and trust in God hold fast
to the belief that God will triumph ultimately. When hope
seems faint, God comes to remind us that He is the God of all
nations. The final victory belongs to Him.

> Lord, there is no one like you among the gods,
> and there are no works like yours.
> All the nations you have made
> will come and bow down before you, Lord,
> and will honor your name.
> For you are great and perform wonders;
> you alone are God. (Ps. 86:8–10)

■

Lord, give me confidence in Your ultimate victory.

THE LAW OF LIFE

Mankind, he has told each of you what is good and what it is the Lord requires of you: to act justly, to love faithfulness, and to walk humbly with your God. —Micah 6:8

Salvation is the gift of God. When a person accepts God's gift, they then assume the responsibility to live the life Christ has called us to, according to His purposes.

Jesus summed up the requirement of the Christian life as "Love the Lord your God with all your heart, with all your soul, with all your strength, and with all your mind;" and "your neighbor as yourself" (Luke 10:27). Centuries earlier, Micah said the same thing—deal justly toward others, be kind to others, and stay close to God.

The person who is willing to implement this formula into their own life will understand the real meaning of the Christian faith. They can then begin to view all the difficult decisions of this life through this lens. We do not always know the plans of the Father, but we do know His will for us: to act justly, to love faithfulness, and to walk humbly with our God. And above all, love as Christ loves us. There can be no greater calling for a Christ follower.

■

O Father, help us to see Your will in the difficult decisions of life and, finding it, to follow it.

BY FAITH

*Finally brothers and sisters, whatever is true, whatever
is honorable, whatever is just, whatever is pure,
whatever is lovely, whatever is commendable—if
there is any moral excellence and if there is anything
praiseworthy—dwell on these things. —Philippians 4:8*

> By faith Moses, when he had grown up, refused to
> be called the son of Pharaoh's daughter and chose
> to suffer with the people of God rather than to
> enjoy the fleeting pleasure of sin. For he considered
> reproach for the sake of Christ to be greater wealth
> than the treasures of Egypt, since he was looking
> ahead to the reward. (Heb. 11:24–25)

The temptation to "enjoy the fleeting pleasure of sin" is ever present. There are times in life when we all find these pleasures to be very real. Our culture and media are full of slogans that seem to undergird this approach to life: Eat, drink, and merry! Live it up! Here today, gone tomorrow. Better make the most of it.

Stories of temptation are nothing new. Temptation has been recorded throughout history, and even before. But the teachings of Jesus are clear on this matter. The shortsighted view of life is not the one He has called His followers to live. To love Jesus means that we will find our freedom when we are in bondage to the will of Christ.

> "But now, since you have been set free from sin and
> have become enslaved to God, you have your fruit,
> which results in sanctification—and the outcome is
> eternal life!" (Rom. 6:22)

*Lord God, help me to live by faith and not by sight, remaining
close to Christ Jesus, who is the author and perfecter of my faith.*

THE COMING GLORY

"The final glory of this house will be greater than the first,"
says the LORD of Armies. "I will provide peace in this place"—
this is the declaration of the Lord of Armies. —Haggai 2:9

The best is yet to come. This is always true for those of us who are Christ followers. No matter how much happiness we have now, Scripture promises us that a greater happiness is to come (2 Tim. 2:10; 2 Cor. 4:17). No matter how much love surrounds us today, a day is coming when love will be perfected.

The psalmist tells us to, "Wait for the LORD; be strong, and let your heart be courageous. Wait for the LORD" (Ps. 27:14). But waiting is hard work. Why is it that God does not hurry? Why does it seem as if His sense of time is so very different from ours?

Yes, it is difficult to have patience. In fact, it is impossible to be patient unless faith and hope are present. God did not forget His house in Jerusalem. With the dedicated help of the people, He promised to bring order out of chaos and meaning out of confusion.

We need a strong faith to help us know that there is no problem beyond the reach of God, and that often what we rebuild on a shattered life is indeed more glorious than anything previously anticipated (Isa. 61:3).

■

Lord, we need Your patience to calm our
hearts and steady our faith in You.

A CHOSEN INSTRUMENT

On that day"—this is the declaration of the LORD of Armies—"I will take you, Zerubbabel son of Shealtiel, my servant"—this is the LORD's declaration—"and make you like my signet ring, for I have chosen you." This is the declaration of the LORD of Armies. —Haggai 2:23

As children, most of us have been chosen to be on a team for a game or contest. Maybe you can remember the joy of being chosen first, or perhaps the sadness and embarrassment of being chosen last. But listen to what Scripture says about those who have been redeemed by Christ:

> But you are a chosen race, a royal priesthood, a holy nation, a people for his possession, so that you may proclaim the praises of the one who called you out of darkness into his marvelous light. (1 Pet. 2:9)

We did not choose God—He chose us! (John 15:16). Our Creator-God calls us by name, and we belong to Him (Isa. 43:1). This is His heart toward His creation. He does not leave any of us out, but we may disqualify ourselves for service by our actions.

Every day the world asks us to choose sides. We already know God's desire is to be reconciled to Him and to bring Him glory. He chooses us, but we must turn to Him in response. So that if God asks us to be one of His chosen instruments we are able to hear Him and say "yes."

Lord, I pray for the courage to submit to Your work in me and through me.

THE KING AND THE CITY

Rejoice greatly, Daughter Zion! Shout in triumph,
Daughter Jerusalem! Look, your King is coming to you;
he is righteous and victorious, humble and riding on a
donkey, on a colt, the foal of a donkey. —Zechariah 9:9

With eloquence and beauty, the prophet Zechariah speaks of the messianic King and the sovereignty and victory of God. It is a time of spontaneous joy, for salvation has come.

Jesus is a picture of contrasts, for His victory is linked forever entwined with humility, power with peace. The royalty of the King is found in His justice, lowliness, and service, and His reign is universal.

When God reigns, our lives are ruled by hope, not fear. And as God's people, we are sheep nurtured and attended by the Good Shepherd. We are the shining jewels in His golden crown (Zech. 9:16).

Many have assumed that to serve God is to be filled with gloom and duty, but the prophet Nehemiah was right when he said, "The joy of the LORD is your strength" (Neh. 8:10). Therefore, it is a privilege to serve Him. And when we do serve, we ought to "do it from the heart, as something done for the Lord and not for people, knowing that [we] will receive the reward of an inheritance from the Lord" (Col. 3:23–24).

Lord, I ask that You would restore unto me the joy of my
salvation, for You are my strength and only true source of help.

THE REIGN OF GOD

On that day the LORD will become King
over the whole earth—the LORD alone, and
his name alone. —Zechariah 14:9

In vivid apocalypse, the prophet depicts the last great battle for Jerusalem and God's divine victory. Here we see the intervention of the heavenly hosts, the redemption of nature, the universal reign of God, and the punishment of God's enemies. It is a new earth where God reigns.

Even in our day, passages like these stir our hearts. God's redemption is for all mankind. He has come for all people. Our common, daily life is sanctified in Him. Nothing is lost from His sight, for to Him all things are holy.

This truth is expressed beautifully in Maltbie D. Babcock's hymn, "This Is My Father's World":

> This is my Father's world,
> And to my list'ning ears,
> All nature sings, and round me rings
> The music of the spheres.
> This is my Father's world,
> I rest me in the thought
> Of rocks and trees, of skies and seas
> His hand the wonders wrought.

"For his invisible attributes, that is, his eternal power and divine nature, have been clearly seen since the creation of the world, being understood through what he has made. As a result, people are without excuse" (Rom. 1:20).

■

Lord, please reveal Yourself to us in all of Your creation.
May we see Your presence with us everywhere.

THE LORD'S COMPLAINT

"When you present a blind animal for sacrifice, is it not wrong? And when you present a lame or sick animal, is it not wrong? Bring it to your governor! Would he be pleased with you or show you favor?" asks the LORD of Armies. —Malachi 1:8

How often we sin by taking God's goodness to us for granted. We presume upon the grace and mercy of God. Like ancient Israel, we become filled with pride and imagine we deserve God's bounty. We assume God is like us and remake Him in our own image, forgetting that He made us in His own. The way we treat one another is always prefaced by our ingratitude toward God.

Malachi, the prophet, confronts us with God's truth. He speaks of God's justice and our infidelity. Moldy bread and imperfect animals do not meet God's requirements, because the cheap gift reflects the cheap heart. Second-rate giving is idolatry in disguise.

King David's cry reflects the conviction of the believer's heart: "No, I insist on buying it from you for a price, for I will not offer to the LORD my God burnt offerings that cost me nothing" (2 Sam. 24:24).

Lord, give me a single eye and an honest heart.

ROBBERY AND RECOMPENSE

"Will a man rob God? Yet you are robbing me!" "How do we rob you?" you ask. "By not making the payments of the tenth and the contributions." —Malachi 3:8

The recognition of man's stewardship under God is a fundamental law of life. It is a basic part of faith and freedom. It is the acknowledgment of the divine source and sustenance of life upon the earth. To ignore or deny this is to rob God and ourselves.

There is a sentence from the ancient Sanskrit which reads: "He who allows a day to pass without generosity . . . is like a blacksmith's bellows—he breathes but does not live." But generosity is not a natural gift. We do not come out of the world and into the world with a natural desire to share. The tiny infant is entirely self-centered; when his desires are frustrated, he lets everybody know it. Generosity is an acquired virtue and must be learned by all Christians and taught by the indwelling Holy Spirit.

There are many motives for stewardship: self-respect and pride, a sense of obligation and duty, the desire to impress others, and the needs of the world. But these are not the primary ones for us as Christ followers. For us, giving is, above all, about loving and being obedient to our gracious God.

I want to have a generous heart like Yours.
Make me more like You, Lord.

A BOOK OF REMEMBRANCE

At that time those who feared the LORD spoke to one another. The LORD took notice and listened. So a book of remembrance was written before him for those who feared the LORD and had high regard for his name. —Malachi 3:16

Who in this life does not wish to be remembered? In our highest moments, we aspire to perform some lasting thing, something which will live beyond ourselves. So we work for years on the making of a book, toil for decades to build a church, labor to steward the lives of the children entrusted to us as parents. In truth, we expend our lives on something outside and beyond ourselves.

In today's text, we find that God remembers. He not only remembers the acts of great moments, but also the cup of cold water, the look of love we turn toward another face, and the small unremembered acts of kindness that fill our days. How good it is to know He remembers, He sees. How comforting it is, oftentimes in the midst of turmoil and frustration, to be told by the prophet that a book of remembrance is written, before God, and that each believer who fears Him and turns their thoughts Godward, will be found and remembered by Him.

God, forgive me when I forget Your goodness to me. I ask for a memory today that would encourage and sustain me.

SPEAK THE TRUTH IN LOVE

*Therefore, putting away lying, speak the truth,
each one to his neighbor, because we are
members of one another.* —Ephesians 4:25

Speaking the truth in love is an identifying mark of the believer. It is the truth that has set us free, and our redemption should cause us to bear witness to this truth. Falsehood is a part of the old life, one we lay aside as we would an old, worn-out garment. We learn to live and speak the truth as revealed to us through God's Word of truth.

There are many kinds of falsehood. We lie by what we say, and sometimes by what we fail to say. Silence can be golden, but it can also be tarnished when we lie by omission. By silence, we can give our approval of something we know in our hearts to be wrong. As believers, we are called to speak what is true; we are called to be people of integrity, honor, and purity.

But when we speak the truth, we must do so with love. The truth must be spoken, but it must be gentle, kind, and life-giving—not judgmental. Orthodoxy and legalism are hard and cold. And so our zeal for earnestness and truth must be tempered by love. Let us remember God is love, and He reveals His truth supremely in One who came to seek and to save that which was lost—His beloved children.

Father, please give me the strength to "speak the truth in love."

GOD'S SUPREME REVELATION

*Long ago God spoke to the fathers by the prophets at different
times and in different ways. In these last days, he has spoken
to us by his Son. God has appointed him heir of all things
and made the universe through him. —Hebrews 1:1–2*

God revealed Himself through the poetic prose of the prophets. He revealed Himself through the wonders of nature. He
made known His message through the strength and wisdom
of angels. But His highest and most perfect revelation was
through His Son, Jesus Christ:

> The Word became flesh and dwelt among us. We
> observed his glory, the glory as the one and only Son
> from the Father, full of grace and truth. (John 1:14)

Jesus is God in the flesh. In Jesus, God came into history
and lived among men, and in Him, revealing to us the goodness, purpose, and righteousness of God, the gentleness and
love of our Creator. God revealed in Christ a way of escape
from our brokenness and sin, and a hope brighter and more
lasting than the stars. Jesus opened our eyes to the truth that
God is a person who came to rescue and to save His children.

*Lord, we earnestly pray that all the earth will become a
part of the redeemed family of God through Christ Jesus.*

GOD'S GREATEST GIFT

*But we do see Jesus—made lower than the angels
for a short time so that by God's grace he might taste
death for everyone—crowned with glory and honor
because he suffered death. —Hebrews 2:9*

If we were asked, "What is the greatest gift you ever received from someone?" we would have difficulty deciding what to answer. But when asked, "What is God's greatest gift to us?" the answer is instantly clear to us as Christ followers. Jesus, God's Son and our Savior, is the greatest gift given to us by our Father. The Bible tells us that while the just punishment for our sin is death, "the gift of God is eternal life in Christ Jesus our Lord" (Rom. 6:23).

Our Scripture passage today tells us why Christ is God's greatest gift. Jesus was made, for a little time, lower than the angels, and died for us that He might lift us above the angels into the family of God. All of mankind had sinned and fallen short of the glory of God, but Jesus had, by His sinless life and His sacrificial death, received great glory and honor. "Therefore, just as sin entered the world through one man, and death through sin, in this way death spread to all people, because all sinned" (Rom. 5:12). Our sin dishonored our God, but the sinless Savior brought the Father honor. Thanks be to God.

■

*Lord, we ask that You will make us able to distinguish
between values, and by faith lay hold of God's greatest gift.*

MAN'S MOST MEANINGFUL EXPERIENCE

"For we have become participants in Christ if we hold firmly until the end the reality that we had at the start. As it is said: Today, if you hear his voice, do not harden your hearts as in the rebellion. —Hebrews 3:14–15

Many meaningful experiences come to us throughout life. Our relationships with our parents, our spouses in marriage, our friends, and our children are all great experiences. Our adventures with those who disciple us and collaborate with us in our walk with the Lord can be uplifting experiences. However, no experience is comparable to our redemption in Christ. This is a relationship and experience entered into by faith. The emotional effects of our relationship with Christ Jesus are determined largely by our background. But, regardless of where we come from, meeting Jesus is life-changing—the most profound experience we as human beings could hope to experience in this lifetime or in the next.

Unbelief often prevents God's people from larger accomplishments in the name of the Lord. The writer of Hebrews warns Christians against unbelief, and he cites the unbelief of those who followed Moses as an illustration. The people followed Moses in the wilderness and then wavered in their faith, failing to enter Canaan's rest and blessing because of their faithlessness. May it not be so with us. For while there is blessing through God, their truly is no greater blessing than knowing the presence and friendship of our God.

Lord, help us to know the joy of being faithful companions with Christ.

LIFE'S GREATEST ASSURANCE

*For we do not have a high priest who is unable to
sympathize with our weaknesses, but one who has
been tempted in every way as we are, yet without sin.
Therefore, let us approach the throne of grace with
boldness, so that we may receive mercy and find grace
to help us in time of need. —Hebrews 4:15–16*

Assurance brings calm and composure. Assurance from the
medical doctor that our health is good produces peace of mind.
Assurance that our vocation and calling are substantial and
meaningful is heartening. Assurance of acceptance by friends
and family relieves anxiety and tension. But our greatest assurance is that we who know God are kept in perfect rest by the
grace and mercy of Him through Jesus Christ.

When we sin or when we face trials and challenges, we
may still boldly approach the throne of grace and receive
mercy—all because of Jesus. Today's text assures us that the
believer has a great High Priest in heaven making intercession for us. That High Priest is Jesus, our Savior and King. As
Christ followers, we have access to God through Jesus who
hears our prayers and petitions, our cries for help and encouragement—because He, too, was tempted as we are, and faced
similar trials and challenges, yet lived the perfect life we could
not.

*Lord, help me to lean into the peace of mind
that can only come from Jesus.*

PURPOSEFUL LIVING

*Although he was the Son, he learned obedience from
what he suffered. After he was perfected, he became
the source of eternal salvation for all who obey him,
and he was declared by God a high priest according
to the order of Melchizedek. —Hebrews 5:8–10*

Learning to live with purpose begins with our most basic relationships and experiences in life. Those of us who are fortunate to be born into a healthy, stable, loving family, and community, may have an initial advantage in relating to God; it is easier to believe our heavenly Father is good when our own earthly father is a good man. But even a good relationship with those around us can lead us astray, encouraging us to think we do not really have need of God when things are already seemingly going well for us.

Our relationship to God is described in our text for today as growing out of "eternal salvation for all who obey" Christ the Savior and High Priest. God is our source of life. Life without God is one which leaves us misdirected. Purposeful living is characterized by usefulness, self-giving, happiness, and joy, because it flows in an unhindered stream from the Heavenly Father. The secret of a purposeful life does not lie so much in educational, social, and financial advantages as it does in our connection with and relationship to a holy God. It is our relationship with Jesus that makes us redeemed and loved and worthy—because He is worthy.

■

*Lord, may those who are confused about the meaning of
life turn to You for salvation and rest through Jesus.*

GOD REMEMBERS

For God is not unjust; he will not forget your work and the love you demonstrated for his name by serving the saints—and by continuing to serve them. —Hebrews 6:10

How different in outlook is God from men! Men remember the evil deeds committed by a neighbor and easily forget the good done. God remembers the good done by true believers because He is just. God remembers to bless those who bless others. As Scripture tells us "Kindness to the poor is a loan to the LORD, and he will give a reward to the lender" (Prov. 19:17).

The text for today indicates that these Hebrew believers had done many labors of love, and that all the works they had done in God's name would not be forgotten. Our text suggests that God would be unjust to forget—something which goes against His very nature (Isa. 30:18).

God assured His people that He could not forget the way they ministered in His name to the saints, having often become "publicly exposed" for God's sake (Heb. 10:33). They suffered afflictions in order to continue their ministry in the world. The Lord takes note of every work of righteousness and the sacrificial spirit in which it is done.

> Whatever you do, do it from the heart, as something done for the Lord and not for people, knowing that you will receive the reward of an inheritance from the Lord. You serve the Lord Christ. (Col. 3:23–24)

■

Lord, help me to never grow tired of serving the Kingdom in Your name, knowing that you see me and know my heart, and that ultimately, You will receive the glory You so deserve.

REMEMBER WHO YOU ARE

"Be on your guard, so that your minds are not dulled from carousing, drunkenness, and worries of life, or that day will come on you unexpectedly like a trap." —Luke 21:34

As the people of God, we must remember who we are in reality—not who the world would tell us we ought to be. The world tells us to be ourselves, to celebrate the individual. But this is not true of those who are Christ followers. More and more, our allegiance to Christ Jesus is frowned upon. Someone who has strong personal convictions on a subject is looked upon as different or uncooperative.

The apostle Paul warned us of this: "Do not be conformed to this age, but be transformed by the renewing of your mind, so that you may discern what is the good, pleasing, and perfect will of God" (Rom. 12:2).

When we try to conform to the ways of this world, to be something that we truly are not, it breaks our heart. We then try to numb the pain, which leads us further away from God in an effort to escape in the unacceptable reality that we, as individuals, have lost our true identity in Christ Jesus.

If we are in Christ, then it is no longer we who live, but Christ who lives in and through us (Gal. 2:20). And so we ought not to worry with what the world thinks of us. The reality is that we belong to another world—an eternal world.

> "Don't you know that your body is a temple of the Holy Spirit who is in you, whom you have from God? You are not your own, for you were bought at a price. So glorify God with your body." (1 Cor. 6:19–20)

Lord, help us to remember who we truly are in You.

THE LAW OF LOVE

*Indeed, if you fulfill the royal law prescribed in
the Scripture, Love your neighbor as yourself,
you are doing well. —James 2:8*

"Love your neighbor as yourself" is described by one translator
as the Scripture's sovereign law. When Christians observe it as
it is taught by Christ, they love without discrimination. They
love the poor, the privileged, the underprivileged, the deserving, the undeserving—people from every nation, creed, and
walk of life. There is no room for exclusiveness, or snobbery, as
James describes it.

How can Christians claim to accept this sovereign law, yet
continue to patronize businesses that exclude others? What
would Jesus do under these circumstances? His actions were
clearly contrary to the ways of His day, and to many of ours.
And so James, the brother of Jesus, admonishes us to not show
any kind of exclusivity: "My brothers and sisters, do not show
favoritism as you hold on to the faith in our glorious Lord Jesus
Christ" (James 2:1).

> "I give you a new command: Love one another.
> Just as I have loved you, you are also to love one
> another. By this everyone will know that you are my
> disciples, if you love one another." (John 13:34–35)

*Lord, help me to see people as you see them,
individually, and in need of You.*

PROOF OF OUR FAITH

You see that a person is justified by works and not by faith alone. . . . For just as the body without the spirit is dead, so also faith without works is dead. —James 2:24, 26

All of us know that love cannot be satisfied with words alone; it must be demonstrated. A couple happily married ten, twenty-five, or fifty years will have performed thousands of acts of devotion and thoughtfulness. Often it will mean sacrifice. This is the kind of language that our hearts really speak and understand. It is also the kind of language God understands.

But just as faith without works does not serve the Kingdom of God, our empty sacrifices and works are meaningless to Him (Isa. 1:11, 13). We cannot earn our salvation, and we cannot earn the love of our God; both are rooted and established in Christ's finished work on the cross. Our God knows the motivation behind our works—even if done "in His name." For "humans do not see what the LORD sees, for humans see what is visible, but the LORD sees the heart" (1 Sam. 16:7).

Our God wants relationship with His people. May He search our hearts and find that true worship, love, and affection for Him reside there.

■

Lord, search me and know my heart. And when You do, I pray You will find the truest of adoration there is for You.

LIVES MARKED BY HOPE

Therefore, with your minds ready for action, be sober-minded and set your hope completely on the grace to be brought to you at the revelation of Jesus Christ. As obedient children, do not be conformed to the desires of your former ignorance. —1 Peter 1:13–14

Someone observed that a reason for the triumphant joy of the early Christians was that they lived in three dimensions. They were grateful for redemption from their past; they were thrilled by the prospect of a future glory with Christ; and they were able, therefore, to bear their present trials with hope and patience.

Today's passage suggests that we should strive to leave corruptible things, from which we have been redeemed by Christ, and devote ourselves to the incorruptible values in which Christ directs us. In this way, may we keep our values in harmony with the holiness of Jesus, who has offered us the gift of unbroken fellowship with Him. And may our present living more resolutely comply with God's command: "Be holy, because I am holy" (1 Pet. 1:16). We, too, need to live in the three dimensions of faith, just as the early Christians did.

With [our] minds ready for action," we must "be sober-minded and set [our] hope completely on the grace" given to us through Christ Jesus (1 Pet. 1:13). May our holy thinking give way to holy living, so that we might truly say along with the apostle Paul, "For me, to live is Christ and to die is gain" (Phil. 1:21).

∎

Jesus, be Lord of all of my life, and all of my heart. My hope is in You alone.

THE MAKING OF MANKIND

*So God created man in his own image; he
created him in the image of God; he created
them male and female. —Genesis 1:27*

It is easy to admire the intelligent, appreciate the beautiful, or
enjoy the cultured. Our difficulty comes when we come into
contact with those who do not share our ideas on what is smart
or pretty or cultured. We have a difficult time with those who
are quite different from us, unless we have an appreciation for
how God created them.

When the psalmist asks his question: "What is a human
being that you remember him, a son of man that you look after
him?" (Ps. 8:4), he spoke of and included all mankind. He then
goes on to answer his own question in the next verse: "You
made him little less than God and crowned him with glory and
honor" (v. 5).

If we are ever prone to look around us and doubt the worth
of our fellow man, or find ourselves despondent and disheart-
ened in life's adventure, the words of the psalmist can help to
reassure us of our worth and the worth of others. God made
us; we are His creation. God made us; we are formed in His
image. It makes little difference what we see in ourselves or in
others. When God looks at us, He sees the intent behind His
original creation, to which He says, "It [is] very good indeed"
(Gen. 1:31).

*O Lord, may we live in such a way as to honor
You, who have made us with a holy purpose.*

DISOBEDIENCE AND DISASTER

I will put hostility between you and the woman, and between your offspring and her offspring. He will strike your head, and you will strike his heel. —Genesis 3:15

One of God's most precious promises is found in 1 Corinthians 10:13:

> No temptation has come upon you except what is common to humanity. But God is faithful; he will not allow you to be tempted beyond what you are able, but with the temptation he will also provide a way out so that you may be able to bear it.

When we read this verse, God tells us that sin is an everyday test in our lives, that it is common to mankind. Then we read the assurance, "But God is faithful." We stand because of God's faithfulness, confident that the temptation will not be too great for us if we seek Him first, and also His way out.

Satan will come into our lives because of the fall. As he comes, he will bring doubt and distrust with him. The doubt can make us stronger if we are honestly seeking God's truth. And distrust can never enter if we overcome the doubt.

Disobedience, however, can bring disaster. At the time disaster comes, we may not recognize it for what it is. God asked Adam where he was, not because he did not know, but because Adam did not realize his own condition following sin. "Where are you?" is always a pertinent question—one the Lord lovingly asks of those He loves.

■

O Lord, we pray not that You would take us out of the world, but that You would keep us from evil as we seek to honor You in it.

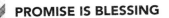

PROMISE IS BLESSING

I will make you into a great nation, I will bless you, I will make your name great, and you will be a blessing. —Genesis 12:2

This is God's call to Abraham, and it is a call to service. The beginning of the adventure of faith, whether it be Abraham's or ours, comes with God's call and His promise. "Go out from your land." Move into another realm, another place. Change your relationships. Sever your ties. A new life lies ahead for you. And when you go, "I will bless you."

How many persons pause at the door to a new life, wanting to move out and change old ties, to become a new creation, but are unable to take the last step for fear of their weaknesses, or for doubt of God's faithfulness. But God's promise to Abraham was not based on Abraham's strength. God said, "I will." The good news we preach today includes not only God's "I will" but also His "I have."

As we share the gospel truth with others, many will answer, "I can't." Then we may testify that we cannot either, but that God can. God never bases our salvation or His blessings on our strength, but upon His strength and faithfulness. The blessing is wherever He has called us to. Let us not tarry in following Him there.

Lord, please strengthen my faith for any and all circumstances that may come my way. And may praise for you always be on my lips.

GOD'S PRESENCE IS PROMISED

"Haven't I commanded you: be strong and courageous?
Do not be afraid or discouraged, for the LORD *your*
God is with you wherever you go." —Joshua 1:9

God's power in human experience is boldly portrayed in the life of Joshua. God's presence is pledged to those who accept His challenge (Josh. 1:2) and follow His truth (vv. 7–8). His presence secures our fragile human strength and courage.

Your biggest problem can be the occasion for God's challenge. This was true in the life of Joshua. He had big shoes to fill in following Moses. To lead Israel to conquer Canaan was a most difficult assignment.

> LORD, you are my portion and my cup of blessing;
> you hold my future. The boundary lines have fallen
> for me in pleasant places; indeed, I have a beautiful
> inheritance. . . . You reveal the path of life to me; in
> your presence is abundant joy; at your right hand
> are eternal pleasures. (Ps. 16:5–6, 11)

◼

Lord, today we echo the words of Joshua's predecessor, Moses,
and say, "If your presence does not go . . . don't make us go up
from here" (Exod. 33:15). You alone know the way to what
you have called us to. We do not want to go where you are
not leading. So we humbly ask that you show us the way.

WHEN JERICHO FELL

*After the seventh time, the priests blew the trumpets,
and Joshua said to the people, "Shout! For the
LORD has given you the city. —Joshua 6:16*

You remember the mental picture from the old spiritual:
"Joshua fit the battle of Jericho . . . and the walls came tumblin'
down." Strange, is it not, that a shrill trumpet and a shouting
people should have such results! Yet it was much more than a
circular pep rally; God was using a special people.

The Bible elsewhere speaks of sounding the gospel like a
trumpet (1 Thess. 1:8). Today, the obedient testimony of God's
people causes modern Jerichos to tremble and fall. There are
walls within our towns and cities that need to come "tumblin'
down." Perhaps there are walls within our hearts or homes,
defending something that is wrong in God's sight. These, too,
must come "tumblin' down."

Let us see the real Jerichos of our area and together encir-
cle them with the Word of the Lord. March around the real
walls of divine and human enmity. Give a clear blast on the
gospel trumpet, rather than an uncertain sound. And together,
with fellow Christians in holy enthusiasm and confidence,
"Shout; for the Lord hath given you the city"!

*Lord, open my eyes to the strongholds in my life and
my community that You have planned to take down.
Use me to blow the trumpet of the gospel against the
darkness in this world. Your power is greater than any
wall and I know that all things are possible through
Your strength. Use me to fulfill Your perfect plan.*

A KING FOR ISRAEL

*Samuel said to all the people, "Do you see the one
the LORD has chosen? There is no one like him
among the entire population." And all the people
shouted, "Long live the king!"—1 Samuel 10:24*

How patient God had been with the people! Yet, they were discontented again and wanted a king to rule over them instead of a judge. God knew the real reason for the demand: The people had forsaken Him and turned to other gods.

This added instance of rebellion was not to stand in the way of God's plan, however. He not only agreed to let the people have their king, but He directed Samuel to choose one of the most outstanding men in all of Israel. In spite of their affront to God, a leader had already been prepared to serve as their ruler.

Saul pleaded that he had come from very insignificant circumstances. Many great men—religious leaders, government officials, educators, and others—have come from similar backgrounds. Often from the humblest surroundings, God calls the very best as instruments of achieving His will.

∎

*Thanking God for individuals whom He has called
and for their wholesome influence on our lives.*

OBEDIENCE IS BEST

Then Samuel said: Does the Lord take pleasure in burnt offerings and sacrifices as much as in obeying the Lord? Look: to obey is better than sacrifice, to pay attention is better than the fat of rams. —1 Samuel 15:22

God had given Saul exceptional leadership ability, but He expected Saul to obey certain basic rules just as any other man. God's plan always allows a great deal of individual freedom, but obedience to His Commandments is necessary if the total pattern of His will is to be accomplished.

Obedience to God places heavy demands on us when we stop to consider the full scope of His Commandments. Included is the full spectrum of everyday temptations, the prejudices and hatreds, the selfishness and the spiritual apathy.

Far more important to God than piously going through the motions of worship is our complete obedience in matters of love of God and love for others. "Sunday religion" is virtually nothing in the eyes of God if throughout the week our lives do not measure up consistently in obedience to God. Men of destiny seek to find out what God expects in every phase of their lives and follow obediently.

Lord, as You give me more responsibility, help me to remember that there will always be a call to obedience on my life. Guide my steps so that I am not tempted to turn away from Your direction. Open my eyes to the places in my life where I have been disobedient and break my heart over the sins that I have committed against You.

THE EYES OF GOD

But the LORD said to Samuel, "Do not look at his appearance or his stature, because I have rejected him. Human do not see what the LORD sees, for humans see what is visible, but the LORD sees the heart."—1 Samuel 16:7

How easy it is to be deceived by outward appearances! A shiny metal case can easily hide a shoddy mechanism; what appears to be tough and durable may not be strong enough to do the job. Unless there is more than the appearance of quality, our investment gives us nothing in return.

Samuel was looking for the man who commanded respect by his physical appearance. Indeed, this needed to be a strong person, one whom others would follow. Samuel was limited to this view, but the Lord could look deeper than he.

It is an uncomfortable feeling to know that while we are glorying in our outward appearance—what others think we are—God sees the inner quality of our lives. God's evaluation is the only one that counts, and before Him we may come to realize we have concentrated on the least important part of life. God's most usable instruments are not those who are simply of good appearance; they are those of a spiritual depth that measure up to God's needs.

Father, I know that I am tempted to focus on outward appearance of both myself and others, but that is not where I should have my focus. Give me Your eyes to see myself and those around me. Help me to recognize what is truly glorifying to You. Lord, use my body as Your vessel, and do not allow me to use it for my own glorification.

PLANNING TO BUILD

The king said to the prophet Nathan, "Look, I am living in a cedar house while the ark of God sits inside tent curtains." —2 Samuel 7:2

A little girl picks a ragged bouquet of wild flowers to give her father; a teenager saves for just the right gift for his current girlfriend; a husband works diligently to give his family the new home he so much wants them to have. Expressions of love and gratitude take many forms.

David had finished his battles; he had ruled the people with the integrity of his heart and the skillfulness of his hands (Ps. 78:72). God had guided and sustained him in many experiences, and now there was an earnest desire to do something for God, to erect a magnificent symbol of his love for God. And while it wasn't in the Lord's plan for David to build the temple, He honored David by promising that His son (Solomon) would someday build Him a temple instead. And so David's royal line would, indeed, continue.

What do you desire to build for God? Perhaps not a house, as David wanted. But there is so much we can plan: to build a life that is dedicated to His service, to develop a capacity for leadership in His church, to nurture a spirituality that will bless the lives of others. Let us ask Him for direction, and trust that He will bless the heart of a servant who wants to honor Him.

■

Our Father, let our every thought, word, and deed show our love for You.

THE HOUSE OF THE LORD

> *"Now, my son, may the Lord be with you, and may you succeed in building the house of the Lord your God, as he said about you. Above all, may the Lord give you insight and understanding when he puts you in charge of Israel so that you may keep the law of the Lord your God. Then you will succeed if you carefully follow the statutes and ordinances the Lord commanded Moses for Israel. Be strong and courageous. Don't be afraid or discouraged."* —1 Chronicles 22:11–13

David's character again proved genuine in his concern for the house of the Lord. Faced with such a frustrated desire, many would have sat down to sulk. But David's love for God was a deep one. He graciously stepped aside and contented himself with gathering together the finest of materials for this work.

Solomon was charged to seek God with heart and soul and to build an "exceedingly great" temple. David had served well; now, he was transferring the responsibility to a new king, his son. Another of God's men of destiny was to carry on the work, but not without the benefit of David's orientation and blessing or of the Lord's guidance.

Each of the kings was to have his own part in building this place of worship. Even to the greatest of the kings of Israel, obeying God's will was far more important than receiving credit and esteem for building His temple.

> *Lord, help me to gladly recognize and accept the Kingdom work You have called me to do.*

GOD CALLS AND EMPOWERS

I chose you before I formed you in the womb; I set you apart before you were born. I appointed you a prophet to the nations. . . . Do not be afraid of anyone, for I will be with you to rescue you. This is the LORD's declaration. Then the LORD reached out his hand, touched my mouth, and told me: I have now filled your mouth with my words. —Jeremiah 1:5, 8–9

Jeremiah need not have doubted that he was unprepared for the job God had called him to do. Other illustrious leaders before him had protested their inadequacy, and many others to this day have felt keenly aware of their own shortcomings and limitations.

To these anxieties, God has always made it clear that we have more than human resources on which to depend. One seldom feels closer to God than when they are faced with extreme difficulty and forced to depend heavily on guidance and power from the Holy Spirit.

God simply does not call us to a task greater than we are able to accomplish, because we are never asked to do anything in our own strength (John 15:5). Relying on God, we draw fully on our human capacity and find that God has expanded it to meet the demands of any and all situations that might come our way.

Our Father, we thank You that You are willing to call and use us, and that You empower us for these tasks.

GOD CALLS FOR OBEDIENCE

So Naaman went down and dipped himself in the Jordan seven times, according to the command of the man of God. Then his skin was restored and became like the skin of a small boy, and he was clean. —2 Kings 5:14

Naaman's obedience brought cure from his dreaded disease of leprosy. Faithful obedience to God always brings rich rewards. When traveling through an unfamiliar terrain or environment, like hiking Machu Picchu, one might come to have a peculiar feeling, unlike any other, for their guide. It is not merely a feeling of companionship, or fellowship, or friendship alone, but a combination of all three. This feeling is produced by obedience to the guide's commands, relying on their expertise, and believing that the guide has our best interests at heart.

Christ, our Guide, once said, "If you keep my commands you will remain in my love, just as I have kept my Father's commands and remain in his love" (John 15:10). Simple obedience to Christ produces in us a feeling of closeness and confidence in Him that all the religious zeal and fervor in the world could not generate without the act of obeying Him, and submitting to His will. Obedience is the key that unlocks the door to our heart so that Christ can dwell within.

Lord, I ask for the realization that the pathway of obedience to Christ is the only pathway that leads to lasting joy and peace.

THE SERVANT OF THE LORD

*"This is my servant; I strengthen him, this is my chosen
one; I delight in him. I have put my Spirit on him;
he will bring justice to the nations. He will not cry
out or shout or make his voice heard in the streets.
He will not break a bruised reed, and he will not put
out a smoldering wick; he will faithfully bring justice.
He will not grow weak or be discouraged until he has
established justice on earth. The coasts and islands
will wait for his instruction." —Isaiah 42:1–4*

Mankind continues to put the hope of the world in terms of
his own power and authority. He increases his power and the
number of his weapons and boldly plays his game "Blind Man's
Bluff" on the international stage. In the midst of it all, tensions
rise and conditions grow increasingly worse. Still, mankind
continues to seek larger dominion over himself and others.

The Israelites sought the peace of God, but even they could
not accept it on God's terms. God promised them a servant who
would bring righteousness and salvation. But they expected a
worldly king. When Jesus came as a servant, they did not have
eyes to see Him for who He was.

Serving God's Kingdom can be rather unpopular in today's
culture. People think those who follow Christ are demanding and judgmental, and in truth, some who call themselves
Christians fit this stereotype. But those who truly follow the
Suffering Servant, our Lord Jesus, know that it is the first who
will be last, the low who will be exalted (Matt. 20:16; Mark
10:32–45). This is what the Kingdom of God is like.

◼

*God, our Father, may we gladly be Your servants. May we
delight in being a part of bringing the gospel to the world.*

GOD'S PROMISE OF PEACE

For a child will be born for us, a son will be given to us, and the government will be on his shoulders. He will be named Wonderful Counselor, Mighty God, Eternal Father, Prince of Peace. The dominion will be vast, and its prosperity will never end. He will reign on the throne of David and over his kingdom, to establish and sustain it with justice and righteousness from now on and forever. The zeal of the LORD of Armies will accomplish this. —Isaiah 9:6–7

Nearly every religious holiday or feast among the Jews of Israel is directly related to the Exodus and the wanderings of God's people in the wilderness. None is more significant than Passover, which, to the Jew, is synonymous with freedom. During the Paschal Supper, the head of each household reads these words from the Haggadah: "In every generation, each person must see himself as though he, himself, has departed from Egypt."

Christ is our Passover Lamb. Through faith in Him, we have been miraculously delivered from bondage to our sinful flesh. As we individually trust in the Lord Jesus, He daily directs our paths through the wilderness of pain and temptation in our world. Our "exodus" is not only a life-transforming experience for now, but it is our spiritual journey into a promised, eternal home with Him in heaven.

■

Lord, we ask for the peace that only You can give us.

GOD'S IMMEASURABLE LOVE

See what great love the Father has given us that we should be called God's children—and we are! The reason the world does not know us is that it didn't know him. Dear friends, we are God's children now, and what we will be has not yet been revealed. We know that when he appears, we will be like him because we will see him as he is. And everyone who has this hope in him purifies himself just as he is pure. —1 John 3:1–3

How great is God's love to us, that He calls us His own children! We are His creation who also bear His image in this world. What's more, those of us who are in Christ Jesus, have been adopted into the family of God, making us co-heirs with God's Son (Eph. 1:5; Rom. 8:17).

Sometimes the Father seems remote and inaccessible. But this is never the case. Because of sin in our lives, we may feel we are far away from Him. But He is always near to us, turning toward us to be our Father and to forgive us, the repentant child. "See what great love the Father has given us!" It is not definable or measurable. It cannot be explained. But His limitless resources are available to those who love Him. Because of this relationship, "what we will be has not yet been revealed," yet abundant life in Christ Jesus is within reach now, today. How tragic that we often do not realize our inheritance on this side of eternity.

■

God, please guide me and empower me to realize fully my true identity in Christ Jesus, as a member of Your forever family.

LOVE ONE ANOTHER

No one has ever seen God. If we love one another, God remains in us and his love is made complete in us. This is how we know that we remain in him and he in us: He has given us of his Spirit. And we have seen and we testify that the Father has sent his Son as the world's Savior. Whoever confesses that Jesus is the Son of God—God remains in him and he in God. And we have come to know and to believe the love that God has for us. —1 John 4:12–16

What does it mean to love others? Does it mean expressing compassion, generosity of spirit, forgiveness? Yes, these and much more.

Have you ever watched the waves wash over a sandy beach, erasing all scars in the sand, day after day, never tiring of obliterating wounds and setting things right? Perhaps this picture is a symbol, a measure, of what it means to love others.

The larger love involves more. In Christian living, we ought to love others not only for what they are, but also for what they can be through Christ Jesus our Lord. It is in such heavenly love that we practice reconciliation with one another, giving us a glimpse into our own redemption through Jesus.

◼

Lord Jesus, help me to forgive as I have been forgiven. Grow my faith that I may experience true reconciliation with my brothers and sisters, echoing the heart of my Redeemer-God.

CHRIST, THE FIRST AND THE LAST

When I saw him, I fell at his feet like a dead man. He laid his right hand on me and said, "Don't be afraid. I am the First and the Last, and the Living One. I was dead, but look—I am alive forever and ever, and I hold the keys of death and Hades." —Revelation 1:17–18

It is easy to play a good game on the sidelines, to be a hero when there is no confrontation in battle, and to great, sweeping promises that cannot be fulfilled in real life. Yet, it is not our words, but our deeds, that count.

Christ not only promises, but He is able to keep the promises He makes. He was there in the beginning, at the creation of the world. Then He came to us, the Word made flesh. And in the Revelation to John, He declares, "I am the Alpha and the Omega . the one who is, who was, and who is to come, the Almighty" (v. 8).

The resurrection authenticated Jesus' promises. As Christ followers, we rejoice not only in His birth, but also His life, death, and resurrection. We can also rejoice in His making possible our own rebirth. Because He lives, we, too, will live by faith in Him (John 14:19).

Whenever the clouds of personal or international crisis hang low, we who know Jesus can still know peace and joy, for He has overcome and lives now and forevermore.

■

Lord Jesus, I pray that I may present my body as a living sacrifice to You, the one who became our sacrifice for sin.

REWARDS OF OVERCOMING

As many as I love, I rebuke and discipline. So be zealous and repent. See! I stand at the door and knock. If anyone hears my voice and opens the door, I will come in to him and eat with him, and he with me. "To the one who conquers I will give the right to sit with me on my throne, just as I also conquered and sat down with my Father on his throne. "Let anyone who has ears to hear listen to what the Spirit says to the churches." —Revelation 3:19–22

There are times when duty and the right require action. Under circumstances like these, we may be faced with pressures, from both man and the enemy, in an effort to halt our action, whatever it is God has called us to do. And when those situations arise, we may be tempted to compromise what we know to be true and right, in order to save face, to self-protect, and even just out of convenience.

When people criticize our actions, or when they fail to understand our motives as Christ followers, it is easy to develop an inferiority complex, thinking, No one appreciates my efforts. No one sees me. I have been forgotten. We are tempted to "throw in the towel" and call it quits. But Scripture reminds us that there are eternal rewards to those who persevere in their faith: "Be faithful to the point of death, and [He] will give you the crown of life" (21:10).

We can rejoice that Jesus was not deterred from His mission to Calvary. Because He overcame sin, death, and the grave, He now enables us to overcome, if we would turn to Him ib repentance.

◼

Lord, I pray You will strengthen me to the point to where I will not grow weary in do what You have called me to do.

DOOM OF CHRIST'S ENEMIES

*Then I heard another voice from heaven: Come out of her,
my people, so that you will not share in her sins or receive
any of her plagues. For her sins are piled up to heaven, and
God has remembered her crimes.* —Revelation 18:4–5

Ancient Israel was once subjected to the tyranny of an evil king.
Jabin, king of Canaan, had a ruthless military captain named
Sisera. This man had nine hundred chariots of iron and a great
host of soldiers. For twenty years, they greatly oppressed the
people of God. In God's own time, however, there was deliverance from the hand of those unbelievers. The record states
simply, but profoundly, that "the stars fought from the heavens;
the stars fought with Sisera from their paths" (Judg. 5:20).

The meaning, of course, is not that suns from other uni-
verses left their courses to come to this small planet and array
themselves in battle against the armies of this wicked man.
The meaning is rather that God is sovereign over all. This is a
moral universe in the sense that God is in ultimate control. In
some miraculous way, God was at work in that critical moment
in human history. He intervened for the good Israel and for the
good of mankind.

God is always at work against evil and for good. The enemies of God are doomed. His obedient people are secure for
and for eternity.

■

*Lord, I ask for spiritual discernment that I may offer myself
as an instrument through which Your good and perfect will
come into fruition. Make me a conduit for Your glory.*

THE BOOK OF LIFE

I also saw the dead, the great and the small, standing
before the throne, and books were opened. Another
book was opened, which is the book of life, and the
dead were judged according to their works by what
was written in the books. —Revelation 20:12

The mental aspects of the gospel have too long overshadowed its moral aspects. God has never been interested merely in a faith that produces works. He is also about the business of bringing people into a personal relationship and experience with Him. He calls us to outward obedience because He is concerned about the inner workings of our hearts; our God is about the work of gospel transformation.

In preparation for that final opening of God's record books when "the dead, the great and the small" will be judged "according to their works" (Revelation 20:12), let us remember that purity is better than sin, that love is better than hate, that peace is better than war, that giving is better than receiving, that integrity is better than popularity, that ideal is more significant than image, and that it is better to suffer for Christ's sake than to compromise with evil.

But to know God as a person, to know Jesus and to experience His presence, is to know that the law He has called us to—the one we cannot live out perfectly on our own, and so we need a Savior—is for our good. We can say with assurance and in agreement with the psalmist that, "The boundary lines have fallen for me in pleasant places; indeed, I have a beautiful inheritance" (Psalm 16:6).

Lord, make me spiritually wise and discerning.
Teach me to love as You love.

LIFE'S SUPREME LOYALTY

"It is written: Worship the Lord your God, and serve him only." —Luke 4:8

Long before the early Christians had that part of our Bible that we call the New Testament, they had a creed. It was the short, simple, profound, inclusive affirmation, "Jesus Christ is Lord." By the name "Jesus," they recognized their Master's humanity. By the name "Christ," they professed their acceptance of Him as the Messiah of Old Testament prophecy. By the third and highest name "Lord," they acknowledged Him as occupying a position of absolute control over them in every area and relationship of their lives.

For Christians today, to reaffirm this ancient truth is to do far more than voice a statement of doctrinal position. "Jesus Christ is Lord" is not just an abstract, irrelevant theological creed. It is a conscious, purposeful commitment to Jesus Christ as the Lord of all life. It is the believer's acceptance of the highest moral challenge to which someone can respond. Life's supreme loyalty belongs not to our institutions or organizations or movements. Life's supreme loyalty belongs to God.

Scriptures says, "Blessed are the pure in heart, for they will see God" (Matt. 5:8). May my commitment to You be single-minded, Lord.

THE KINGDOM IS AT HAND

In those days John the Baptist came, preaching in the wilderness of Judea and saying, "Repent, because the kingdom of heaven has come near!" For he is the one spoken of through the prophet Isaiah, who said: A voice of one crying out in the wilderness: Prepare the way for the Lord; make his paths straight! —Matthew 3:1–3

The Kingdom of God is at hand! What extraordinary news! John was not speaking of a national or political institution, but of the reign of God in one's heart. The Kingdom that God had promised through the Messiah was seeking to break through a world of evil. There was no time to be wasted. Something must happen to mankind. In order for us to enter this Kingdom of righteousness, peace, truth, light, love, life, and joy—we must repent.

To repent means to have true godly sorrow over our sin. It is to see sin as God sees it and to hate sin as God does. The only way into the Kingdom of God is through tears of repentance coupled with faith in the Son of God.

The meaning of the word *repentance* (from the Greek word "metanoia") is "change of mind." It is the literal turning away from our sin and turning toward God. For the Christ follower, it is this turning of heart that allows us to return to our God. He is ever present, but we are prone to wander. Thanks be to God, that He calls us to repentance, and through repentance, to relationship with Him.

Thank you, God, that it is Your kindness and love for me that leads me to repentance (Rom. 2:4).

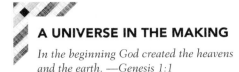

A UNIVERSE IN THE MAKING

In the beginning God created the heavens and the earth. —Genesis 1:1

We live in a marvelous world. How did it come about? Does some spiritually blind person say: "It just happened. There is no intelligence or purpose to back it up"? Surely, to look around us, we know this to not be true. "For [God's] invisible attributes, that is, his eternal power and divine nature, have been clearly seen since the creation of the world, being understood through what he has made. As a result, people are without excuse" (Rom. 1:20).

The author of Genesis, guided by God's Holy Spirit, went to the heart of the whole matter. How wonderful that the Bible begins with the words, "In the beginning God"! Not a defense mechanism, blind force, nature, matter endowed with a self-creative process, polytheism, pantheism, dualism, agnosticism, deism, atheism—but God! If we want to know the whole truth about the universe, we find it in His Word, and also in the expression of His creation—"In the beginning God"!

> "The heavens declare the glory of God, and the expanse proclaims the work of his hands." (Ps. 19:1)

■

I pray that God may open the eyes of any person whoever thinks of this world as anything other than God's.

IN GOD'S IMAGE

*So God created man in his own image; he
created him in the image of God; he created
them male and female. —Genesis 1:27*

God gave us a heart to love Him, a mind to think His thoughts,
and a will to obey Him. Scripture tells us we were made in the
likeness of God, to live God's life joyfully and lovingly of our
own free will. Created in holiness, we were indeed the glory of
the universe, the jewel in God's crown (Zech. 9:16).

But, alas, mankind chose to sin, and the image of God went
out of us. Only through the incoming of the Spirit of Christ
into our lives can God's image be restored.

A portrait of Dante, painted on a wall in Florence, Italy, was
once lost. One day an artist carefully cleaned dirt and white-
wash off of the wall, where lines and colors, which had long
been hidden, began to appear. Then the grave, lofty, noble face
of the great poet again looked upon a world of light. And so it is
with us; Christ restores the likeness of God in us, bringing the
divine image to light again.

■

*As we bear Your image, Lord, may it not be darkened by
our sin, but instead may shine more and more brightly.*

SAFETY IN THE ARK

And Noah did this. He did everything that God had commanded him. —Genesis 6:22

There was a new beginning with Noah. God looked and saw that the earth was corrupt, and He decided to bring about the end of all flesh. But Noah found grace in His sight. And so God commanded Noah to build an ark and to gather together his wife, his sons and their wives, and two of every kind of fowl and cattle and creeping thing into it. They were to take plenty of food. Noah did this, and the flood came upon the earth. It rained for forty days and nights, and the waters prevailed for a hundred and fifty days. But Noah and his family were safe inside the ark.

Is it any wonder that Noah's ark has become a symbol of salvation? Every person needs a refuge from the power of sin and Satan. Isaiah says that a man "will be like a shelter from the wind, a refuge from the rain, like flowing streams in a dry land and the shade of a massive rock in an arid land" (Isa. 32:2). Who is that man? He is none other than Jesus Christ, God's Son. The winds may howl without, the storm clouds may grow black, and the terrible tempest may break. But all who find their shelter in Jesus Christ are safe within the ark.

■

Lord, may we turn to You and seek to find protection in Your presence.

THE FIRST ALTAR

Then Noah built an altar to the LORD. He took some of every kind of clean animal and every kind of clean bird and offered burnt offerings on the altar. When the LORD smelled the pleasing aroma, he said to himself, "I will never again curse the ground because of human beings, even though the inclination of the human heart is evil from youth onward. And I will never again strike down every living thing as I have done. —Genesis 8:20–21

How many people there are who, after some great deliverance, forget the aid which heaven sent! Jesus once sadly asked, "Were not ten cleansed? Where are the nine?" (Luke 17:17). Only one out of the ten healed lepers returned to thank Him. The truly grateful always acknowledge that the deliverances of life come from the loving care of the heavenly Father.

Noah could have easily lost sight of divine providence over him. But, no! He gratefully acknowledged God's merciful deliverance. He built an altar to thank God for His gracious protection, and to pray for His mercy to come. Noah was commanded to build an ark, not an altar. The truly thankful person does not have to be told to build an altar. Noah proved himself worthy of being entrusted with the care of a new world.

How many altars of gratitude have you built? What about your family altar?

Lord, I ask for the grace of gratitude for all of the mercies You have given me, and to be worthy of serving You in my generation.

THE WRONG WAY TO HEAVEN

And they said, "Come, let us build ourselves a city and a tower with its top in the sky. Let us make a name for ourselves; otherwise, we will be scattered throughout the earth." —Genesis 11:4

The work of all Babel-builders is doomed to failure. As men abide under the awful power of evil, they grow worse and worse. As the men sought to build a city and a tower whose top would reach heaven, they actually raised a monument of human sin and folly. They undertook to make for themselves a name. They erected a monument to their own glory to show forth their greatness. This was the most daring form of iniquity.

Their wild and selfish ambition demonstrated that they had become a providence to themselves, and that they felt no need of God. But man's pride can lead him only so far. God brought them suddenly and unexpectedly to judgment. It never occurred to them that God would stop their labors in such an extraordinary way as the confusion of their speech.

They had taken the wrong road to heaven, and we, too, are prone to make the same attempt. We cannot reach heaven by glorifying ourselves, but only by glorifying God by faith in Jesus Christ.

■

God, forgive us when we try to go our own way. Please take away the selfish ambition from our hearts and give us the spirit of true and devoted followers of our Lord, Jesus Christ.

THE BLOOD OF THE COVENANT

Moses took the blood, splattered it on the people, and said,
"This is the blood of the covenant that the LORD has made
with you concerning all these words." —Exodus 24:8

Deeds, contracts, wills, or any legal papers are invalid without the signatures of the contracting parties. They are merely forms, pieces of paper. Only when the signature is affixed, does it signify approval of the agreement. Only then is it binding.

The Lord gave Moses the laws for the people, and Moses wrote them down. When he called the people together, he read the laws aloud to them. And the people agreed to do all that the Lord had said.

Moses then sprinkled the blood on the people, which was the bond of agreement. It was an act of faith, an outward expression of obedience to God's will, and it gave them claim to His promises.

God loved us and Christ died for us to save us from our sin. We believe in Christ and are given reconciliation with God and an everlasting life spent in His presence. It is our faith in God and obedience to His that will make us heirs to His Kingdom. Our salvation comes not by strength or by might, but by His Spirit (Zech. 4:6).

■

God, help us show our faith in You by our obedience to Your will.

A PLACE FOR GOD

"They are to make a sanctuary for me so that I may dwell among them. You must make it according to all that I show you—the pattern of the tabernacle as well as the pattern of all its furnishings." —Exodus 25:8–9

Every effective leader must identify themselves in a very real and personal way with those they lead. The best-loved leaders of our country and churches have been those persons with whom the people felt a strong personal relationship.

God was leading His people along by personally instructing them in the minutest details of life. Moses spent forty days with Him, listening as He outlined an offering of gifts the people were to bring. These gifts were to be used in the sanctuary, a place where God might dwell among His people.

God instituted the plan. He was the architect and interior decorator of the first house of worship. The tabernacle was built according to His specifications, and He was the Author of the order of service.

Today, our places of worship, the order of service, and the conduct of worshipers should be in keeping with the majestic holiness of God.

■

God, only You know what You intend of us in worship. Teach us to praise You, worship You, and seek You as we should.

CHILDREN OF THE KINGDOM

*Therefore, whether we are at home or away, we make
it our aim to be pleasing to him. For we must all
appear before the judgment seat of Christ, so that
each may be repaid for what he has done in the body,
whether good or evil. —2 Corinthians 5:9–10*

We sometimes hear people speak of "planting" a light post or
a telephone pole. It is odd, the thought of planting anything
inanimate; it is as if we should expect to see limbs or flowers
growing on a flagpole.

God plants the children of His Kingdom in this world that
they may grow. The sweetness and fragrance of their growth
attract the children of this world to the "Lily of the Valley" and
the "Rose of Sharon."

Too often, God's children are like telephone poles—rigid,
standing tall, and always in place—but never sprouting or
enlarging. Then, some of them are out of line or have decayed.
And so since they cannot be trusted to support a wire, there
can be no communication. Some are like totem poles, an
object of curiosity, but judgmental and, therefore, unattractive.
In fact, the top man on the totem pole may be the ugliest of all.

Despite the presence of innumerable weeds, the Gardener
will someday present an attractive arrangement for His own
glory, if we are willing to be cultivated.

Lord, cultivate us for Your garden and for Your glory.

MARCHING ORDERS

Whenever the cloud was lifted up above the tent, the Israelites would set out; at the place where the cloud stopped, there the Israelites camped. At the LORD's command the Israelites set out, and at the LORD's command they camped. As long as the cloud stayed over the tabernacle, they camped. —Numbers 9:17–18

Waiting on God's timing is not time wasted. The truest evidence of belief in God is not action, but faithfulness. True men and women of faith do not attempt to proceed ahead of God. It is an act of submission to our God to sit contentedly when our situation requires it.

God is no slave driver, but we must follow His Word and live by His Spirit. At His command, we will move or rest, as did the Israelites. At the command of the Lord they journeyed, and at His command they waited. The Lord was faithful to always abide in their presence.

We are assured of God's power and spiritual victory only when we go with God. "A person's steps are established by the LORD, and he takes pleasure in his way. Though he falls, he will not be overwhelmed, because the LORD supports him with his hand" (Ps. 37:23–24).

■

Lord God, please teach us to wait on You, for the assurance of Your will and power.

FEARS OF FAITHLESSNESS

They reported to Moses: "We went into the land where you
sent us. Indeed it is flowing with milk and honey, and here
is some of its fruit. However, the people living in the land
are strong, and the cities are large and fortified. We also
saw the descendants of Anak there. —Numbers 13:27–28

All of us have moments when our faith is weakened and seems very small. We know that sin never gives up an inch of conquered territory without a fight. We see the seemingly impregnable fortresses of organized crime, teen pregnancy, materialism, social injustice, and addiction running rampant the world over. And we feel that we, as Christians, are little, weak, and inconsequential in the face of these things. There are times when we feel that we are grasshoppers under the feet of giants, and so we back off and do nothing. But this is more than timidity and cowardice: it reveals a weakened faith.

But our God is able to make good on His Word. He goes before us and has undertaken more than we could dare accomplish in our own strength—more than we could ever ask or imagine Him to do on our behalf (Eph. 3:20).

We can go forth and possess the land—as we travel the way of faith, as we pray, as we love, as we share the gospel, and as we follow the footprints of Christ to the summits of sacrifice.

■

Lord God, we ask that you deliver us from our
timidity and cowardice, and give us the courage for
a relevant witness against the issues of our day.

A MINORITY FOR GOD

"If the Lord is pleased with us, he will bring us into this land, a land flowing with milk and honey, and give it to us. Only don't rebel against the Lord, and don't be afraid of the people of the land, for we will devour them. Their protection has been removed from them, and the Lord is with us. Don't be afraid of them!" —Numbers 14:8–9

Many people look at things from the point of view of their own happiness, comfort, spiritual, and even enjoyment. This led the Israelites to murmur against Moses and the God who had led them out of captivity.

When our lot is not as pleasant as we might wish, we have a tendency to blame God for our difficulties and misfortunes. But the Bible does not promise us that becoming Christians will put an end to our suffering and hardships. Jesus promised us we would face trials of all kinds (John 16:33).

Christ suffered to make salvation possible. We join in His sufferings to bring glory to His name and to share the gospel with those who have yet to know Him. We dare not retreat because there are difficulties in the way.

Who are the Joshuas and Calebs among us today? Not the masses who follow the popular movements of society and seek their own comforts and prosperity, but those who realize that as Christ followers, we have a call on our lives to love everyone on Earth without prejudice or favoritism, and to share the gospel message with the whole world.

Lord, forgive us when we look at our circumstances and believe they are too much. In our strength they are, but with You, all things are possible.

GREATNESS AT FAULT

But the LORD said to Moses and Aaron, "Because you did not trust me to demonstrate my holiness in the sight of the Israelites, you will not bring this assembly into the land I have given them." —Numbers 20:12

There are times when God's commands are not in line with our mood or disposition of the moment. It is certainly not always easy to follow His will. What then? Are we to act out of our anger and passion?

Moses was commanded to speak to the rock at Kadesh, that it might bring forth water. Instead, he spoke harshly to the people and smote the rock.

Christians are commanded to give evidence of God's power, mercy, and grace in our lives. If we follow our call immediately and do not vary from our instructions, God will reveal His power as He works through us.

Unbelief is our greatest transgression. Our failure to trust God hinders our sharing of the gospel. But we know firsthand that God's rebuke and judgment are necessary in the divine discipline of human life; they call us home to Him. And the promised land is denied to the unbelieving.

Lord, today we ask that You strengthen our spiritual leaders who sometimes become tired, weary, and burdened. We also ask that You forgive our unbelief in our moments of despair.

THE SERPENT OF BRASS

*Then the LORD said to Moses, "Make a snake image and
mount it on a pole. When anyone who is bitten looks at it,
he will recover." So Moses made a bronze snake and mounted
it on a pole. Whenever someone was bitten, and he looked
at the bronze snake, he recovered. —Numbers 21:8–9*

When venomous snakes attacked the Israelites in the wilderness, Moses was commanded to make a brazen serpent and to lift it up for all to see. The Israelites who lifted up their eyes to the serpent of brass and turned their hearts to their Father in heaven were healed. This is a foreshadowing of things to come—a striking emblem of the crucified Savior.

All who are wounded by "that old serpent, the devil," can look in faith to Christ and be delivered. Christ said, "Just as Moses lifted up the snake in the wilderness, so the Son of Man must be lifted up, so that everyone who believes in him may have eternal life" (John 3:14–15).

Receiving Christ as Lord and Savior removes the venom, the lust, and the passions that inflame our soul. The Israelites looked and lived, and we, by faith, look unto Jesus and live. Thanks be to God.

*Lord, in Your power and strength, may we go forward
continually proclaiming the saving work of Jesus on
the cross to all who would hear and believe.*

CHOSEN FOR LEADERSHIP

The LORD replied to Moses, "Take Joshua son of
Nun, a man who has the Spirit in him, and lay your
hands on him. Have him stand before the priest
Eleazar and the whole community, and commission
him in their sight." —Numbers 27:18–19

Moses prayed for a successor. He begged earnestly that the work
of God might be carried on. Envious souls do not love their successors. Moses was not one of these. He had a tender concern
for his people and a believing dependence upon his God.

After Joshua was ordained by the priest, Moses transferred
the leadership to him. Joshua was then charged with the
responsibility of leading the people of Israel. As he proceeds
to govern them and to conquer Canaan, he must do so under
God's divine counsel and leadership.

It is reassuring to know that God's work will go on. The
scepter of leadership must be passed from one to another. God
Himself is ever at work grooming and preparing successors in
a thousand ways we know nothing of. God is more concerned
about His work than we are. He will accomplish it all.

> I declare the end from the beginning,
> and from long ago what is not yet done,
> saying: my plan will take place,
> and I will do all my will. (Isa. 46:10)

Thank You, God, for calling and preparing spiritual leaders.
We pray for their protection from the evil one today.

TRADITION AND CHRISTIAN DUTY

"I am the gate. If anyone enters by me, he will be saved and will come in and go out and find pasture. A thief comes only to steal and kill and destroy. I have come so that they may have life and have it in abundance." —John 10:9–10

Purity is to be sought in the soul, not externally. Jesus was more concerned with purity of heart than keeping the external observances required by rabbinical tradition. He taught that the things which issue from the heart defile the man. For "a good person produces good out of the good stored up in his heart. An evil person produces evil out of the evil stored up in his heart, for his mouth speaks from the overflow of the heart" (Luke 6:45).

Holiness is a matter of the heart, and not of alleged clean or unclean food or hands. The things that are harbored within— evil thoughts, malice, hate, carnal lust, envy, jealousy, pride, covetousness, and self-indulgence—are the things which defile a man. It then becomes far too easy to charge others for breaking God's laws, all the while transgressing God's laws in a greater way by judging their behavior.

A corrupt fountain can only spew forth a geyser of bitter water. Therefore, "Guard your heart above all else, for it is the source of life" (Prov. 4:23).

God grant us the grace to honor Christ in all we do.

LIFE'S TRUE TEST

"Every good tree produces good fruit, but a bad tree produces bad fruit. A good tree can't produce bad fruit; neither can a bad tree produce good fruit. Every tree that doesn't produce good fruit is cut down and thrown into the fire. So you'll recognize them by their fruit." —Matthew 7:17–20

As every farmer knows, and even the amateur gardener is aware of, the weeds may look better than the planted seed at first. It may be difficult to know what to hoe and what to leave standing. As in Christ's parable of the wheat and the tares, it may be necessary for both to grow together until the harvest. Then, the difference stands revealed, and it is obvious. The corn, tomatoes, and beans are known by the fruit they have borne, while the weed has produced nothing useful at all.

People who ask, "Does the Christian faith work?" may ask in the wrong spirit, having already made up their minds that no evidence will convince them. To the honest question, however, there is this answer: Christian faith does work. It is based on the experience of reality. It is involved with the deepest needs of life. All the while the Christian is producing their fruit, they grow among those who do not share their faith. Both are subject to the same law; that they shall be known by their fruits. And in this way, God gives testimony for the world to see.

We praise You, God, that by Your Spirit, You are the One who produces good fruit in us.

BE NOT AFRAID

Immediately Jesus spoke to them. "Have courage!
It is I. Don't be afraid." —Matthew 14:27

The hand of the Lord often touches our lives in ways we do not expect. Life seems to be going along smoothly, even prosperously, when the unexpected happens. This may be the loss of a job, or the opportunity of a better one. The unexpected may be the death of a loved one, or a new relationship with some other person. The unexpected event could be a serious illness, or a miraculous recovery. Because we do not know what each day holds for us, we could easily give ourselves up to a fear that would stifle our joy and choke our productivity in life.

Instead of dwelling on the future and plotting our own plans, we must cultivate our faith in Jesus, who gives enough for each day (Matt. 6:31–34). We must accept life joyfully, knowing that God desires the best for His children, and is actively working on their behalf and for His glory (Rom. 8:28).

In retrospect, we can look back at the unexpected events in our lives, both good and bad, and say, "That was the hand of God directing my life on that day." Such reflection helps us to be joyful and at peace in all circumstances, eagerly reaching out to gain the best from each new experience in life.

Thank You, God, for Your continued guidance
and for increased faith in Your goodness.

OUT OF THE HEART

"Don't you realize that whatever goes into the mouth passes into the stomach and is eliminated? But what comes out of the mouth comes from the heart, and this defiles a person. For from the heart come evil thoughts, murders, adulteries, sexual immoralities, thefts, false testimonies, slander. These are the things that defile a person; but eating with unwashed hands does not defile a person." —Matthew 15:17–20

Have you ever made an embarrassing slip of the tongue? Perhaps you said what you did not intend to say. Nevertheless, it is possible you said what you really believed. Such a slip may reveal more of our true nature than a carefully worded sentence ever could.

Psychologists have spent much time helping people see how their actions are related to their thoughts. If a person continually acts as a show-off, it is probably because he feels inferior to other people and is trying to prove himself worthy.

The only effective way to improve our behavior is to improve our thoughts. We must stock our minds as we would stack shelves in a closet. In one place, we hide the words of the Bible. In another stack, we keep the essence of great books we have read. Back here, we keep good thoughts about experiences with our friends. In this place, we cherish the lovely memories of our childhood. Daily, we remove resentment and hate by relinquishing it to the Holy Spirit. Daily, we ask for God's help in keeping the hidden places of our mind well stocked.

∎

Lord, we ask for Your help in filling our minds with thoughts of You, Your Kingdom, and Your purposes. Help us to keep our eyes fixed on You.

A FAITH THAT STANDS

*"But you," he asked them, "who do you say that I
am?" Simon Peter answered, "You are the Messiah,
the Son of the living God." —Matthew 16:15–16*

A faith that lets you down is worse than no faith at all. You
think you are prepared for every emergency, but at the crucial
moment, your faith collapses.

We see an example of a faith that endures in today's text. But
that faith did not come from current, in-the-moment thought.
If it had, it would have passed on as quickly as it came.

But how did this faith form with such solidarity in the
soul of Peter? The answer is clear. He received a witness
from Andrew, and his association with Jesus had been constant. He listened to the words of Jesus and walked with Him.
Through this association, God revealed to Peter a faith that
stood, because Peter's faith was in the immovable Son of God
Himself (Matt. 16:17) .

Peter's faith was not perfect, as indicated by his denial. But
in trial, persecution, and witnessing, Jesus—the object of his
faith—never let him down, sustaining Peter to face whatever
circumstances came his way.

■

*Jesus, You are the source and perfecter of our faith. Therefore,
let us look to You in sharing our faith with others. Attempting to
share the gospel in our strength would be to share a false gospel.*

TESTS OF GREATNESS

"Whoever wants to become great among you must be your servant, and whoever wants to be first among you must be your slave; just as the Son of Man did not come to be served, but to serve, and to give his life as a ransom for many." —Matthew 20:26–28

Jesus was well acquainted with the mind of mankind. By our human standards, the greatest among us is the person with the greatest authority. It may be political authority—the President, the Prime Minister, or a dictator. It may be the authority of knowledge—a professor or a researcher. It may be the authority of wealth which can command yachts, palaces, servants, and the best of material things this world has to offer.

But by this standard of living, Jesus was shockingly different. He taught that the greatest man is the man who renders the greatest service. Who can argue with this? In order to have greatness, we must be childlike in our faith. The child is characterized by humility, open-mindedness, and enthusiasm. She is free of prejudice and has a great capacity to love and trust. These characteristics are essential to learning and service. Without them, there is no true greatness, only ego and self-ambition.

■

May we keep in mind all the truths taught by You Lord, and seek Your greatness through true humility.

IN FULFILLMENT OF PROPHECY

"This took place so that what was spoken through the prophet might be fulfilled." —Matthew 21:4

Some people would have us believe that Jesus was simple a man through whom God revealed Himself in wonderful ways. These people go on to say that Jesus was as divine as any other human being can be divine. Others might go so far as to dare say that we do not really need a true Savior; the historic Christ is more than enough.

The witness of the apostles who knew Jesus is different. Jesus is not just man; He is the God-man. According to Galatians 4: "When the time came to completion, God sent his Son" (v. 4). His coming was announced by the prophets. His life and death were foretold. He fulfilled the intricate pattern of prophecy as no one else did or ever could. No wonder the apostles were awestruck at Jesus' words. He spoke as one having authority, because He is the ultimate Author. The apostle Paul, a Hebrew scholar, saw it and exclaimed, "He is the image of the invisible God, the firstborn over all creation. For everything was created by him, in heaven and on earth, the visible and the invisible, whether thrones or dominions or rulers or authorities—all things have been created through him and for him" (Col. 1:15–16).

We praise You, God, for Your eternal Son, Jesus Christ, who has brought us back into relationship with You.

SOURCE OF PURITY

"Woe to you, scribes and Pharisees, hypocrites! You clean the outside of the cup and dish, but inside they are full of greed and self-indulgence. Blind Pharisee! First clean the inside of the cup, so that the outside of it may also become clean." —Matthew 23:25–26

Purity definitely does not begin from the outside. No one is ignorant enough to think that the color of a pump gives any assurance that the water is pure. The Pharisees wore robes indicating their purity and righteousness. "But inside," said Jesus, "they are full of greed and self-indulgence" (Matt. 23:25). These men were sure to scrub themselves clean on the outside, but the inside the neglected and left filthy.

"Don't eat a stingy person's bread, and don't desire his choice food, for it's like someone calculating inwardly. 'Eat and drink,' he says to you, but his heart is not with you'" (Prov. 23:6–7). Jesus answered the quest for the source of purity when he said to Nicodemus, "Do not be amazed that I told you that you must be born again" (John 3:7). The new birth from above is our only hope for purity, but it is a hope that is sure and steadfast, not because of us but because of Jesus.

Anyone who recognizes their own impurity and turns from it and to our Lord in faith has the promise of eternal life. That is the source of the purity Jesus revealed. "If we confess our sins, he is faithful and righteous to forgive us our sins and to cleanse us from all unrighteousness" (1 John 1:9).

■

We confess our sins to You, Lord, and we are confident that You will forgive us and cleanse us from all unrighteousness.

PREPARED FOR HIS COMING

"Therefore be alert, because you don't know either the day or the hour." —Matthew 25:13

The second coming of our Lord is foretold in the same Bible that tells us of His first coming. It is declared with the same authority and assurance. The apostles were ever watchful for His coming. And just before the final benediction of the New Testament comes these words: "'Amen! Come, Lord Jesus!'" (Rev. 22:20).

The most important thing about the second coming of our Lord, so far as we are concerned, is to be prepared. To be watchful and ready. Some people want just enough religion to get them into heaven. But they do not intend to be troubled with a particle of faith more than that. But today's passage makes it clear that no less than our total commitment of faith is enough.

> "Not everyone who says to me, 'Lord, Lord,' will enter the kingdom of heaven, but only the one who does the will of my Father in heaven. On that day many will say to me, 'Lord, Lord, didn't we prophesy in your name, drive out demons in your name, and do many miracles in your name?' Then I will announce to them, 'I never knew you. Depart from me, you lawbreakers!" (Matt. 7:21–23)

■

Lord Jesus, we look forward to Your return, and pray we may tell others about You so they may receive Your gift of redemption.

THE GREAT BETRAYAL

While he was still speaking, Judas, one of the
Twelve, suddenly arrived. A large mob with swords
and clubs was with him from the chief priests
and elders of the people. —Matthew 26:47

"What are you willing to give me if I hand him over
to you?" (Matt. 26:15)

With those words, Judas, overcome and blinded by great greed,
bargained with the chief priests of the Jews. For thirty pieces
of silver, the price of a slave, he agreed to deliver Jesus into
their hands. With a kiss as the sign, Judas committed his infamous act of betrayal.

To this day, we still betray our Lord for a price. Our thoughts
are consumed with what the world tells us to pursue: How
much money can I make? Will my social prestige or my standing be advanced? What is the easiest way to get ahead? And
in this way, we bargain with the world and deny our faith in
Jesus Christ. Overcome by covetousness and greed, we reenact Judas' sin again and again.

Judas discovered that his deed could not be undone, and
with remorse, he hanged himself. On the cross, Jesus provided
the remedy for Judas' guilt, and ours, too. In His love, we all
find forgiveness for our sin. Thanks be to our God.

◼

Lord God, please forgive me for trading You for the comforts
and distractions of this world. Deliver me from the power
of greed, which so easily tempts me and leads me to sin.

DYING FOR ME

But Jesus cried out again with a loud voice and gave up his spirit. Suddenly, the curtain of the sanctuary was torn in two from top to bottom, the earth quaked, and the rocks were split. The tombs were also opened and many bodies of the saints who had fallen asleep were raised. And they came out of the tombs after his resurrection, entered the holy city, and appeared to many. —Matthew 27:50–53

Jesus died. The facts of His death are recorded by several who saw Him die on a cross. And so it is easy to prove from these accounts of history that Jesus of Nazareth once lived. It is also easy to show that He died on a cross.

It is often true that people die needlessly, tragedies which were caused by carelessness. But, in the providence of God, His Son was crucified for a special purpose. Every believer is familiar with that purpose and may say, with deep feeling, "He died for me."

Jesus said, "No one has greater love than this: to lay down his life for his friends" (John 15:13). He must have been looking toward His death, which was truly on behalf of His own friends, and it was for us also. By His death, Jesus showed unmistakably His love for all mankind.

◼

Lord, I ask for an abiding consciousness of and gratitude for the purpose of the Jesus' death. May I never grow numb or ambivalent of His gift of salvation.

VICTOR OF DEATH

*The angel told the women, "Don't be afraid, because I
know you are looking for Jesus who was crucified. He
is not here. For he has risen, just as he said. Come and
see the place where he lay. Then go quickly and tell
his disciples, 'He has risen from the dead and indeed
he is going ahead of you to Galilee; you will see him
there.' Listen, I have told you." —Matthew 27:5–7*

One of the significant events of Jesus' crucifixion was that His
body was taken from the cross and laid in a new tomb belonging to Joseph of Arimathea; this is why it has been referred to
as a borrowed tomb. The body of Jesus was to require the use
of it for a short time only.

There was no doubt that Jesus was dead when His body
was placed in that tomb. The angel of the Lord stood beside
the open tomb to announce to the two women the resurrection
of Jesus in such a forthright manner that the women could
never doubt it.

"The angel told the women, 'Don't be afraid, because I know
you are looking for Jesus who was crucified. He is not here. For
he has risen, just as he said. Come and see the place where
he lay'" (Matt. 28:5–6). How the hearts of those two women,
Mary Magdalene and Mary, who loved the Savior so much,
must have been filled with joy upon hearing those words!

Jesus' victory over death brings real assurance to those who
believe in Him and call on His name.

■

*Lord, I ask that You would grant me a greater realization
of Jesus' love for me, and a fuller understanding
that, with Him, there is victory over death.*

"WHAT SHALL I DO WITH JESUS?"

Pilate asked them, "What should I do then with Jesus, who is called Christ?" They all answered, "Crucify him!" Then he said, "Why? What has he done wrong?" But they kept shouting all the more, "Crucify him!" —Matthew 27:22–23

A time for decision had come. The mob demanded that Jesus be put to death, and Pilate faced the most significant decision of his life. It seems strange to us that the judge, who was accustomed to making important decisions should ask a perjured mob what he should do about the matter. Here was a judge who forsook his responsibility, letting an unruly crowd have its way—against his better judgment.

Since Pilate asked his question, countless souls have faced life's most important decision, often asking someone else what we should think about Jesus. Some have followed good advice in their decisions to follow the Savior, but not all people know where the best advice may be found. We do well to remember that the Bible is the authoritative Word of God on salvation.

■

Today, as people consider Jesus and the cross, they do not sit where Pilate sat. They have no power to release or kill our Savior. Yet, what we decide about Jesus sets the eternal destiny of our souls. Lord, have mercy on our souls.

THE BATTLE CRY OF FAITH

David said to the Philistine: "You come against me with a
sword, spear, and javelin, but I come against you in the name
of the LORD of Armies, the God of the ranks of Israel—you
have defied him. Today, the LORD will hand you over to me.
. . . Then all the world will know that Israel has a God,
and this whole assembly will know that it is not by sword
or by spear that the LORD saves, for the battle is the LORD's.
He will hand you over to us." —1 Samuel 17:45-47

Most people have a rallying cry that calls them to action. It
may be money, prestige, a desire to serve, or a loved one.

The person concerned with service to mankind ask few
questions before acting. They need only the knowledge that
someone is in need, and that something must be done to help
that someone.

What was the difference between the people of Israel and
their enemies? God was on the Israelites' side. They went forth
to meet the challenge with confidence, and they enjoyed the
Lord's support in their efforts. All the shining armor of Goliath
could not blind David's simple faith. He met and defeated the
powerful Philistine in the strength of the Lord.

Lord, please give me the courage to face important
matters head on, and for wisdom and courage to make the
decisions I encounter. May my faith in You be renewed as
I trust You more and more each day for these things.